MONOPOLY®

MONEY, AND YOU

MONOPOLY

MONEY, AND YOU

HOW TO PROFIT FROM THE GAME'S SECRETS OF SUCCESS

PHILIP E. ORBANES

Mc
Graw
Hill
Education

NEW YORK   CHICAGO   SAN FRANCISCO

LISBON   LONDON   MADRID   MEXICO CITY   MILAN

NEW DELHI   SAN JUAN   SEOUL   SINGAPORE

SYDNEY   TORONTO

1 2 3 4 5 6 7 8 9 0   QFR/QFR   1 9 8 7 6 5 4 3

ISBN 978-0-07-180843-9
MHID   0-07-180843-4

e-ISBN 978-0-07-180844-6
e-MHID   0-07-180844-2

Design by Lee Fukui and Mauna Eichner

This publication is designed to provide accurate and authoritative information in regard to the subject matter covered. It is sold with the understanding that neither the author nor the publisher is engaged in rendering legal, accounting, securities trading, or other professional services. If legal advice or other expert assistance is required, the services of a competent professional person should be sought.

—From a Declaration of Principles Jointly Adopted by a Committee of the American Bar Association and a Committee of Publishers and Associations

Library of Congress Cataloging-in-Publication Data

Orbanes, Philip.
  Monopoly, money, and you : how to profit from the game's secrets of success / by Philip E. Orbanes.
    pages cm
  Includes bibliographical references.
  ISBN-13: 978-0-07-180843-9 (alk. paper)
  ISBN-10: 0-07-180843-4 (alk. paper)
  1. Finance, Personal. 2. Monopoly (Game) I. Title.
  HG179.O73 2013
  332.024—dc23

                                                                2012045756

MONOPOLY® and © 2013 Hasbro, Inc. Used with permission.

The MONOPOLY® name and logos, and the distinctive design of the game board, the four corner spaces, and the playing pieces, the MONOPOLY name and character, and each of the distinctive elements of the board and the playing pieces, are trademarks of Hasbro for its property trading game and equipment. Used with permission.

McGraw-Hill books are available at special quantity discounts to use as premiums and sales promotions or for use in corporate training programs. To contact a representative, please e-mail us at bulksales@mcgraw-hill.com.

This book is printed on acid-free paper.

I dedicate this book to Leo and Kyle . . .
and all of their generation who apply its lessons.

CONTENTS

It's not so important who starts the game but who finishes it.
—John Wooden, coach

ACKNOWLEDGMENTS

The following people enhanced the content of this manuscript:

Kevin Tostado, producer of *Under the Boardwalk: The Monopoly® Story,* meticulously documented and recorded the 2009 championship games depicted in this book. Kevin's thoughtful assistance, along with that of coproducer Craig Bentley, is greatly appreciated.

Tim Vandenberg, outstanding teacher in the Hesperia Unified School District of California, kindly provided and gave permission to reprint his Monopoly Speed Die Probabilities chart. Tim's use of Monopoly to teach math in his classroom is becoming the stuff of legend. His success demonstrates the effectiveness of the game as a storehouse of real-life lessons.

Matt McNally, former Monopoly champ and founder of an impressive Monopoly players' association, was a valued source of insight and comment throughout. He is featured among the nine Game Changers found throughout this book and also contributed the winning strategy for Monopoly: The Mega Edition.

Sincere thanks to Joe Sequino for his help with the online surveys and charts.

A tip of the Top Hat to the Game Changers: Jason Bunn, Jerry Dausman, Jim Forbes, Will Lusby, Yutaka Okada, Gary Peters, Dana Terman, Leon Vandendooren, and Matt McNally, all former Monopoly champs, who graciously offered their recollections and advice for you, my reader.

My sincere appreciation to Jonathan Berkowitz, Kim Losey, Nicole Agnello, Cameron Nixon, Jane Ritson-Parsons, and Margie Chan-Yip of Hasbro; my literary agent, Rob McQuilkin; and especially my visionary editor, Casey Ebro, of McGraw-Hill Professional, along with the McGraw-Hill team, Mary Glenn, Stacey Ashton, Courtney Fischer, Ann Pryor, Ty Nowicki, Peter McCurdy, Maureen Harper, and Jane Palmieri.

GETTING READY TO PLAY THE GAME

Once again, I find myself in the charming community of Marven Gardens, standing before *his* door. I was last here many years ago when I wrote *The Monopoly® Companion*. Memories swirl. I tap on the shiny brass ring of the handsome oak portal.

It opens and there he stands. Mr. Monopoly. I rub my eyes in disbelief; he doesn't look a day older, despite the passage of 25 years. It's been said that a virtuous life remains long protected by fortune's power. A virtual life is even better, it seems. He offers me his hand.

"You're back! What took you so long? Come in, come in. This way. Hang up your coat; we'll sit. Can't wait to talk money." His voice is warm and as commanding as ever.

I take a posh seat and admire his expansive den, its rich wood panels accented by framed awards and glass cases filled with objets d'art: large gold-plated irons and shoes, battleships and racecars. The carpet is embossed with locomotive icons woven out of golden threads. And—just for my satisfaction, perhaps—the wall safe is open, so I can't help but notice how filled it is with colorful Monopoly money. In his realm, Mr. Monopoly clearly wields a Midas touch.

You might suppose that Mr. Monopoly's money is as trivial as the sayings that play on it, like "Don't worry, it's only Monopoly money," or "You're spending cash like it's just Monopoly money." But the principles of making money in his classic game are remarkably applicable to making real dollars.

This is the reason why I've returned to Marven Gardens: to bring to light the financial lessons so easily absorbed while playing the game and their parallels in the world you and I contend with. The one that is often harsh, confusing, and not always virtuous. Who can't use a bit of help?

"If you learn to play my game to win," Mr. Monopoly offers, as his pleasant wife, Madge, enters with a tray bearing a pitcher of tea and tall, ice-filled, Monopoly-decorated glasses, "you'll see how making smart financial decisions improves the odds that you will prosper and not lose your shirt. This applies in business as well as to your own hard-earned money."

I concur. One thing I know from long experience in judging Monopoly championships is that for most of us this legendary game provides the seminal opportunity to handle money and practice the art of negotiation. Much like the basic knowledge Robert Fulghum conveyed in *All I Really Need to Know I Learned in Kindergarten,* Monopoly's lessons lay the groundwork for sound financial judgment—provided we pay attention to them.

I realize too, after many years in business, that I owe a good measure of my own success to the knack I developed, early in my career, to "game" each problem and opportunity that came my way. Playing Monopoly sparked this instinct. It has compelled me to challenge my business teammates to figure out the range of rewards and potential penalties before making any key financial decision. It has schooled me in the need to set goals, expect setbacks, and recognize trends before they become obvious.

And so, after a rousing discussion that lasted until the wee hours of the morning, I came away with Mr. Monopoly's maxims to link to my own experiences. As we said goodbye, he left me with this remark:

Life is richer when you play a game.

Especially mine!

MONOPOLY MAKES YOU THINK

. . . ABOUT MONEY

Money. We have difficulties when we don't have it, and problems when we do. Most of us would rather have the problems.

Why don't we show our money the same care and attention as we shower on every other important relationship in our lives?
—SUZE ORMAN, FINANCIAL ADVISOR

I t goes without saying that it takes *commitment* if you want to become good at anything. That means a lot of practice, trial and error . . . and education. Yes, it takes all three; there are no shortcuts, especially when money is involved. I've seen many a brilliant academic mind, hired at a high level into a firm, really muck up its business. I've seen laborers build a good life by virtue of their own hands, but never figure out how much more they could make if they trained others to do the hard work for them. I've seen doctors and lawyers build flourishing practices, earn upwards of $750,000 a year, and fall deeper and deeper into debt.

Why do these mistakes occur? I think it's because most of us receive very little—or no—practical training in financial management. (It's been said that there is no difference between theory and practice . . . until practice.) We try to learn as we go and often endure the consequences of mistakes: budgets out of whack, an inability to see the merits of doing without now in order to reap a reward later, not understanding the difference between saving and investing. Worse yet, we become vulnerable, prone to listen to silver-tongued individuals intent on separating us from our money through the lure of a "sure thing." By the time we recover from basic avoidable mistakes, we're in the hole and need to devote more of our financial resources just to get back to breaking even. I've been there.

Imagine being challenged to operate a giant construction crane, having only read the owner's manual before being thrust into the operator's seat. (Okay, maybe your uncle, a retired forklift operator, gave you a few vague pointers.) Suddenly, the controls are in your hands and you're on your own. Do you think your first lift would go smoothly? Or are you more likely to drop the load?

That's what handling money is like for many of us after we come out of school, start earning a respectable salary, and find that the controls are now in our grip. Sure, we might instinctively apply (or avoid) our parents' financial habits. More instinctively, we want *everything* today (solution: credit cards). We fall into debt. Time marches on, and hopefully we recover from our early mistakes (pay off those cards) and gain some wisdom to protect our money. We come upon good advice along the way and apply it if we wise up. If we don't, we remain stuck in a rut with no savings for the bulk of our working lives and must place our trust in government largesse, especially after we're retired. But if you read the news, you know a crisis is coming because the weight of promised government entitlements is unbearable. (It already dwarfs the alarmingly large national debt.)

More than ever, worry about money dominates our lives, and the message is clear: you need to acquire it through your own hard work, save as much as you can, and constantly nurture and grow a nest egg to "win the game."

What about that good financial advice I mentioned? The problem for most us (me included when I was starting out) is that we can't *feel* this advice. It's as abstract and academic as Avogadro's number. (If you had high school chemistry, you might remember this term, but who remembers the number of molecules it signifies?) In order to make good financial decisions, you need the benefit of experience to drill home the basic lessons. This comes at a price—literally. Fortunately, there is a playing field's worth of experience at your disposal that enables you to feel the impact of both good and bad financial decisions, joyously, without penalty.

Yes, it's the classic version of Monopoly. Monopoly puts you through a financial wringer without real-world loss. Once you get the hang of how to win it, you'll *feel* the game's secrets of success and see how they apply to real life—sometimes verbatim, always in principle.

Since Monopoly is a money game, it is *denominated*. Filled with numbers. Every component of this amazing game is built of bricks related by addition, subtraction, and sometimes multiplication and division. These simple operations can, if you're a true enthusiast, lead to a study of the kind of probabilities, tables of statistics, and future value analysis that would make any Wall Street financial guru salivate. In fact, this parallel demonstrates the great value of Monopoly in honing your real-world investment skills. You need to do numerical analysis to understand the impact of key financial decisions in your personal life or business. It can be fun to do this. ("Gamification" will be discussed in Chapter 10.) Many successful people I know view money like points in a game. The more points earned, the more they feel they're succeeding. Money is a scorecard of sorts. Increasingly, it's becoming a virtual scorecard because we actually don't see or touch our money. It exists in accounts, represented by digits (points, as my friend would say). We access it on our mobile devices, making it easier than ever to count our money and know our "score."

You may not have a degree in finance or have ever thought of becoming an investment banker on Wall Street, but that doesn't mean you don't have the smarts to make a good investment. By playing Monopoly, you pick up the basics the pros paid a handsome sum to learn in advanced schools: rate of return, payoff odds, likelihood of a big return, cash management, diversification (not to mention the art of negotiation).

These skills apply equally well to your everyday financial decisions. Here's a chart that demonstrates five such disciplines:

Topic	Monopoly	Life
Budget	Maintain a balance between cash, properties, and buildings.	Compile a monthly budget. Classify items by "essential," "savings," and "desired." Meet your savings goal before you spend on "desires."
Track spending	Learn to visualize or record your balance sheet to know where you stand.	Stick to it; monitor your investments and their growth.
Reduce debt	Don't deplete your credit (that is, your ability to mortgage and sell assets if needed).	Pay off debt, especially high-interest debt. Try to become debt free.
Maintain a cash reserve	Don't go bankrupt by having no cash, or assets to convert into cash.	Protect against loss; carry insurance. Maintain a rainy-day savings fund.
Deal effectively	Trade to get the most income potential.	Bargain wisely; get what you need without overpaying.

Here's the big idea. To make money, you have to steadily think about and apply yourself to making money. Amassing play money to win at Monopoly requires a high level of attention (one dumb move might bankrupt you). By developing a winning discipline in the game, you'll be inspired to diligently protect and grow your real cash. Devotion to your money should be akin to regard for a valued family member, for whom you want only the best, an absence of threat, and success beyond measure. You wouldn't treat such a loved one with neglect or casual disregard. Hold money in the same light. Think about this.

Monopoly immerses you in financial decision making. All those colorful bills lie at the core of the game. Nearly everything is related to them: the value of the spaces on the board, the cost of buildings, the messages on the cards, the investments and rentals on the deeds. The bills provide the game with its rhythm; it ebbs and flows with each cash exchange. Just as important, the amount of cash you possess affects how others perceive you at any moment (with respect or awe, hopefully not with apathy).

The game's lessons are acute because you can't win by playing it safe (translation: by holding on to all your pretty bills). You must invest a good deal of them, rather quickly, in order to win, thereby placing them at risk. The danger you subject your money to is palpable. This sense of vulnerability means that money controls you during the game. You may feel like its master, but you are its servant. (That's often the role we let real money maneuver us into.)

In Monopoly, money creates and destroys. At times it brings players together, while they are making deals, but more often than not it drives them apart—because only one player can win the game, the one who gains *all* the money. Games are like that. There can be but one victor.

Fortunately, real life stresses cooperative effort to get rich (win-win). You won't need to bankrupt your neighbor to come out ahead. (But if you try too hard to emulate his glitter, he could bankrupt you!) The game's need of a clean, decisive outcome results in well-structured rules that permit, condone, and assure that one player (hopefully you) will win everything. For this reason, its lessons are vivid and clear. This is why the principles of winning Monopoly aren't difficult to figure out, apply, or learn from. Alas, the "rules" in life are constantly evolving, and their lessons are more difficult to discern in a timely manner. But believe me, you gain an edge when you accept that there are rules and you begin to figure them out.

Handling money in the Monopoly game triggers a broad range of human emotions. You might laugh, shout for joy, grit your teeth—or cry—because of its changing impact on your fortune. This range of drama is a key reason why players come back to play time and again. We like the roller-coaster ride. And that's why we *feel* its lessons. We relish joy on the way up and a heightened sense of fear on the way down. Recovery brings relief, but only temporarily. The money game in real life is much the same, when you think about it.

Game Changer 1—
Playing It Safe Is a Sure Way to Lose

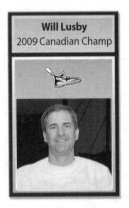

Will Lusby
2009 Canadian Champ

It's been said that you can't win by playing it safe. Will Lusby won a key playoff game, on his way to the 2009 Canadian Championship, because he traded safety for game-winning potential.

Lusby: "As much as I like the Railroads for their safe income, they are rather worthless unless you are diversified, meaning you also have a developed color group to knock out your opponents. Late in this game, I realized I could not hope for both. So when a cash-starved opponent came looking for a deal to bolster his income, I decided to trade away my two Railroads—giving him all four—in exchange for two Yellow properties, gaining me the Yellow color group. I developed it quickly. In short order, my two remaining opponents landed on my Yellows and I bankrupted them. I must admit, this game-winning deal was a challenge to complete, but I have this philosophy: bend but don't break, be polite, don't shake. I held firm and waited for my opponent to come around to my point of view."

Will Lusby applies his Monopoly savvy daily in his dealings with real-life "opponents" on the other side of his financial transactions.

Lusby: "My favorite negotiating tactic is the 'reverse the deal.' If I am in a dire situation relative to a prospective trading partner, or when we are both in dire situations, I say, 'Let's do the deal in reverse—you take everything I have and you give me everything you have, cash included.' If he or she will not, I then ask, 'Okay, how can you logically expect me to accept a trade when you wouldn't in my position?' If my opponent is rational and accepts this reasoning, we both give up what is fair."

Will's advice is a good tactic in real life—put the other person into your shoes. Often, he or she will see things much more sympathetically and you'll both come away with a sense of gain.

2

THE BOARD

AND WHERE YOU STAND

Keenly focus on the board. It becomes your world until the final toss of the dice. Distraction is your enemy.

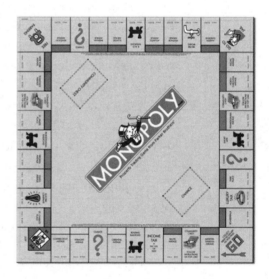

Why did I succeed? I viewed each decision like a move on a game board and I was determined to win.

—GEORGE S. PARKER, GAME ENTREPRENEUR

The Monopoly board is much like the path you follow month by month in your life. It has a beginning, a series of challenges and opportunities along the way (not all of which will come to fruition), events that are not entirely unexpected, a few surprises (good and bad), and periodically a payoff (a salary, if you're not sidetracked or unduly taxed).

In life, you can mark time and respond to what fate serves up, day by day, month by month, while awaiting the next paycheck (perhaps thinking, "I have to slog it out until I reach GO"). Or you can muster your resolve, gain some savvy, and make money work for you. Doing so successfully enlarges your payoff because you will earn *more* than a salary by investing wisely.

Much like the confines of real life, the board offers limited choices each round, according to where you land. Making the best within the limits is the most you can hope for. You might earn some extra money (Second Prize in a Beauty Contest: $10) or incur an unfortunate bill (Pay Hospital Fees: $100). You might delight an opponent by landing on her space and paying a rent (Illinois Avenue: $20) or have an opportunity to buy a space yourself (Marvin Gardens: $280), thereby putting some of your cash at risk in an investment capable of earning a whopping return. Our daily routine progresses much like a game of limited choices. We work, we play, we pay bills, we interact with others. On some days, we earn a reward for our efforts. And if we don't spend it all, we can answer the door when opportunity knocks (by investing the surplus).

People who successfully build wealth have realized that merely passing GO and earning a salary can pay for one's daily routine and keep the roof securely in place, but not much more. For most of us, a salary won't make us rich. We need to do more than just work for money. We must hold on to whatever we can and make it work for us. That's an important insight, don't you think?

As we advance around the Monopoly board, more and more of our money gets converted. With a reasonable amount of luck, our investments grow in value and suddenly we are no longer facing limited choices. We can think beyond the space landed on. Do you want to build houses and increase your potential return? Do you want to trade Marvin Gardens for Illinois and $100? Likewise, once you have real dollars working for you, your daily shuffle is no longer a limiter. Build an investment portfolio and manage it at your discretion. Thanks to modern communications technology, it doesn't matter where you may be within your daily routine or monthly schedule.

The odds of a particular event happening in daily life range from likely (going to work, eating lunch) to improbable (winning the lottery, enduring a flood). We anticipate the likely and, if we're capable and wise, prepare for the improbable.

Monopoly's range of outcomes is just as dramatic. Some are good, some not so good. Its board features a track precisely 40 spaces long. Twenty-eight of those spaces are properties, all owned by the bank at the game's start, but destined to be sold before too long. The other 12 spaces create events, like drawing a card, going to Jail, resting, paying taxes, and earning one's salary.

The game board teaches an important lesson. In life, not everything is equally likely to happen, and we must adjust to the odds, or be "adjusted" *by* them. Let's now examine the Monopoly board by first looking at it as it appears, and then as it might appear if it were adjusted for "reality."

Here's the actual game board. Each of its four corners is a square, while each of the 36 interior spaces is an identically sized rectangle. Such beautiful symmetry. You might think of it as a roulette wheel, where each space is equally likely to be landed upon, right?

Wrong. Let's look closer.

SECRET 1: The odds of landing on any space of the board are not equal. There are four reasons for this:
- Drawing cards that move tokens to certain spaces
- Going to jail
- Rolling doubles (especially three doubles in a row)
- The new Speed Die (explained in Chapter 6)

Remove these four game changers and the Monopoly board would be much the same as a roulette wheel, upon which (tampering aside) the bouncing white ball has an equal chance of landing in any one of its 38 slots (37 in Europe).

But contend with game changers we must. They happen in life. Every day offers something new and unexpected. A bold request from a friend, a nasty mistake on a bill (who relishes dealing with a robotic voice and multiple button presses on a phone?), rain when you need sunshine, a terrific sale on something you wanted to buy a month from now (get it now on credit?). Likewise, game-altering events happen suddenly in Monopoly. They make the game what it is: endlessly variable, eternally fresh, and continually suspenseful as you bounce from space to space.

Is there a way to better visualize this secret? Indeed. Let's look at the board if it were laid out to represent the frequency with which each space gets

The MONOPOLY game board
with each space resized
according to its likelihood
of being landed on.

landed upon (the higher the frequency, the wider the space, and vice versa). Note how the spaces stretch and contract.

The lovely symmetry was actually an illusion. Now, to make it even easier to visualize which spaces get landed on the most, and least, here's the Monopoly board scrambled again, this time with its spaces ordered from highest to lowest landing frequency.

The MONOPOLY game board with its spaces reordered from the most to the least landed upon.

This diagram makes it obvious which properties are better investments, because a property that gets landed on more often is more likely to collect rents. Right? (Given a choice, would you rather own Park Place or New York Avenue?)

Just as the pleasant symmetry of the Monopoly board belies the unequal likelihood of landing on any space, the supposed predictability of our daily routine is not perfectly symmetrical. Something always seems to shake it up. Benefiting or recovering from such a disruption adds a measure of satisfaction to life, even if the lesson is a harsh one.

Traveling around the Monopoly board teaches you that adversity not only lurks, it happens. The board is a vehicle that carries you from decision point to decision point. If you make the most of each choice encountered, you improve the odds of winning the game. And as you'll see in the pages to follow, learning how to make the best decisions really does separate the merely good from the truly great players.

You can be a great player. Read on.

Game Changer 2—
Risk vs. Reward vs. Reserve

Gary Peters
1987/91 US Champ

It's been said that no sooner do you put money away for a rainy day than it rains unexpectedly. Balancing a risk to earn a big reward with a reserve set aside for a rainy day was a firm goal for eventual 1987 United States Monopoly champion Gary Peters.

Peters: "After each of us traded and gained a color group, the race was on to build houses. I decided to purchase six houses, two for each for my Red properties. I was very aware of the need to hold on to some cash in case I had a bad roll and a 'rainy day' occurred. After all, tearing down houses inflicts extra pain—you only get half their value back from the bank. But when an opponent landed on Virginia Avenue, exactly seven spaces prior to my Kentucky Avenue, I realized I had to take a risk and give up my security, because 7 is the most likely roll. I used my cash to build a third house on Kentucky, playing the odds he'd roll a 7. He obliged me and couldn't pay the $700 rent. (He would have only owed $250 if I'd played it safe with two houses.) After taking over his holdings, I was in the driver's seat and rode my reward to victory."

+ $450!

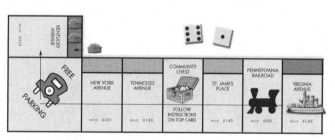

Peters: "Monopoly reveals the peril of taking money lightly. Every time you spend, ask yourself: 'Do I really need this?'"

3

THE RULES

WHY IT IS ESSENTIAL TO LEARN THEM

First, you need to learn the rules of the game. And then, to win, you have to use them and play better than anyone.

By the time the fool has learned the game, the players have dispersed.
—AFRICAN PROVERB

Rules can be a drag. You have to read them, digest what they mean, endure a scolding by an opponent when you misinterpret one, and otherwise learn to live within their confines. (Why can't I move backwards?) On the other hand, master them and you'll have a leg up on those who don't take the time to do likewise.

Life is bound by rules and regulations. The government creates most of these, but there are social conventions, requirements like paying bills on time, circumstances we hardly think about until we get in trouble by ignoring the rules (leave your windows open when it rains and your car's interior gets soaked), and of course the ever-present rule ("law") of unintended consequences (like the effect of encouraging subprime mortgages, which triggered events leading to the financial crisis and the enduring foreclosure mess). The point is, by mastering the rules of a game like Monopoly, you can better grasp the importance to improve your understanding of the rules and their consequence in everyday life. Fortune tends to favor those who know the way and prepare appropriately for the journey.

Let's start with some basics about Monopoly's rules. You begin with $1500. You might question the significance of this rather modest sum. Why not start with millions? Well, it's all relative. You can imagine your $1500 as being $1,500,000 if you like. But $1500 is simply more practical for game purposes. It makes for easier math during play, and it is closer in scale to the kind of cash we might handle during a week or month.

Once the dice begin to fly, your cash will be converted into investments. Spend it wisely. How do you do this? Well, imagine yourself as owning a business—a real estate investment business. You turn cash into properties, develop them, and earn rents. Now can you visualize your role in the game?

START YOUR OWN COMPANY

Greetings, real estate magnate! Proudly consider yourself to be a tycoon, a wheeler-dealer, a shrewd investor, a big spender—whichever expresses the inner you. You own a company, with $1500, represented by its icon: a shiny metal token. Every trip around the board earns you a further $200. Your cash will enable you to buy several properties, the cheapest of which, Mediterranean, costs $60, while the most expensive, Boardwalk, is listed at $400. An opponent landing on your property must pay you rent. Your rents will escalate if you collect like-colored sets of properties and add buildings to them. The value of your company can jump by leaps and bounds if you make good choices and have a bit of luck. Your goal is to *bankrupt* all opponents and gain all their cash. If you win a four-player game, you'll likely end up with $6000 or so. Six thousand dollars is four times the investment you began with. What investor wouldn't be delighted with a 400 percent return in the time it takes the clock to tick off an hour or so? When you play Monopoly, you want to earn a high return on your firm's investment capital, just as you would in real life. The alternative (a negative return) spells doom and eventual bankruptcy. Ouch! There's no middle ground.

Like any business, yours will have assets and eventually liabilities (debt). Your assets consist of *cash*, *deeds*, and *buildings* (little green houses and red hotels). Your liabilities will be *mortgages*. The difference between the sum of your assets and total liabilities is your *net worth*. As long as your net worth is positive, you are in the game. If your net worth goes "in the red" (turns negative), you go bankrupt! Goodbye. Your current net worth is, of course, $1500, because you have $1500 in cash (assets) and zero liabilities (no mortgages).

In real life, a business with plenty of assets and no debt is enviable. It possesses the means to invest and gain credit with the bank. It may use its credit to borrow money to invest in even more assets, hoping to earn even more money. It is good to have a stellar credit rating. As comedian Bob Hope once said, "A bank is a place that will lend you money [only] if you can prove that you don't need it." Can you take on too much credit, have too much debt? Absolutely, as millions heartbreakingly learned during the recent financial crisis. To amplify Hope's quip, it's also been said that a banker is a friend who eagerly loans you an umbrella for a fee, then asks for it back the moment it starts to rain. (Witness this decade's mortgage meltdown.) The bank in Monopoly operates according to a similar principle. The instant you can't repay a debt to it, it will seize your collateral. Yes, it is dangerous to have too much debt. The lesson taught by Monopoly is: incur debt at your own peril.

The only collateral the Monopoly bank will loan against is a property deed. When you decide you need to raise money, the bank will loan you one-half its value. You will gain this amount in cash and turn your property deed facedown to signify that it has become mortgaged. While you can hold on to this mortgage as long as you like, the property will cease earning income for you. And when you want to lift the mortgage, you must repay the bank the money borrowed plus a stiff 10 percent of the mortgage value (interest). In the remote event that you cannot pay a debt to the bank (for example, for a tax or a fee on a Chance card), the bank will call in its umbrella—it will take all your deeds—and immediately auction them off to the highest bidder. And you are forced to retire from the game.

The moral is: mortgage wisely to leverage your earning power or, if desperate, to stay alive in the game.

YOUR TOKEN

Before play begins, you select one of the charming metal tokens to represent your firm and place it on GO. "Charming" is an apt word. The metal charms we all know and love were inspired by charm bracelets. Your monetary empire will be represented throughout the game by the likes of a racecar, top hat, shoe, or thimble.

A recent survey among Monopoly players revealed fascinating differences in personality among those who favor each venerable token. This personality seems to carry over in real life. In Chapter 5, you'll see how you match up with the profile associated with your favorite token, and in Chapter 11 you'll learn how to make the best of your tendencies when dealmaking—around the board or in the real world.

Once every player has selected a token (dice rolls settle disputes), they are placed on GO. The order of play is determined by rolling both dice. The high roller goes first. (Should two or more players tie for high roll, they reroll until the tie is broken.)

The game's objective is to bankrupt every other opponent. You can't win if you don't achieve this goal. Think about this for a moment. Monopoly, like all games, has a clear aim. How about you? What's your real-life financial goal? Why not set one, so you can measure your progress and know when it's reached?

To win the Monopoly game, you need to play by the rules. We've established this. But what rules will you follow to make steady progress toward achieving your goal?

Here's the goal and rules I've established:

My goal: Have enough money saved upon retirement to maintain a comfortable standard of living without touching my nest egg.
Rule 1: Know, monthly, where I stand. Every month, total my assets and liabilities to gauge my net worth.
Rule 2: Avoid debt. Minimize or pay down any debt, especially high-interest debt.
Rule 3: Pay myself first. This means, after covering the cost of necessities, to save before spending money on things I don't really need.
Rule 4: Maintain a high credit score. Today, this is more important than ever.
Rule 5: Invest excess savings. Savings provide for potential emergencies and are readily available. Investments are aimed to grow in value and are not readily (or advisedly) converted into cash.
Rule 6: Diversify my investments. "Don't put all your eggs in one basket" is truer than ever.
Rule 7: Insure. Carry insurance, protect against loss—especially home, auto, and life.
Rule 8: Don't own more home than I can afford. Look forward to owning a bigger, nicer home when paying for it is not a burden.
Rule 9: Never take money for granted. Think clearly about money. Avoid the temptation to buy or invest on a whim. Do the homework; stay the course.
Rule 10: Have fun. When interim accomplishments are attained, enjoy a reward and celebrate the achievement.

The "game plan" I've lived by works well for me. How about you?

WHAT IS YOUR GOAL?
WHAT ARE YOUR RULES TO REACH IT?

Fill in the form that follows after thinking about your personal goal and financial rules. The process of writing it down helps to commit to it—like an oath solemnly written in your own hand. Do so even if you decide to adopt my plan. Writing it down will make it yours.

My goal:
Rule 1:
Rule 2:
Rule 3:
Rule 4:
Rule 5:
Rule 6:
Rule 7:
Rule 8:
Rule 9:
Rule 10:

Suggestion: don't file this away. Refer to it often until it becomes as essential to you as waking up and every other discipline you adhere to in your daily life.

Now let's get back to Monopoly. The city awaits.

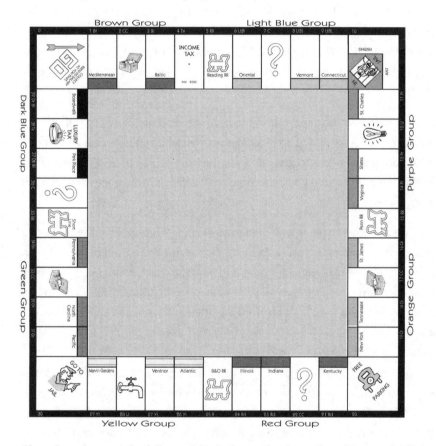

I've already waxed philosophical about the board and its symbolism, how it is pristine and balanced at the start. We can think of it as a small city about to be developed. Its 22 empty streets are nicely paved; 2 utilities are ready to service them. Its 4 railway lines are spiked and laid, awaiting the first trains to arrive.

But once the first player rolls the dice and moves his token, the scales sway. Each decision made, and luck, tips them back and forth. Risk is in the air; you sense it with every breath you take, you feel it in your stomach. So now is a good time to have a few words about risk, and to distinguish between *risk management*, *risk tolerance*, and *risk avoidance*.

Risk management is the art of making wise investments in the face of the inevitable uncertainty within a market. Just as a "sure thing" is usually an illusion in the real world, there are no surefire investments in Monopoly. But some investment decisions are clearly less risky than others. If you evaluate the risk/reward of an investment, you'll know if it makes sense over other alternatives. This applies to Monopoly, but it especially applies to real-world investments. Risk management is a principle by which you can make "the rules" work for you. Think about this.

Risk tolerance is the level of risk appropriate to your age and income needs. If you are young, your risk tolerance level should be much higher than when you are near retirement. There is time for your investments to grow and weather inevitable ups and downs. When you are at or close to your financial goal, you should have low risk tolerance as you'll want to preserve your net worth.

Risk avoidance, on the other hand, is a technique of avoiding a hazard by either engaging in an alternate activity or ending exposure to a specific risk. It can be used beneficially. An example is shifting one's investment from stocks and bonds to bank savings at retirement. But risk avoidance is often used as an excuse to disengage prematurely. This occurs in personal lives as well as in businesses. It stems from a tendency to avoid as much situational risk as possible. As noted, it can be wise to avoid risk, but usually "playing it safe" means giving up the chance to win the game.

Here are two examples. Bob has reached his retirement goal and is financially able to move to a lovely condo facing the Atlantic Ocean in Florida, his lifetime dream. However, as he's aged Bob has become increasingly aware of the threat of hurricane damage in Florida. He decides to avoid this risk and "play it safe" by staying in New York state and enduring the harsh winters he's yearned to escape from. Similarly, the We Make What You Need firm decides not to hire any more employees because of the aggravation of red tape and growing liability for employee benefits. The business avoids these burdens, but stops growing, and its competitors scoop up the sales it can't handle. Realistically, Bob would do better by moving and buying insurance for the potential hurricane loss, while the We Make What You Need firm should conduct a risk/reward analysis to see if the added employees will sufficiently augment sales and profits to justify the perceived drawbacks.

I've come to learn, through my many years in business, that the greatest risk is to take no risk at all. Risk avoidance has its place, but it's a small place in my estimation.

———

Risk management, risk tolerance, and risk avoidance come into play several times in the pages to follow. Stay tuned.

One more clarification. You may have noticed the term *systemic risk* frequently popping up in financial discourse. This kind of risk is out of your control; it is the danger of an entire market or financial system collapsing. (No need to recount the events of 2008, right?) *Nonsystemic risk* relates to the hazards of a specific investment. You protect yourself from nonsystemic risk through diversification.

Returning to Monopoly, let's examine the game's mechanics. Its procedure is straightforward. You roll; you land on a space; you deal with its impact. (It's especially exciting to land on an unowned property space and purchase its deed!) Your turn then ends unless you can and wish to initiate a special transaction. For example, you might want to offer an opponent a trade involving one or more properties, perhaps with some cash thrown in. You might decide to mortgage or unmortgage some of your properties. Even better, you might be able to convert some cash and build houses or hotels—to increase the income potential of a complete set of like-colored properties. Alas, if you landed on a big rent, you might be forced to tear down some of your precious buildings (*always* painful) to meet an opponent's rent bill.

Okay. The first game is finally ready to go. Take a seat. You'll be playing.

4

GAME ONE

FRIDAY NIGHT MONOPOLY

The first Monopoly game I played with my brothers,
I hated losing so much, I just had to beat them.
—DREW CAREY, ENTERTAINER

The players you're competing with in this game are friends. You know them better than I do, but I have heard you enjoy bankrupting each other whenever the mood strikes! I suspect a rousing game lies ahead.

Some of those watching may not know the rules; I'll explain them as we go. (For those who know how to play Monopoly, there are many key insights to absorb.)

Twenty-two secrets are revealed, essential to mastering the game. Their real-world parallels will be drawn and after the game its main financial lessons will be further illuminated.

Tokens are selected first. The Shoe, Top Hat, and Racecar are nabbed quickly by your friends, so you take the Scotty. Each player rolls the dice to see who will go first. The 11 rolled by the Shoe is the highest throw, so the Shoe will move first, followed by the Top Hat to his left, then the Racecar, and finally you, the Scotty. (Since I'm here as a happy observer, I volunteer to be the banker, but normally one of the players assumes this role and pulls double duty.)

Take a look at the game illustration shown here. The pulse of the game will be felt through this graphic, as it will be used to depict every key move in each game. You will see the dice rolls, the tokens moving from space to space, and the current finances of each player's firm. You'll instantly know what deeds are held in the bank and which ones each player has purchased. The title bar of each property's space is empty when the game begins, because all are unowned. Each will be filled in once its deed is purchased.

ROUND ONE—THE GAME BEGINS

The early rounds of the game constitute an *investment* phase, with players parting with cash and accumulating property deeds. This phase is akin to what you would do in real life after you've built up enough savings to begin investing and therefore accepting a higher risk/reward ratio (perhaps in mutual funds or real estate).

The Shoe begins. He picks up the dice and rolls them on the game board. They come up a 9, and he advances nine spaces (clockwise) to Connecticut Avenue—a Light Blue property. The Shoe purchases it for its printed value, $120. After he hands me his cash, which I deposit in the bank, I give him the deed for Connecticut and he places it face up before himself.

Note: the deed for each group's "premier" property is marked with an asterisk (*) in the illustrations. Connecticut is the premier property of the Light Blue group. It costs more and earns higher rents than its cousins Vermont and Oriental.

The Top Hat rolls a 7 and lands on Chance; she draws the top card from its deck. It advances her to Illinois Avenue. Basking in this good fortune, she purchases its deed for $240. *Chance cards usually advance you to another space, much like gaining a special opportunity in real life.*

The Racecar rolls a double (3,3), which moves him six spaces to Oriental Avenue—another Light Blue property. He purchases it for $100.

SECRET 2: Buy every property you land on, especially if another player owns a deed (or deeds) in this group. (There are only a few exceptions to this rule, as explained later.) Since the Shoe owns a Light Blue property—Connecticut—the Racecar knows he must be included in any trade discussion involving this color group.

It is good to gain influence in the game and it helps attract real-world opportunities. This can be daunting, especially when you are starting your career. You're on the bottom looking up. If you want to climb and improve your income, you need to be noticed. Yet the only influence you may have is your character and your smarts. Good superiors encourage development of subordinates because they know it takes some of the load

Game 1 Round 1

rolls: 🎲🎲
Shoe: 9
Top Hat: 7
Racecar: 6
(3,3), then 7
Scotty: 9

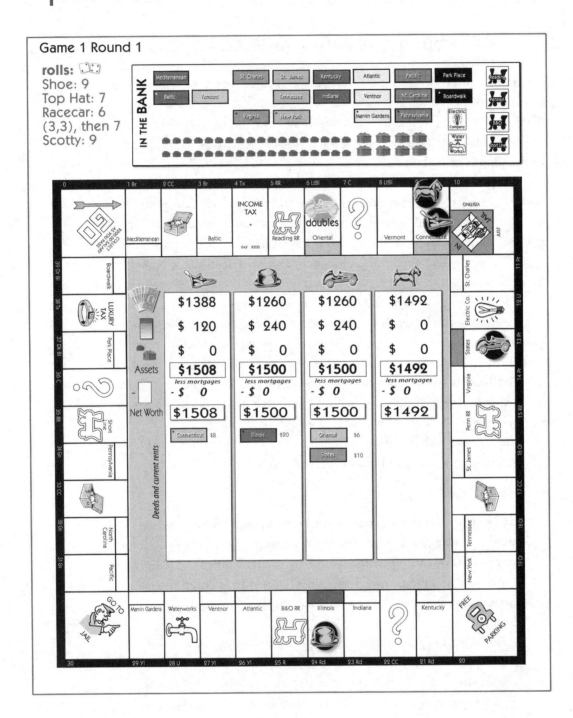

off their backs and improves their department's performance. (Hopefully you have a good boss.) Once you move up, you automatically gain influence because your position requires more people to go through you to get things done. Use this wisely, not to take advantage of others. You never know when someone in your orbit will alert you to an opportunity (a promotion, a great project, perhaps a job elsewhere) that can truly accelerate your career progress. More income equals more investment capital.

SECRET 3: **Don't risk an auction early in the game when bidding will most likely be irrational.** If the Racecar elected not to purchase Oriental Avenue, its deed would not languish in the bank. The rules require the banker (me) to auction it and sell it to the highest bidder. The Racecar could bid on it during the auction, but chances are its final price would go above $100, so why take the risk? (I suspect the Shoe would bid aggressively.)

In the real world, investors (and speculators) gradually lose objectivity when a market or stock seems to be rising without pause. An irrational urge to own it carries them away. Witness the amazing rise in the price of oil in the summer of 2011 when bids went from $80 a barrel to over $140. Predictions were rampant that it would keep going to $200. Instead, it reversed course and dropped to $60 and fortunes were washed away. Likewise, in the spring of 2012, it seemed everyone wanted to own Facebook's newly offered stock. It briefly touched $45 before bidding dried up and the price crashed to $18 per share.

The Racecar picks up the dice and rolls again, because doubles are rewarded with a free turn in Monopoly. The dice tumble to a halt, showing a 7—the most likely number to be thrown with two dice (we'll also talk about odds later). This throw advances the Racecar to States Avenue. He hands over cash and purchases this Purple property for $140. It costs more and has a higher potential return than a Light Blue property, so it is a somewhat more coveted investment.

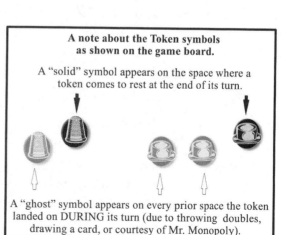

A note about the Token symbols as shown on the game board.

A "solid" symbol appears on the space where a token comes to rest at the end of its turn.

A "ghost" symbol appears on every prior space the token landed on DURING its turn (due to throwing doubles, drawing a card, or courtesy of Mr. Monopoly).

It's now your first turn. You let the dice fly, they come up 9, and you move your Scotty to Connecticut. The Shoe happily asks you for rent in the amount of $8. Sorry, but there's an increased likelihood of landing on an owned property if you go last in a four-player game. Typically, two or three properties will have been purchased before the fourth player rolls the dice for the first time. (Luck tends to balance this disadvantage later on, thanks to doubles and messages found on several cards.)

ROUND TWO

The second round begins with the Shoe rolling a 5,1 and advancing six spaces to the Pennsylvania Railroad. Without a moment's hesitation, the Shoe pays $200 for its valuable deed. The Railroads are high-yield investments, especially if you own several. The rent for one is a mere $25, but if you own two Railroads, this doubles to $50. Acquire three and you make a cool $100 whenever one of them receives a visitor. Own all four and you'll rake in $200 for each hit. That's as much as for passing GO! Further, the Railroads are landed on more often than any other group. That's because there are more of them (four) and several cards direct players to move to a Railroad.

> **SECRET 4:** **Owning the Railroads is like owning a cash machine.**
> You want them for the cash they produce. While you cannot win the game without developing a color group, the Railroads may provide the funds needed to build up your group.
>
> *The Railroads are akin to bonds or high-yield CDs in real life. In "normal" economic times, their yields pay much more than bank savings. Given the miracle of compound interest over time, you'll multiply your principal.*

The Top Hat rolls 6,4 and advances 10 spaces to Pennsylvania Avenue ("Big Green"). Many players associate the Greens with riches because of their alluring color and because, when developed, their rents are huge. But the Top Hat is a savvy player and she is aware of the trap posed by investing in the Greens. Namely, a small fortune ($2720) is required to acquire and develop them to the three-house level (a key benchmark, as you'll learn). Considering that each player only begins with $1500, it will take $1250 in

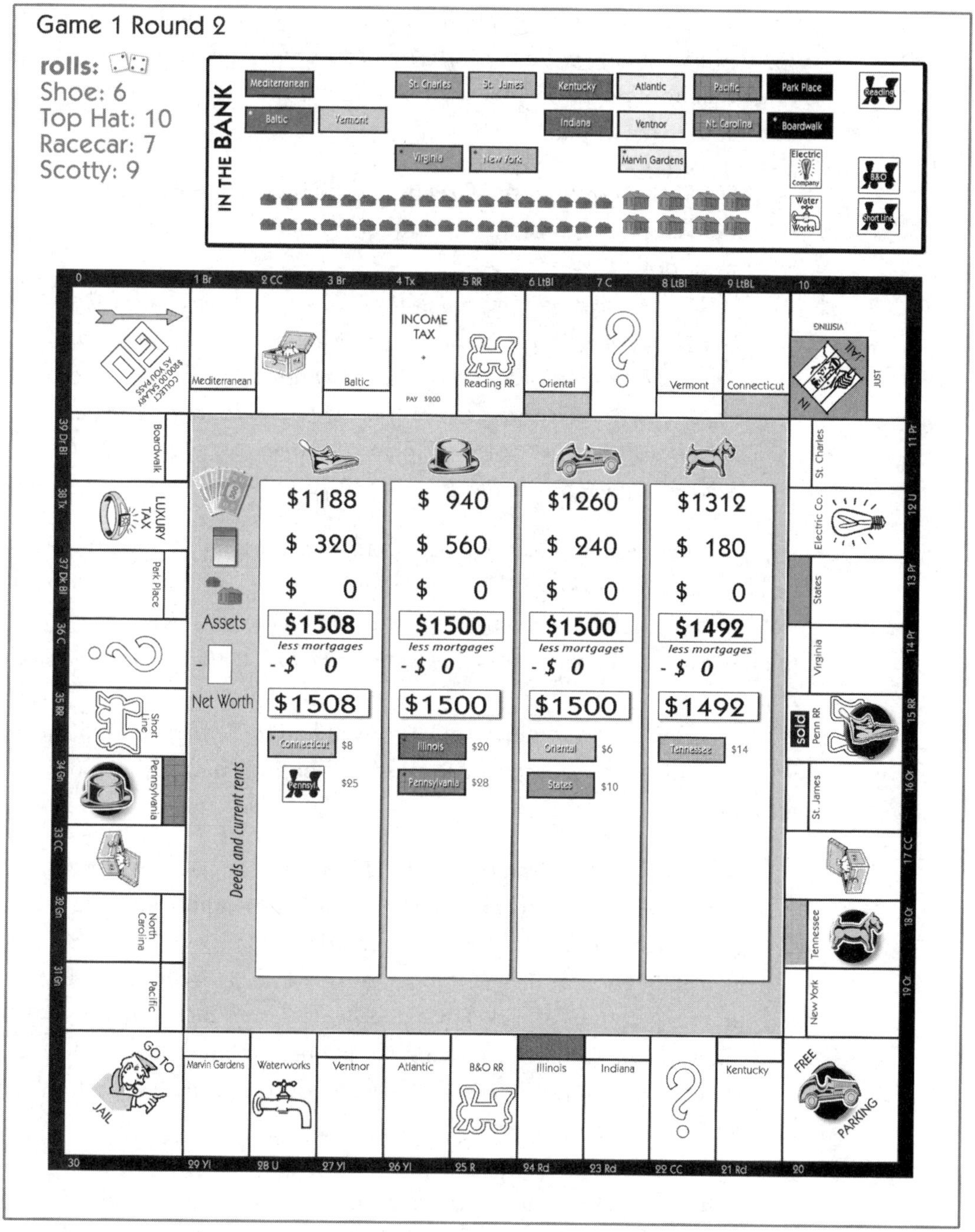

Game 1 Round 2

rolls:
Shoe: 6
Top Hat: 10
Racecar: 7
Scotty: 9

IN THE BANK

Deeds and current rents	Shoe	Top Hat	Racecar	Scotty
	$1188	$ 940	$1260	$1312
	$ 320	$ 560	$ 240	$ 180
Assets	$ 0	$ 0	$ 0	$ 0
	$1508	**$1500**	**$1500**	**$1492**
	less mortgages	*less mortgages*	*less mortgages*	*less mortgages*
−	− $ 0	− $ 0	− $ 0	− $ 0
Net Worth	**$1508**	**$1500**	**$1500**	**$1492**

Shoe: Connecticut $8, Pennsyl. $25
Top Hat: Illinois $20, Pennsylvania $28
Racecar: Oriental $6, States $10
Scotty: Tennessee $14

profits to fully finance such a building project. Nonetheless, the Top Hat buys Pennsylvania Avenue because she has a good supply of cash and she knows that another player may end up owning the other two Greens and will want to make a deal.

> **SECRET 5:** **Caution: the Greens are the most expensive group to develop.** Circumstance will determine if they are worth the risk or not.
>
> *You need to decide for yourself if you first want to own established "blue chips" in your real investment portfolio, or potential blue chips, often available at a lower price. Do your homework. Well-known, large companies with a consistent record of rising profits are iconic blue-chip stocks—companies like Google, Amazon, and Merck, as opposed to "hot" but unproven companies, like Zynga and Zipcar.*

The Racecar rolls a 7 and advances to Free Parking. While Free Parking is the setting for the game's most popular house rule (see Chapter 14), nothing happens here when playing by the official rules. It is a space to rest, much like any quiet place. *Use the opportunity to study the board and think about what lies ahead.*

You throw a 6,4 and move your Scotty ahead to Tennessee. This property is one of the treasured Oranges, so you happily part with $180 to acquire its deed.

> **SECRET 6:** **The Oranges get landed on more than any other color group.** Why? Because players go to Jail steadily during the game, and whenever a player is released from Jail his token must pass through or over the Orange group. Certain dice rolls occur more often than others. For example, 6, 7, and 8 are the most likely throws. Voilà. Six spaces from Jail lies St. James Place (Orange property), while eight spaces removed is Tennessee (the second Orange property).
>
> *The Oranges are like a great stock that pays a good quarterly dividend and grows steadily in value to boot. Prosperous companies like PepsiCo, Kellogg, Altria, General Mills, and Clorox are known for their higher dividend yields. Publicly traded funds like Duff and Phelps Select Income Fund usually offer high dividends in return for higher risk.*

Tip: learn the odds of throwing any number from 2 through 12. This will help you determine the likelihood of landing on each space in front of you. Here are the basics. Rolling a specific double, like 1,1, equals one chance out of 36 rolls. A 3 or an 11 equals two out of 36. A 4 or a 10 equals three out of 36. A 5 or a 9 equals four out of 36. A 6 or an 8 equals five out of 36. A 7 equals six out of 36. (This means, on average, that you will throw a 7 every sixth roll.) *The lesson: some events are more likely to occur than others.*

ROUND THREE

The Shoe rolls another 7 and lands on Chance. The card drawn advances his token all the way to St. Charles Place. Quite a move! Instinctively, the Shoe buys St. Charles for its modest $140 price. In the course of advancing to St. Charles, the Shoe passed the GO corner. Whenever a player completes a passage around the board and either lands on or passes over GO the bank rewards this player with a $200 salary. So in a sense, the Shoe purchased St. Charles for free and got another $60 in cash! (That is, $200 for passing GO minus $140 for purchasing St. Charles equals $60 net cash.)

The Top Hat's roll of 8 advances her beyond GO as well. She lands on Community Chest, whose card requires a payment of $50 to the bank. Deducting $50 from her $200 salary, I pay the Top Hat $150 in cash. There are 16 cards each in the Chance and Community Chest decks. Some are beneficial, some are costly, and a few are neutral, according to the circumstance.

> **SECRET 7:** **Nine Community Chest and only two Chance cards pay you money. Nine Chance and only one Community Chest move you to another space.** Since there are 16 cards per deck, there is a 56 percent likelihood of collecting money in the Community Chest deck (9 out of 16), and the Chance deck is equally likely to move you elsewhere (these cards are featured in Chapter 10).
>
> *The lesson: position yourself for improved return on your existing investments while keeping your eyes open for a "big move" opportunity. What does this mean? Deciding which investments you'd liquidate in the event something more promising lands in your lap. It's a smart idea to pick your sell candidates well before you need to sell. This discipline prevents impulsive, last-minute decision making. Perhaps a sudden drop in*

Game 1 Round 3

rolls:

Shoe: 7
Chance: to St. Charles

Top Hat: 8
CC: -$50

Racecar: 3

Scotty: 4
Chance: back 3

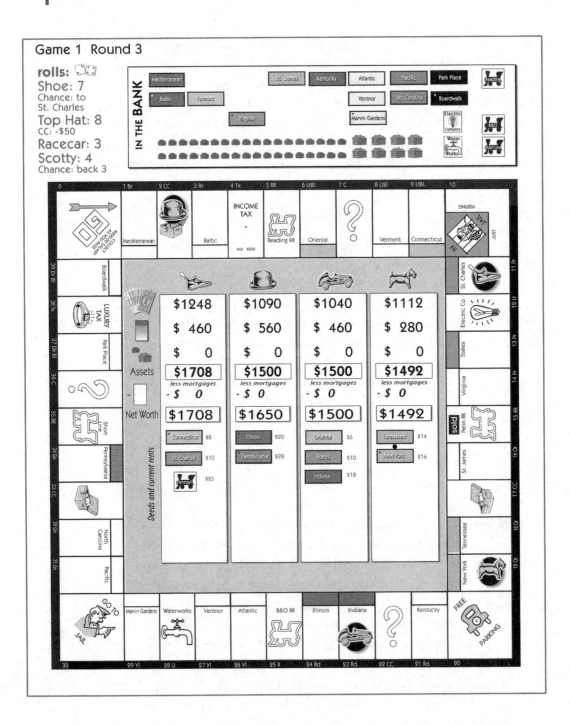

a certain stock's price brings about the golden opportunity because some short-term event spooked investors. For example, let's say a Chinese factory had a fire and Apple couldn't get enough mobile devices for a month; its stock might take a nasty hit and drop many points. Since you've noticed the resiliency in the price of Apple stock, you know the stock typically recovers from such a jolt. Perhaps you can't pass up this chance to buy.

The Racecar rolls a puny 3, but this lands him on Indiana, the first Red property to be touched. Since the Red group is one of the best to acquire, the Racecar invests $220 to own Indiana.

SECRET 8: **The Reds are landed on almost as frequently as the Oranges. The Yellows are not landed on as much, but are still solid investments.** Illinois Avenue, the premium Red property, is the most landed-on property on the board (due to a combination of its location in front of Jail on the path and a Chance card that advances a player to its space). There is another reason why the Oranges and Reds are desired color groups. They are cost-efficient. That means they can be developed to the three-house level within most budgets. For example, the Oranges require an investment of $1460 to do so, while the Reds require $2030. (While $2030 is much more than $1460, so are the rents on the Reds compared to the Oranges.)

Ask yourself: would I rather invest $100 per month in a mutual fund, or wait five years, accumulate $6000, and then buy 100 shares of a $60 stock? (If you invest in the fund, you'll have money working for you after week one!)

You roll a 4 and land on Chance. You'll recall that nine Chance cards move you to another space. One of these ("Advance to St. Charles") has already been drawn. The one you now draw compels you to move your Scotty back three spaces. This is a reason for cheer. Three spaces behind this Chance space is New York Avenue, the premium Orange property. You are already the owner of neighboring Tennessee, so you gladly buy New York for $200. In two rounds' time, you have recovered from your bad luck of paying a rent on Connecticut and have a commanding ownership in the board's most desired group! *You endured a small adversity and came out ahead.*

The New Speed Die

The newest enhancement to the Monopoly Game is the Speed Die. A player rolls it, along with the white dice, on every throw *after* completing one circuit of the board. And it *does* speed up play.

Here's what each of its six sides look like. Three sides de-

pict ordinary numbers (1, 2 and 3), while two sides have a picture of Mr. Monopoly; the final side depicts a Bus. You'll see all its possibilities revealed during the next few turns. (Chapter 6 has a lot more to say about the Speed Die.)

What Else Is New?

Luxury Tax now requires a payment of $100, Income Tax is fixed at $200 (rather than $200 or 10 percent of net worth), and the first color group has changed to Brown, from Dark Purple. A few cards have altered messages. Otherwise the game is unchanged.

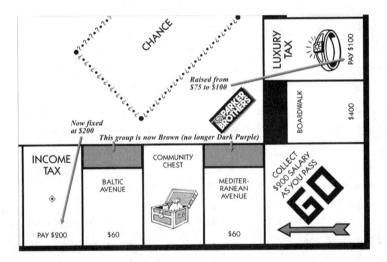

In the real world taxes always seem to rise, so Monopoly seems to be keeping pace. Many players lament the removal of the "10 percent of assets" alternate calculation for Income Tax, but thanks to Congress many of us are hit with the Alternative Minimum Tax each year. Its intention was originally only to make sure that the very wealthy could not avoid paying any tax. (Talk about an unintended consequence.)

The charts shown here are for your reference. You might want to check out these financial facts as you follow the game in progress.

Tip: any investment you consider should be evaluated on as many financial facts as you can gather to determine whether it has merit. Examples are the firm's balance sheet (what is its net worth per share?), the amount of debt it owes, its profit per share, its sales, and its earnings projections going forward.

MONOPOLY PROPERTY INVESTMENT COSTS

-Group-	Property	Price	Mortgage	each House	Hotel 4 Houses +	Resell to bank per building
Brown	Mediterranean	$ 60	$ 30	$ 50	$ 50	$ 25
	Baltic	$ 60	$ 30	$ 50	$ 50	$ 25
Light Blue	Oriental	$ 100	$ 50	$ 50	$ 50	$ 25
	Vermont	$ 100	$ 50	$ 50	$ 50	$ 25
	Connecticut	$ 120	$ 60	$ 50	$ 50	$ 25
Purple	St. Charles Pl.	$ 140	$ 70	$ 100	$ 100	$ 50
	States	$ 140	$ 70	$ 100	$ 100	$ 50
	Virginia	$ 160	$ 80	$ 100	$ 100	$ 50
Orange	St. James	$ 180	$ 90	$ 100	$ 100	$ 50
	Tennessee	$ 180	$ 90	$ 100	$ 100	$ 50
	New York	$ 200	$ 100	$ 100	$ 100	$ 50
Red	Kentucky	$ 220	$ 110	$ 150	$ 150	$ 75
	Indiana	$ 220	$ 110	$ 150	$ 150	$ 75
	Illinois	$ 240	$ 120	$ 150	$ 150	$ 75
Yellow	Atlantic	$ 260	$ 130	$ 150	$ 150	$ 75
	Ventnor	$ 260	$ 130	$ 150	$ 150	$ 75
	Marvin Garder	$ 280	$ 130	$ 150	$ 150	$ 75
Green	Pacific	$ 300	$ 150	$ 200	$ 200	$ 100
	North Carolina	$ 300	$ 150	$ 200	$ 200	$ 100
	Pennsylvania	$ 320	$ 160	$ 200	$ 200	$ 100
Dark Blue	Park Place	$ 350	$ 175	$ 200	$ 200	$ 100
	Boardwalk	$ 400	$ 200	$ 200	$ 200	$ 100
Railroads						
	Reading	$ 200	$ 100	-	-	-
	Pennsylvania	$ 200	$ 100	-	-	-
	B&O	$ 200	$ 100	-	-	-
	Short Line	$ 200	$ 100	-	-	-
Utilities						
	Electric Co.	$ 150	$ 75			-
	Waterworks	$ 150	$ 75			-
	total	$ 5,690				

MONOPOLY PROPERTY RENTS

-Group-	Property	basic rent	doubled	1 house	2 houses	3 houses	4 houses	hotel
Brown	Mediterranean	$ 2	$ 4	$ 10	$ 30	$ 90	$ 190	$ 320
	Baltic	$ 4	$ 8	$ 20	$ 60	$ 180	$ 320	$ 450
Light Blue	Oriental	$ 6	$ 12	$ 30	$ 90	$ 270	$ 400	$ 550
	Vermont	$ 6	$ 12	$ 30	$ 90	$ 270	$ 400	$ 550
	Connecticut	$ 8	$ 16	$ 40	$ 100	$ 300	$ 450	$ 600
Purple	St. Charles Pl.	$ 10	$ 20	$ 50	$ 150	$ 450	$ 625	$ 750
	States	$ 10	$ 20	$ 50	$ 150	$ 450	$ 625	$ 750
	Virginia	$ 12	$ 24	$ 60	$ 180	$ 500	$ 700	$ 900
Orange	St. James	$ 14	$ 28	$ 70	$ 200	$ 550	$ 750	$ 950
	Tennessee	$ 14	$ 28	$ 70	$ 200	$ 550	$ 750	$ 950
	New York	$ 16	$ 32	$ 80	$ 220	$ 400	$ 800	$ 1,000
Red	Kentucky	$ 18	$ 36	$ 90	$ 250	$ 700	$ 875	$ 1,050
	Indiana	$ 18	$ 36	$ 90	$ 250	$ 700	$ 875	$ 1,050
	Illinois	$ 20	$ 40	$ 100	$ 300	$ 750	$ 925	$ 1,100
Yellow	Atlantic	$ 22	$ 44	$ 110	$ 330	$ 800	$ 975	$ 1,150
	Ventnor	$ 22	$ 44	$ 110	$ 330	$ 800	$ 975	$ 1,150
	Marvin Gardens	$ 24	$ 48	$ 120	$ 360	$ 850	$ 1,025	$ 1,200
Green	Pacific	$ 26	$ 52	$ 130	$ 390	$ 600	$ 1,100	$ 1,275
	North Carolina	$ 26	$ 52	$ 130	$ 390	$ 600	$ 1,100	$ 1,275
	Pennsylvania	$ 28	$ 56	$ 150	$ 450	$ 1,000	$ 1,200	$ 1,400
Dark Blue	Park Place	$ 35	$ 70	$ 175	$ 300	$ 1,100	$ 1,300	$ 1,500
	Boardwalk	$ 50	$ 100	$ 200	$ 600	$ 1,400	$ 1,700	$ 2,000

Railroads		1 owned	2 owned	3 owned	4 owned
	Reading	$ 25	$ 50	$ 100	$ 200
	Pennsylvania	"	"	"	"
	B&O				
	Short Line				

Utilities		1 owned	both owned
	Electric Co.	$4 x roll	$10 x roll
	Waterworks	"	"

ROUND FOUR

The Shoe, having passed GO, qualifies to include the Speed Die in all future throws. He picks up all three dice and gives them a shake. They turn up 3 and 3 on the white dice along with a 2 on the Speed Die. This means the Shoe will advance a total of eight spaces (all three dice being added together if the Speed Die shows a number). This roll carries the Shoe to New York Avenue, where you politely ask for $16 in rent, thank you. Since the white dice comprise a double (3,3), the Shoe has also earned a free throw. Doubles are only based on the white dice (meaning that any number showing on the Speed Die is ignored when determining if doubles have been thrown).

The Shoe rolls again, and miraculously throws the same result (3,3 plus a 2 on the Speed Die). He again moves ahead eight spaces, landing now on Ventnor Avenue. The Yellows, being a good group to own, cause him to exchange $260 for Ventnor's deed. Once again the Shoe picks up the dice and rolls 1,1 and a Bus. *Uh-oh.* Doubles again! Whenever doubles are thrown *three times in succession*, the rolling player forfeits the third roll in its entirety and moves back to Jail. (I'll explain the Bus later. Meanwhile, pardon me while I admit the Shoe to his cell and lock the door.) *Clang!*

The Top Hat rolls a 6 (3,2+1) and advances to Vermont, which she purchases. All three Light Blues are now owned, evenly split between three players.

The Racecar rolls a 5 (3,1+1) and lands on Waterworks. There are two Utility spaces on the board, and this one is now up and running in the time it takes him to hand over $150. Is it worth it? Should the Racecar have invested a full 10 percent of his initial cash in this solitary utility property?

SECRET 9: Owning both Utilities is a so-so investment. Why is the Utility monopoly a so-so bet? It's because they don't get landed on much (there being only two of them). True, owning both Utilities compels another player to pay you 10 times the amount of his throw if he lands on one. (The average you can expect is 7 times 10, or $70.) Owning one Utility is not a good investment because you only earn four times the throw of the un-

Game 1 Round 4

rolls:
Shoe: 3,3+2,
3,3+2,1,1=Jail!
Top Hat: 5+1
Racecar: 5
Scotty: 7

IN THE **BANK**

Mediterranean St. James Kentucky Pacific Park Place Reading

Baltic Nt. Carolina Boardwalk

Virginia Marvin Gardens Electric Company B&O

Short Line

$ 972	$ 990	$ 890	$ 868
$ 720	$ 660	$ 610	$ 640
$ 0	$ 0	$ 0	$ 0
$1692	**$1650**	**$1500**	**$1508**
less mortgages	less mortgages	less mortgages	less mortgages
- $ 0	- $ 0	- $ 0	- $ 0
$1692	**$1650**	**$1500**	**$1508**

Assets

Net Worth

Deeds and current rents

Connecticut $8	Vermont $6	Oriental $6	Tennessee $14
St. Charles $10	Illinois $20	States $10	New York $16
Pennsy. $25	Pennsylvania $28	Indiana $18	Atlantic $22
Ventnor $22		Water Works 4x roll	

Board squares (outer ring):

0 | 1 Br Mediterranean | 2 CC | 3 Br Baltic | 4 Tx INCOME TAX PAY $200 | 5 RR Reading RR | 6 LtBl Oriental | 7 C | 8 LtBl Vermont | 9 LtBl Connecticut | 10 JUST VISITING / IN JAIL

39 Dr Bl Boardwalk
38 Tx LUXURY TAX
37 Dk Bl Park Place
36 C
35 RR Short Line
34 Grn Pennsylvania
33 CC
32 Grn North Carolina
31 Grn Pacific
30 GO TO JAIL

11 Pr St. Charles
12 U Electric Co.
13 Pr States
14 Pr Virginia
15 RR Penn RR sold
16 Or St. James
17 CC
18 Or Tennessee
19 Or New York doubles
20 FREE PARKING

29 Yl Marvin Gardens to Jail | 28 U Waterworks sold | 27 Yl Ventnor doubles | 26 Yl Atlantic | 25 R B&O RR | 24 Rd Illinois | 23 Rd Indiana | 22 CC | 21 Rd Kentucky | 20

lucky opponent. But you need to own one before you can own two, and you just might land on the other. Or you might gain the second in a future trade. (The Utilities are often fodder thrown in to make a bigger trade happen.)

The game's Utilities are akin to very safe, boring, and low-return bank savings. You need savings, for sure. But you might be able to find safety with a better return. Examples are a three-year CD at your bank with a rate bump for current account holders, or an annuity, or a government bond selling at less than par (that is, if you hold it to maturity, you are guaranteed to be paid par value). Ironically, one of the higher-yielding classes of stocks is real utilities, including utility mutual funds. But like any stock, their value fluctuates in line with economic events.

You throw a 7, advance to Atlantic Avenue, and buy it for $260. Round over.

ROUND FIVE

The Shoe pays $50 to get out of Jail. There is a well-accepted maxim in Monopoly: always pay to get out of Jail if deeds remain in the bank. *(You can't land on their spaces if stuck in Jail; likewise, if you sit on the sidelines in real life many desirable investment opportunities will pass you by. That's known as **opportunity cost**—the difference in return between two choices. For example, you leave your investment money in the bank and earn 1 percent versus buying a government bond paying 3 percent. The opportunity cost here is 2 percent. Alternately, you hesitate and don't compete for that new job opening. Here, the opportunity cost could be far-reaching, perhaps years of delayed career progress.)* The Shoe needs to be moving around the board to get his fair share of the 14 left unowned. If it were later in the game, when only rents awaited the Shoe on the path, he would stay in Jail for three turns (hoping not to roll doubles beforehand). Having paid his fee, the Shoe slides to Just Visiting and rolls a 6 (3,2+1). This throw advances him to St. James—the only Orange property whose deed remains in the bank. Eagerly, the Shoe parts with $180. His purchase blocks you from completing the Orange group on your own. You're going to have to deal with the Shoe to own them all.

The Top Hat rolls a 5 (3,2) on the white dice and Mr. Monopoly. Here's what happens when Mr. M is rolled. First, the Top Hat moves according to the white dice. She taps out five spaces and lands on States Avenue. The Racecar asks for and collects $10 rent. Now Mr. Monopoly provides a free move, and it's a good one. The Top Hat is obliged to move ahead to the next *unowned* property. Looking at the bank, the Top Hat sees that the next unowned deed belongs to Kentucky. So she hops her token over to Kentucky. Will she buy it or put it up for auction? Since she already owns a Red property (Illinois), there's no hesitation. She buys Kentucky for $220. This move shows how Mr. Monopoly works on the Speed Die while the game is young—he sees to it that all properties get sold without undue delay.

- **Mr. Monopoly always advances a player to the next unowned property,** provided there is at least one deed remaining in the bank. So what happens, you ask, after all properties are owned and the bank is out of deeds?

- **Thereafter, Mr. Monopoly advances a player to the next *rent* he must pay.** Uh-oh! (We'll see this happen in a few more moves.)

The Racecar rolls a 9 (5,2+2) and moves forward to Park Place, which he purchases for $350. This is the land of the rich, right? The Dark Blue properties (Park Place and Boardwalk) bear the highest rents in the game, and even their basic rents are meaningful—$35 for Park Place, $50 for Boardwalk. (Compare these with the lowly $2 for Mediterranean and $4 for Baltic Avenue.) A hotel on Park Place earns a staggering $1500—the equivalent of your starting cash! So the Dark Blues must be great investments, right? Perhaps not.

SECRET 10: **The Dark Blue properties are more intimidating than rewarding.** The mere sight of houses rising on Park Place and Boardwalk will rattle opponents and distract them with worry. After all, the potential financial pain of landing on one can be fatal. But their bark is often worse than their bite. There are only two of them, so the group is less likely to get landed on than three-property groups (even after allowing for the Chance card that advances a player to Boardwalk). So should a player buy a Dark Blue when opportunity knocks? Yes, because it's not

Game 1 Round 5

rolls:
Shoe pays$50:6
Top Hat: 5+
Racecar: 9
Scotty: 8

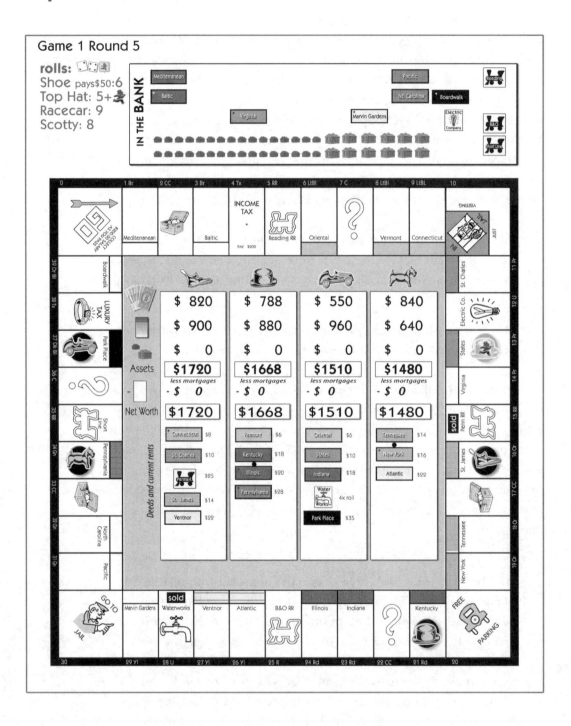

	Shoe	Top Hat	Racecar	Scotty
	$ 820	$ 788	$ 550	$ 840
	$ 900	$ 880	$ 960	$ 640
	$ 0	$ 0	$ 0	$ 0
Assets	**$1720**	**$1668**	**$1510**	**$1480**
	less mortgages	*less mortgages*	*less mortgages*	*less mortgages*
	- $ 0	- $ 0	- $ 0	- $ 0
Net Worth	**$1720**	**$1668**	**$1510**	**$1480**

Deeds and current rents

Shoe		Top Hat		Racecar		Scotty	
Connecticut	$8	Vermont	$6	Oriental	$6	Tennessee	$14
St. Charles	$10	Kentucky	$18	States	$10	New York	$16
Pennsyl.	$25	Illinois	$20	Indiana	$18	Atlantic	$22
St. James	$14	Pennsylvania	$28	Water Works	4x roll		
Ventnor	$22			Park Place	$35		

wise to allow it to go to auction, especially at this point in the game.

Investment choices in real life can also be a mixed bag. If financial markets are in retreat, buying the best blue-chip stock will likely lose you money for a while. But if you are patient, it should gain in the longer term. Likewise, if the market sells off suddenly, short-term gains can be made if it snaps back. But beware of trying to time the end of a downtrend. A snapback is a quick chance to gain, but if the trend remains down it is foolish not to sell quickly. Sometimes, the best you can hope for is preservation of capital, not sustained gains.

You roll an 8 (6,1+1) and land on Pennsylvania, paying the Top Hat a handsome $28 rent.

Eleven out of the game's 28 properties remain in the bank. Mr. Monopoly will inevitably cause all to be purchased in the next few turns. How they divide will significantly influence the fate of each player. On to round six.

ROUND SIX

The Shoe rolls a 9 (4,3+2) and advances to the B&O Railroad, which he buys. He now owns two of the game's four railroads and will collect $50 each time one is landed on. Given that he's paid $400 to own both, each rent will earn him a 12½ percent ROI (return on investment). (If he can acquire a third railroad, he will rake in $100 in rent each time one is visited.)

The Top Hat rolls a 7 (5,1+1) and pays a rent on Waterworks to the Racecar. Note how this is calculated. The owner of a single utility is entitled to collect four times the amount of the throw that landed his opponent on its space. Four times seven is 28, so the Top Hat forks over $28 to the Racecar, after calculating this in his head, saying, "Show me the money." But what if the Racecar forgets to ask for his rent?

SECRET 11: You do not have to pay a rent if your opponent fails to ask for it in time. What's this? Yes, you are never obliged to pay a rent; your opponent must *ask* for it. How much time does he or she have before the rent is excused for tardiness? The answer is: two player turns.

Game 1 Round 6

rolls:
Shoe: 7+2
Top Hat: 6+1
Racecar: 6+🏃
Scotty: 5+2

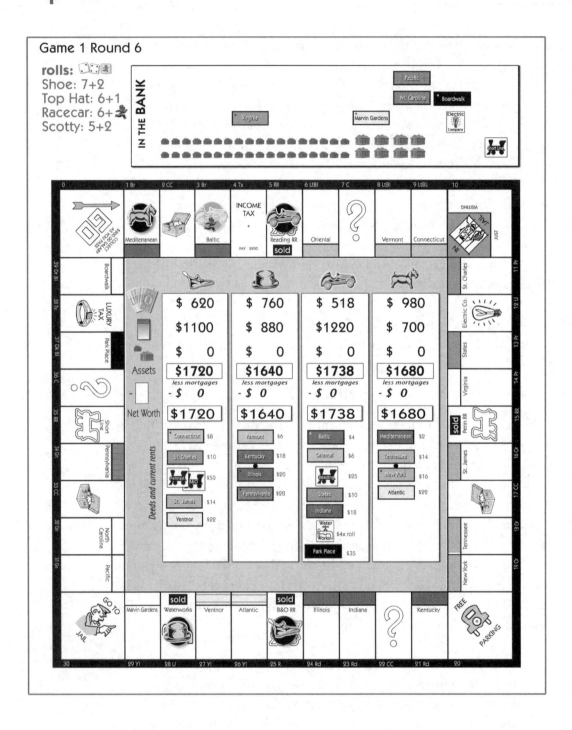

Here's an example. The Top Hat lands on Waterworks, but its owner, the Racecar, is busy talking to you and doesn't notice this. The Top Hat's lips are sealed as she hands the dice to the Racecar, who rolls and moves. The Racecar then hands the dice to you, and you shake and let them fly. The moment the dice leave the hands of the "second player following" (in this example, you), the rent is void. Perhaps the Racecar wakes up and yells, as the dice hit the board, "Hey, Top Hat, where's my rent? You owe me . . . twenty-eight dollars." Sorry, Racecar. You're too late; you weren't paying attention. If the Racecar had asked for his rent up until the time the second player following was shaking the dice in hand, he would be entitled to collect his rent. But not after they leave this player's hands.

Note: it is unsportsmanlike to alert a player that he or she is due a rent. (In tournament play, this action can be penalized by forcing the player who does so to pay the rent instead!)

What's the real-life equivalent to "missing a rent"? Vigilance. Always be watchful that you are billed correctly. For example, you can get hit with a charge on a credit card bill that you didn't authorize or didn't realize was a repeating charge. If your credit card bill is automatically paid from your bank account, you might not be taking the time to inspect its accuracy month by month.

The Racecar, having collected his $28, rolls a 6 on the white dice and Mr. Monopoly on the Speed Die. He lands on Baltic, passing GO in the process, collects $200, and buys Baltic Avenue for $60. Now, thanks to Mr. Monopoly, he advances to the next unowned property (Reading Railroad). He gladly purchases this railroad for $200.

You roll a total of 7 and advance to Mediterranean Avenue. You collect $200 for passing GO and invest $60 of this into the purchase of "the Med."

Four color groups are now owned among the players. This is enough for trade talk to heat up. But the Shoe cannot convince the Top Hat and Racecar to part with Vermont and Oriental, to give him the Light Blue group. And the Top Hat can't pry Indiana away from the Racecar (the Reds would be great to own right now). Likewise, you would love to get St. James away from the Shoe to complete your Orange group—but no dice. There is good reason to hold tight; seven properties still remain in the bank.

SECRET 12: **The Light Blues and Purples are good early investments, provided that the more powerful groups are split or**

underdeveloped (possessing no more than two houses each). Game Three is testament to their worth, as you'll see.

Significantly, there's a time when your nest egg will need easy-to-purchase small investments, like a few shares in a mutual fund, and a time when—given the amount of capital you have to invest—you will need to consider private offerings, like expensive units of a real estate investment trust (REIT).

ROUND SEVEN

The Shoe rolls the Bus on the Speed Die, the first player to do so (his complete throw being 4,2+Bus). The Bus provides a welcome choice in the game. The Shoe has earned the privilege of moving either of the white dice, or their total. After studying the board, he realizes that a 2 will advance him to Yellow Ventnor Avenue, which he already owns, while a 4 will advance him to its unpurchased mate, Marvin Gardens. The total of both dice is 6, and six spaces ahead lies Pacific Avenue. The Top Hat owns the only Green property in play, so purchasing Pacific will block her potential formation of the Green color group. Defensive moves are often wise. But the Shoe decides his best decision is to play offense, so he moves four spaces and purchases Marvin Gardens for $280. Marvin is the premium Yellow property, and the Shoe now owns two of the three Yellows. The Yellows are a good group, located on the "right" side of the Go to Jail corner (they get landed on more often than the Greens on the other side).

The Top Hat rolls an 8 and advances from Waterworks to Chance. Here she draws a Get Out of Jail Free card to hold for future use.

The Racecar rolls a 7; the Electric Company calls him over. If he buys it, he will own the utility monopoly outright; $150 secures its deed. The Racecar will now collect 10 times the roll of an opponent landing on either of his utility spaces. Consider that the average roll with the Speed Die is an 8. This means, on average, that the owner of the Utility monopoly will collect $80. Since the investment to acquire both is $300, that's a more than 25 percent ROI with every hit. The owner of both Utilities typically recovers his investment after four hits. But there are only two of these spaces, so hits aren't as

Game 1 Round 7

rolls: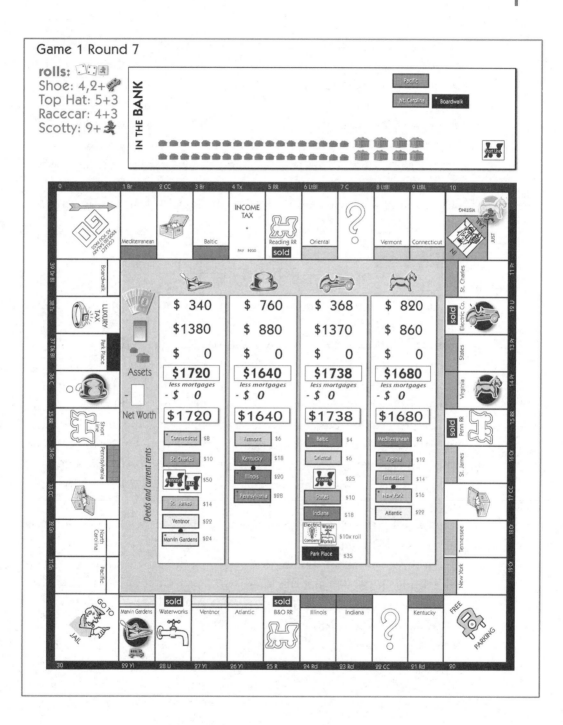
Shoe: 4,2+🚃
Top Hat: 5+3
Racecar: 4+3
Scotty: 9+🏃

frequent. (Yes, there's also a card in the Chance deck that advances a player to the nearest utility.) All in all, the Utilities do generate cash, but of a much lesser magnitude than the four Railroads.

Fortunately, safe, better-yielding investments are available to all to us: real-life utility stocks and funds, the best-yielding certificates of deposit, certain bond funds. Do your analysis and don't settle for lesser alternatives of comparable risk.

You roll a 9 plus Mr. M. First you advance your Scotty nine spaces to the Just Visiting corner, then ahead to the next unowned property, which is Virginia Avenue—the premier property in the Purple group—and purchase it for $160.

ROUND EIGHT

In the prior round, the Shoe decided to move to Marvin Gardens, courtesy of the Bus. He now shakes and rolls a 5 plus Mr. M. The 5 advances him to Pennsylvania Avenue, whose owner, the Top Hat, alertly asks for $28 rent. Then Mr. M carries the Shoe ahead to the next unowned property, which happens to be another railroad: the Short Line. The Shoe parts with $200 cash and a third railroad enters his empire. Speaking of which . . .

The Top Hat picks up the dice and rolls an 8 and comes to a halt on one of the Shoe's railroads: Pennsylvania. The Shoe is delighted with the quick payoff and asks for $100. The Top Hat reluctantly parts with a $100 bill.

The Racecar rolls a 5 and advances to Community Chest. He wins second prize in a Beauty Contest and earns a hefty $10!

You roll a 9 and your Scotty finds itself on Indiana Avenue. The Racecar demands his $18 rent.

At this point in the action, every player's net worth is up nicely. The Shoe leads with $1792, but the Racecar has nearly caught up, with $1766. Your net worth is $1662, while the Top Hat trails the pack with $1574.

Notice how, during the investment phase of the game, every player is richer than when the game started. If you plow money steadily into savings, the same result will occur. Soon the Monopoly properties will need to turn in big rents to justify their purchases. Likewise, you'll need to look beyond the bank and CDs to make your money work harder.

Game 1 Round 8

rolls:
Shoe: 5+🏃
Top Hat: 8
(3,3+2); 9+2
Racecar: 5
CC: +$10
Scotty: 8+1

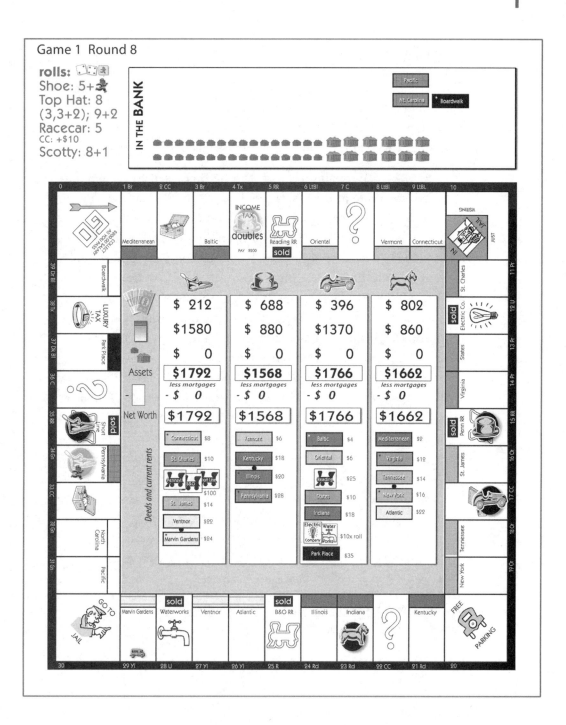

Borrowing Power

The strategy of buying every property you land on has nearly depleted the bank of deeds, but it has also drained the cash of every player, some more than others. But as the investment phase of the game nears its end, it is necessary to explain another important financial concept: *borrowing power.*

SECRET 13: A player's cash can be increased by as much as half the value of the assets acquired. As you look at the balance sheet for each company, note the amount of its money invested in deeds and buildings. This investment determines the extent of the borrowing power of each player's company. For example, at the end of round eight, the Top Hat owned $880 worth of deeds. Her borrowing power is therefore $440 (one-half of this amount). Note that if fully utilized, the borrowing power of the Top Hat would increase her cash on hand from $688 to $1128.

Have you calculated your real-life personal or business borrowing power? It's an informative exercise. How do you figure it? It is the sum of what lenders are willing to provide, especially if you pledge an asset against the loan. Credit lines for credit cards are part of your borrowing power (the most expensive, so beware). If you own a home, you can raise money with a home equity line if your home has risen in value. You can raise some money with a personal loan based on your monthly budget and available free funds to make a monthly repayment. You can borrow against your investments. If you do the math and put together the sum of all these options, you'll determine your borrowing power. Warning: your borrowing power is not to be abused; it's there for emergencies and unique opportunities (buying a home, perhaps).

Borrowing power becomes a significant consideration as the game enters its development, or "build 'em up," phase.

ROUND NINE

The Shoe rolls a 7, passes GO, and lands on Community Chest. He must pay $100 to the bank for hospital fees. I perform shorthand and pay him a net of $100 rather than handing over $200 for passing GO and then asking for $100 back. Note: you can also request that each transaction be separated, to assure accuracy. The bank can never cheat a player or fail to pay its obligations. A player is entitled to collect $200 for passing GO, without time limit, if the player and the banker fail to take notice when it is due.

The Top Hat rolls a double 4 plus a 2 on the Speed Die. She moves ahead to the B&O Railroad and the Shoe asks for $100 in rent. Doubles entitle the Top Hat to roll again. This time she rolls a 6 plus Mr. M. The six carries her to Pacific; she quickly determines that Mr. M will advance her token to its neighbor, North Carolina. Since the Top Hat owns Pennsylvania, the third Green property, the opportunity is within grasp of the Top Hat to own the entire color group! She pays $300 for the deed to Pacific, then moves ahead one space to North Carolina and is eager to buy it. Wait a minute! She doesn't have enough cash. She began the turn with $688, had to pay $100 rent on the B&O, and paid out another $300 to buy Pacific. She's $12 short of the $300 needed to buy North Carolina. Should she auction it instead? No! Instead, she'll draw on her borrowing power to raise cash.

> **SECRET 14: Draw on your borrowing power, if need be, to acquire a color group.** How? In this case, the Top Hat need only mortgage one deed.

Mortgaging

Mortgaging a deed (or selling back to the bank a building previously purchased) raises cash. Either of these actions converts half of its value to cash. The Top Hat needs a mere $12. She could gain this by mortgaging Vermont for $50, or Kentucky for $110, or Illinois for $120. She won't consider mortgaging a Green, as she will now be entitled to collect double rent on each of its (unmortgaged) properties. The Top Hat makes the easy decision: mortgage Vermont for $50. The bank pays her, and the Top Hat flips over

Vermont's deed to indicate that it is now indeed mortgaged. While mortgaged, a property—like Vermont in this case—cannot earn rent; Vermont's $6 rent is canceled for any player landing on it so long as it is mortgaged. (We'll discuss *unmortgaging* a property a little later.)

> **SECRET 15:** **When you must mortgage, try to do so in this order: single properties first, then a single Utility, and then a single Railroad.** If you need to mortgage further, the utility group should be mortgaged before a second property in a color group or another railroad.
>
> *The mortgaging lessons in this game are the same as in real life: when you incur debt, try to minimize its effect on your income. If possible, take on debt only to leverage the possibility of increasing your income via further investment (like the Top Hat is doing in this instance). Buying a home at less than replacement cost in a promising market is an excellent example of using debt wisely. Overpaying for a showy home in a volatile market is not. Most important, don't add to debt merely to consume. This is a lose-lose proposition.*

With $338 in cash, the Top Hat pays the bank $300 and acquires the deed to North Carolina. All the Greens are hers.

You roll an 11 plus Mr. M. Your dog advances to Pennsylvania Avenue and you pay the Top Hat $56 (double rent because the Greens are grouped) and then advances to the board's last unowned property, Boardwalk, which you strategically purchase for $400.

All deeds are now owned and Mr. M's purpose on the Speed Die changes from advancing a token to the next unowned property to advancing it to the next rent due!

Monopoly's Three Phases: Buy, Build, and Bankrupt!

Many classic games progress through three phases: beginning, middle, and end. Entire books have been written about the play of chess during any one of its three phases. Monopoly's three phases—investment, development, and payoff—are often nicknamed the "three Bs"—*buy, build,* and *bankrupt.*

In a similar light, your lifetime financial plan typically consists of three lengthy phases: accumulate, grow, and withdraw. While that will take decades to fully play out, the Monopoly game is an opportunity to experience its highly compressed equivalent, time and again, to see the implications of phase transitions and their requirements.

Typically, the "accumulate" phase in your life continues until your major financial obligations subside (for example, when your kids' educational costs are funded). This might also coincide with the paydown of your mortgage and advancement in your career. If so, you suddenly have far more surplus income each month.

This is when your "grow" phase takes over. Not only are you investing more each month, but you are also gaining far more compounded income on your investments. For example, if you increase your investments from $100,000 to $300,000 in 10 years, your assets have not only increased by $200,000 but by the added income on this $200,000. Let's say your portfolio earns 8 percent annually during this time. The first $100,000 doubles itself, and the added $200,000 earns another $100,000 (assuming you invested it evenly throughout these 240 months). You end with $500,000 instead of $200,000!

The final phase, "withdraw" begins after you retire and stop earning a paycheck. Your pension and Social Security checks will cover some portion of your monthly expenses and the amount you withdraw from your investments will cover the remainder. The less you expect from the former, the more you need of the latter. This is another reason why it is essential to anticipate the three phases and set a target age for each—you need to know decades in advance your expected withdrawal needs.

But back to our game. The attention of the players turns to the game's second phase, building, initiated by the need to trade for and develop color groups. Typically, a trading panic ensues after the first such group is formed.

In our game, all three Greens are now owned by the Top Hat. Will a panic now ensue? Not yet. The reason is the Top Hat's dearth of cash. The Top Hat has but $94 and will need $200 to buy just one house for the Greens. While she appears to have $740 of bargaining power, she can't afford to mortgage a Green. All properties of a group must be unmortgaged before any can be built upon. The Top Hat could raise $230 by mortgaging Kentucky and Illinois (Vermont is already mortgaged), and then build one house. If she placed it on Pacific or North Carolina, it would earn a rent of

Game 1 Round 9

rolls:
Shoe: 4,2+2
Top Hat:5,2+
Racecar:5,3
Scotty: 5,4+

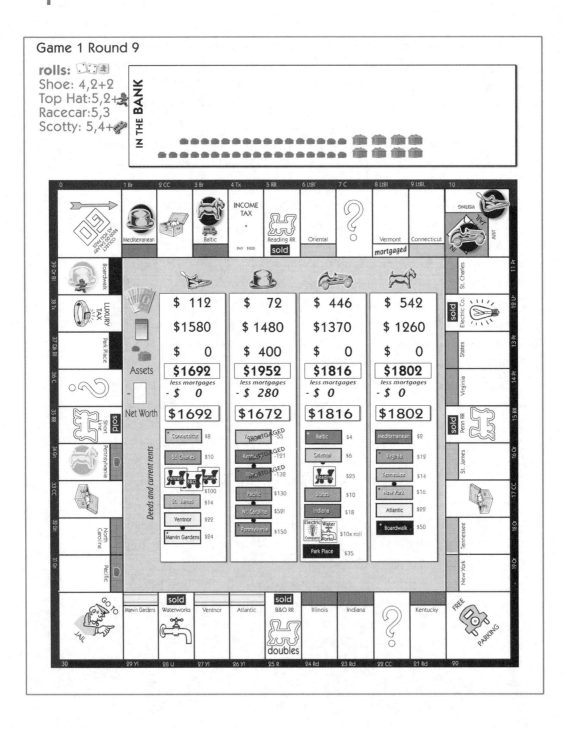

$130. On Pennsylvania Avenue it would earn her $150. But the Top Hat respects another of my secrets and decides to wait.

SECRET 16: **It is better to roll before building on one's turn.** The logic is obvious. You have nothing to gain by building before rolling, and much to lose if you roll unfavorably. The Top Hat might land on a rent or one or even both tax spaces. To pay, she could be forced to tear down her lone house, losing half its value before it could snare even one rent.

If you can gain added information before making an investment, do so, provided the opportunity doesn't slip by while you dig. What does this mean? It means not basing your decision solely on the recommendation of brokers or rating services, but rather also seeking other resources tapped into the pulse of a company you wish to invest in. I've seen analysts within my industry wooed by a strong presentation, often staged in company boardrooms and promising a bright future. You read their reports and feel good. But if you go to the front lines and talk to retailers, salesmen, and industry veterans, you might get a different picture. The products so highly touted in the presentations might not be selling as hoped. Inevitably, when the "street" learns the truth of an overpromise, it downgrades a company. Investors are stunned and often outraged. The stock's price plummets and those published reports are hastily revised. Too late for you, perhaps. I don't mean to imply that this is typical, or that well-researched recommendations are always suspect, but rather that there's a chance they don't reflect current facts. A little extracurricular digging can save your hard-earned money. On the brighter side, the prospects for a company may have improved beyond those expected. If a new product is selling well above expectations and the analysts haven't updated their reports, you'll be able to get in before the good news is out. Instant profits!

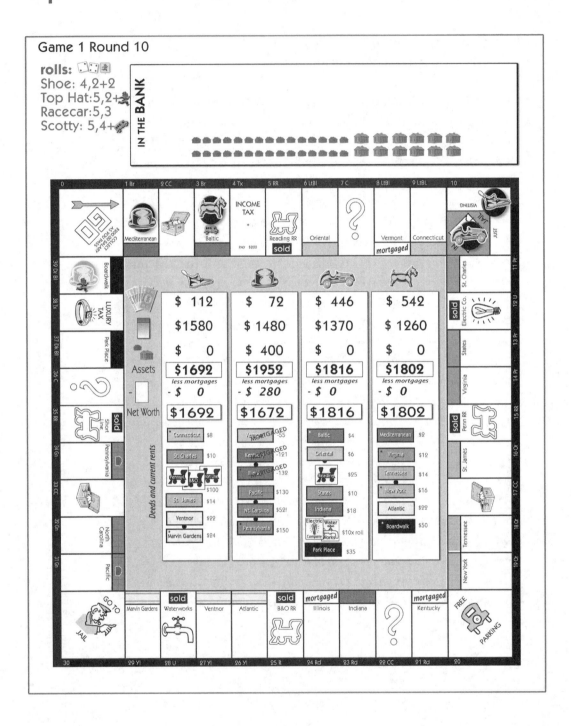

Game 1 Round 10

rolls:
Shoe: 4,2+2
Top Hat: 5,2+
Racecar: 5,3
Scotty: 5,4+

IN THE **BANK**

	Shoe	Top Hat	Racecar	Scotty
	$ 112	$ 72	$ 446	$ 542
	$1580	$1480	$1370	$1260
	$ 0	$ 400	$ 0	$ 0
Assets	$1692	$1952	$1816	$1802
	less mortgages	*less mortgages*	*less mortgages*	*less mortgages*
-	- $ 0	- $ 280	- $ 0	- $ 0
Net Worth	$1692	$1672	$1816	$1802

Deeds and current rents

Shoe
Connecticut $8
St. Charles $10
Pennsy B&O Short L $100
St. James $14
Ventnor $22
Marvin Gardens $24

Top Hat
Vermont MORTGAGED
Kentucky MORTGAGED -121
Illinois MORTGAGED -132
Pacific $130
Nt. Carolina $52!
Pennsylvania $150

Racecar
Baltic $4
Oriental $6
Reading $25
States $10
Indiana $18
Electric/Water Works $10x roll
Park Place $35

Scotty
Mediterranean $2
Virginia $12
Tennessee $14
New York $16
Atlantic $22
Boardwalk $50

ROUND TEN

While the Top Hat is contemplating, the trade talk among the other players loses steam and the Shoe rolls. His 8 takes him to Just Visiting, where he cools his heels.

Next, the Top Hat blows on the dice and rolls a 7 plus Mr. M. She moves ahead to Boardwalk and pays $50 rent to you. Mr. M carries her past GO to Mediterranean, where you demand another $2 in rent. Having earned $200 for passing GO, the Top Hat now has $242 in cash. Before ending her turn, she decides to mortgage Kentucky and Indiana to raise that $230. Armed with a total of $472, she converts $400 into two houses, placing one on Pacific and one on Pennsylvania.

The Racecar rolls an 8 and happily goes off to Jail.

You roll a 5,4 plus Bus. You decide to move the 4 and pay a $4 rent to the Racecar on Baltic. (You could have moved nine spaces and paid no rent, but you are not eager to get any closer to the Greens.) Oh yes: you also collect $200 for passing GO. Nice.

ROUND ELEVEN

The Shoe proposes a new deal with you: St. James for Atlantic and Mediterranean. The Shoe will end up with the Yellow color group and the Med to help balance the deal (so persuades the Shoe), and you'll get the Oranges, purportedly the top group in the game. But you decline, because it doesn't strike you as a fair deal with the Shoe gaining a more powerful group to develop against you. The Shoe rolls the dice. The 6,3+1 carries him to Free Parking and another rest.

In Chapter 11 you'll learn many insights into the art of negotiation, but for now it is important to note that in the real world, as in the game, you should never make a deal that doesn't improve your situation. Think objectively, not emotionally, before deciding.

The Top Hat rolls an 8 and lands on Connecticut, paying the demanding Shoe $8.

The Racecar tries and fails to swing a deal involving the Light Blues and the Purples. He rolls both white dice, hoping not to roll doubles because he wants to remain safely in Jail. He stays put after rolling a 3.

You roll an 8 plus Mr. M and first advance to St. Charles. The Shoe is not asleep and asks for $10 in rent. Thanks to Mr. M, your Scotty also moves to the next rent you must pay—which is the very next space, Electric Company. You pay the expectant Racecar $80 (10 times your roll of 8).

You are about to pass the dice but decide to first try one more time to swing a trade. All four players get involved and suddenly the Light Blues enter the discussion. But there's a catch; the Top Hat would have to unmortgage Vermont in order for the terms of the proposed multiplayer trade to come off.

Unmortgaging

A player may unmortgage a deed during his turn (or in between the turns of other players if he asks for a pause). The penalty to unmortgaging is the requirement to pay interest, which is calculated at 10 percent of the mortgage's value. Vermont's mortgage value is $50. So the Top Hat would need to pay the bank $55 (the original $50 mortgage plus $5 interest). Once unmortgaged, a deed is flipped face up and once again is entitled to collect rents.

The Top Hat demand $455 for Vermont, but that cools the proposed deal and the turn ends without the tempting trade being consummated.

> **SECRET 17**: **Unmortgage in reverse order of the mortgaging priorities in Secret 15.**
>
> *Pay off your most costly debts first. This may seem obvious, but many people tend to think it is better to reduce the number of debts than reduce the most possible interest per month. For example, let's say you have one big credit card debt, a small department store debt, a monthly car payment, and an installment of a furniture purchase. You now have enough money to pay off the last three. Seems logical to do so, right? Then you'll only need to make one payment per month toward the credit card balance. However, the three minor debts carry interest rates of 10 percent or less, while the major debt is burdened with a 22 percent rate. So the right decision here is to pay down as much of the imposing credit card debt as you can and keep the three lesser debts for the time being. It is far more advantageous to shed higher-cost debt first.*

Game 1 Round 11

rolls:
Shoe: 6,3+1
Top Hat:4,3+1
Racecar:2,1
Scotty: 5,4+

IN THE BANK

ROUND TWELVE

The Shoe rolls an 11 and—with displeasure—shuffles ahead to Pacific Avenue. The Top Hat is delighted and asks for her $130 rent. The Shoe mortgages Connecticut out of necessity.

The Top Hat now rolls an 8 and lands on Chance. Her luck is good; the card advances her token to GO. Suddenly, she has $394 in cash. Emboldened, she buys a house and places it on North Carolina.

Building Evenly

Houses must be built as evenly as possible when developing a color group. This means each property in the group must have one house on it before any can be further developed with a second house. Once all have a second house, each may receive a third house. A fourth can be built on each once all have three. Hotels may be built thereafter. There is no restriction on which property may receive the first of a new row of houses. In the case of the Greens, the Top Hat would likely choose Pennsylvania for her next house because it is the premier property in the group and will yield her a hefty $450 in rent. The rule of building evenly leads to the game's most important secret.

> **SECRET 18: Build three houses on each property of your color group as soon as possible. Mortgage single properties to do so, if necessary.** The investment wisdom of going from two to three houses per property is amplified in Chapter 8.
>
> *The three-houses-per-property principle identifies the investment sweet spot of a group. Likewise, you'll want to add to profitable investments, once you experience them, until you reach a point where the need to remain safely diversified causes you to halt. Savvy investment advisors recommend that you weight each class of assets in your portfolio according to the greater economic outlook—sometimes more stocks than bonds, at other times more cash than usual. If your best investments go up so much that the recommended ratio becomes distorted, it's time to add to the "underweighted" classes in order to regain balance.*

Game 1 Round 12

rolls:
Shoe: 5,4+2
Top Hat: 5,1+2
Racecar: 5,2
Scotty: 6,3+

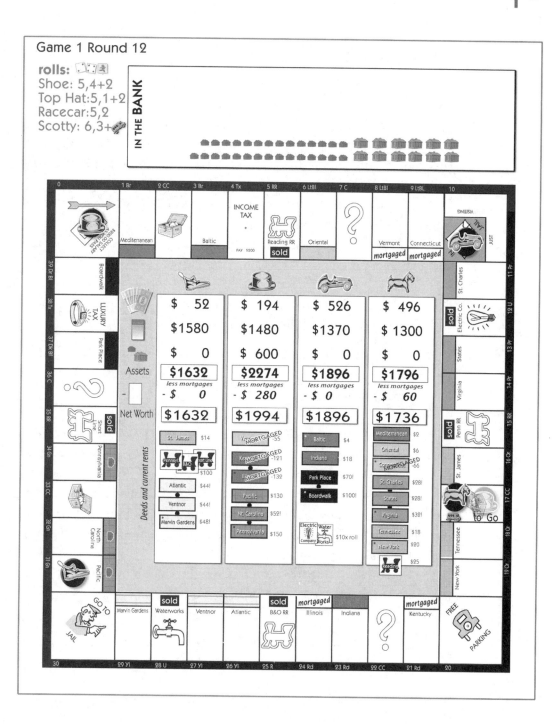

The Trading Panic

The prospect of a second house on Pennsylvania causes the "trading emergency" beacon to flash and the inertia dissipates. The Shoe, Racecar, and you get serious. First, the notion of a trade with the Top Hat, involving either the Light Blues or the Reds, is placed aside. That leaves five groups worthy of discussion: the Browns, the Purples, the Oranges, the Yellows, and the Dark Blues.

The Shoe is stubborn and will not part with St. James; he is determined not to see the Oranges opposing him with houses on them. You shrug but keep your cool. Finally a trade evolves that is acceptable to all three players. Deeds are now exchanged:

- The Shoe will trade St. Charles and Connecticut to you in return for Atlantic, gaining the Shoe the Yellow color group.

- The Racecar will trade Oriental, States, and Reading Railroad to you in return for Boardwalk. This gives the Racecar the Dark Blues and you the Purples.

You remember the mention of the oil price spike in 2011? That's a perfect example of a real-world trading panic. Whenever there's an urge to "make something happen," be sure you're not swept away by a tide of emotion. You came away well in this trade.

The Racecar rolls a 7 and again stays put in Jail. But he is not restricted from other actions and builds one house on each Dark Blue property.

You roll a 6,3 plus Bus. You decide to try your luck on Community Chest. Luck is kind; you make $50.

The idle chatter abates. Many players are contemplating building houses. The city is about to develop before our eyes.

ROUND THIRTEEN

Before the Shoe can roll, you announce that you intend to build. You spring into action by mortgaging the Reading Railroad and Oriental, and then decide to include Tennessee as well. You gain $240 from the bank in return ($100, $50, and $90, respectively). Your cash total momentarily swells to $736. After a bit of further contemplation, you decide to build seven houses. Two each rise on States and Virginia; three go up on St. Charles.

The Racecar notices that the Shoe is an ideal six spaces away from Park Place and eight spaces from Boardwalk. He mortgages Indiana, gains $110 from the bank, and has enough cash to build one house on Park Place and two on Boardwalk.

The Shoe shakes the dice and rolls a 6 (3,2+1), and finds himself on Park Place, owing a rent of $175. Gnashing his teeth, he mortgages St. James and the B&O Railroad, raising $190, handing $175 to the Racecar.

The Top Hat picks up the dice and rolls 8 plus Mr. M. The 8 is no problem, as the Top Hat owns the mortgaged Vermont Avenue. But Mr. M poses a big problem. The next property where the Top Hat will owe a rent is St. Charles, and three houses interrupt its skyline. The rent is a steep $450, and the Top Hat can only raise it by knocking down all three of her houses on the expensive Greens. She obtains $300 from the bank and the debt is paid, leaving her with a mere $44 in cash.

> **SECRET 19: When building the next row of houses on a group, place the first house on the property most likely to be landed upon.** This is what you did by placing a third house on St. Charles, rather than on States or Virginia (despite Virginia's higher rent). Of the three, St. Charles was most likely to be landed on because of the influence of Mr. Monopoly on the Speed Die. With all the four intervening properties mortgaged, the odds were 100 percent that any player landing on any property from Baltic through Connecticut would be directed to your St. Charles and pay the rent due there.
>
> *Likewise, when adding to your current investments, pick those with the best chance to rise in value. I know this sounds simplistic, but it's not. The challenge is to discern which are the most promising. The Monopoly*

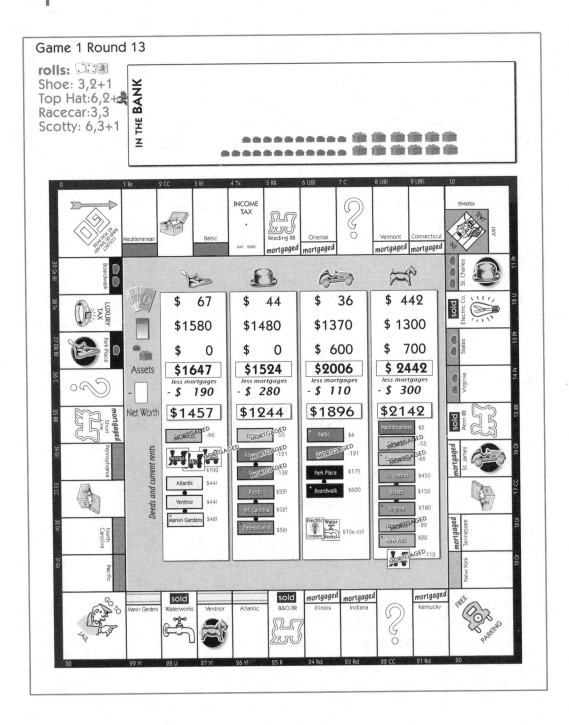

game features printed, unchanging payoffs on its deeds. Achieving them is a matter of building to a certain level and hoping your opponents land on your spaces. There are no such "deeds" in the real investment world, which is dynamic, often volatile. Nonetheless, financial pros double down by identifying investments that have reversed a lengthy down or flat trend and begin moving up. For example, if a stock has fallen from $20 to $10 per share because of negative news, then bounces back to $12, down to $10, and then above $12, this movement would attract a lot of "technical" attention. It could signal that the company has good news coming and therefore the trend reversal is justified. Deere & Company provides a good example. This venerable and well-run farm equipment company saw its stock price fall from $90 to $30 during the bad days of 2008–2009. It then rallied to $46, fell back under $30, then rallied again to $46 and remained between $46 and $35 for several weeks. In November 2009 it finally climbed above $46. The pros moved in. Deere rewarded its shareholders by advancing beyond $90 by the spring of 2011.

It's round three in Jail for the Racecar and he is required to exit. Should he roll a double, he does not pay $50 to leave. If he does not roll a double, he must pay $50. In either event, he moves the total showing on the white dice. Note: if he does roll a double, he doesn't get another free throw. (And as a reminder, a player does not throw the Speed Die while in Jail.) The Racecar does have one timing option. He may decide to pay $50 *before* he rolls. Why would he do so? Because, having paid to get out of Jail, he will be entitled to throw again if he rolls double, and include the Speed Die in this throw. The Racecar knows that the Speed Die might increase his move, thereby leaping him over your Purple group, but he has only $36, so he doesn't pay $50 before he throws. The result is a 3,3. Whew! He avoids paying to get out of Jail, and moves to St. James, which the Shoe has mortgaged.

You roll 6,3+1 and land on Ventnor, paying the Shoe a rent of $44.

ROUND FOURTEEN

While it may not be apparent, the game is in its third "B" phase: bankrupting. Enough buildings are present on the board to bring about the game's conclusion.

The Shoe rolls an 8 and lands on Reading, which is mortgaged. He earns $200 for passing GO.

The Top Hat rolls an 8 plus Mr. M, lands on Tennessee, which is mortgaged, then advances to New York, where she pays you a mere $16 rent.

The Racecar rolls a 2,2+2. Unfortunately, one of the white dice has rolled off the board, so this marvelous triples roll does not count. The Racecar must roll the dice again.

No Throw

The dice roll does not count if one or more of the dice lands cocked against a card deck, or on top of it, or touches the table surrounding the board. If a die is leaning over the edge of the board but not touching the table, it is considered valid. A die that rolls completely off the board negates the throw. When a "No Throw" occurs, the player picks up all the dice and rolls them on the board once more.

Triples

The rare triples roll—three 1s, 2s, or 3s—entitles the roller to pick up his token and move ahead to any space of the board, where its turn ends (despite the inclusion of the doubles within a triple). If a player had rolled two previous doubles before rolling a triple, he or she does not go to Jail. Triples are a unique throw. This ability to move anywhere includes the option to move to the Go to Jail space in order to move back into Jail. If a player decides on this choice, he or she forgoes $200 if GO was passed during the leap. Note: the odds of rolling a triple are 1 out of 216.

> **SECRET 20:** Take advantage of triples—a rare throw—to move to the space that will bring you the most advantage.

Game 1 Round 14

rolls:
Shoe: 4,2+2
Top Hat:6,2+
Racecar:6,1+1
Scotty: 4,3+3

IN THE **BANK**

| | 0 | 1 Br | 2 CC | 3 Br | 4 Tx | 5 RR | 6 LtBl | 7 C | 8 LtBl | 9 LtBl | 10 |

GO — COLLECT $200 SALARY AS YOU PASS

Mediterranean

Baltic

INCOME TAX
PAY $200

Reading RR
mortgaged

Oriental
mortgaged

?

Vermont
mortgaged

Connecticut
mortgaged

VISITING JAIL JUST IN

Boardwalk

LUXURY TAX

Park Place

mortgaged
Short Line

Pennsylvania

North Carolina

Pacific

Assets

-

Net Worth

Deeds and current rents

$ 267	$ 28	$ 36	$ 233
$1580	$1480	$1370	$ 1300
$ 0	$ 0	$ 600	$ 700
$1847	**$1508**	**$2006**	**$2233**
less mortgages	*less mortgages*	*less mortgages*	*less mortgages*
- $ 190	- $ 280	- $ 110	- $ 300
$1657	**$1228**	**$1896**	**$1933**

MORTGAGED -99

Pennsyl B&O MORTGAGED $100

Atlantic $44!

Ventnor $44!

Marvin Gardens $48!

MORTGAGED -55

Ke MORTGAGED -121

Il MORTGAGED -132

Pacific $52!

Nt. Carolina $52!

Pennsylvania $56!

Baltic $4

MORTGAGED -121

Park Place $175

Boardwalk $600

Electric Company Water Works $10x roll

Mediterranean $2

MORTGAGED -55

MORTGAGED -66

St. Charles $450

States $150

Virginia $180

MORTGAGED -99

New York $20

MORTGAGED -110

11 Pr	St. Charles
12 U	Electric Co.	SOLD
13 Pr	States
14 Pr	Virginia
15 RR	Penn RR SOLD
16 Or	St. James mortgaged
17 CC	
18 Or	Tennessee mortgaged
19 Or	New York

| 30 | 29 Yl | 28 U | 27 Yl | 26 Yl | 25 R | 24 Rd | 23 Rd | 22 CC | 21 Rd | 20 |

GO TO JAIL

Marvin Gardens

Waterworks sold

Ventnor

Atlantic

B&O RR sold

Illinois mortgaged

Indiana mortgaged

?

Kentucky mortgaged

FREE PARKING

When fortune unexpectedly smiles, try to maximize your benefit. Lightning doesn't strike on command. For example, an uncle passes away and leaves you his home. You love the idea of a second house in the mountains of Colorado and are tempted to keep it. But the upkeep and taxes will prevent you from achieving your monthly savings goal. There is a good market for your uncle's home. If you sell it promptly, you will be able to add to your investment nest egg, not see it stagnate.

The Racecar picks up all three dice and rolls them successfully, on the board this time. His 8 lands him on Illinois, which is mortgaged. So he lodges rent-free.

You hesitate before you roll. Park Place and Boardwalk beckon with their increased rents. You shake and silently chant before throwing a 10, which almost carries you onto dreaded Park Place. Fortunately, it deposits your Scotty on the Chance space preceding it. You draw the top card; the news is not good. Building repairs are required on each of your houses and the rate is $25 per house. That means you must part with $225 in cash and delay consideration of adding to your housing on the Purples. (Hmmm.)

ROUND FIFTEEN

You call another halt, thinking, "Damn the torpedoes." You decide to build a third house on both States and Virginia, thus depleting your cash (and safety reserve).

The Shoe rolls an 8 plus Mr. M and lands first on States, then on Virginia. The double whammy costs him $950. The Shoe could raise $600 by mortgaging his five face-up deeds, but when that is added to his $267 in cash, he would still be $83 short. If he could raise the shortfall from another player via a trade he could remain in the game. But the Top Hat and Racecar are also strapped for cash and neither come to his rescue. The Shoe gracefully bows out and turns over all his properties, as is, to you. Wow! Your decision to buy a third house on Virginia proved wise indeed. *Remember the adage: you must constantly think about your money in order to make money? Here is proof.*

Note: by getting St. James in the Shoe's bankruptcy, you finally own the coveted Orange group. New York, its unmortgaged property, will earn you double rent: $32.

Going Bankrupt to Another Player

1. You can try to swing a trade to obtain the cash you need. But you can't make the trade(s) unless it results in sufficient cash to pay your debt. If it can't make enough cash, you must go bankrupt "as is."

2. "As is" means you do not disturb your remaining unmortgaged deeds. Rather, you hand them face up to the player to whom you owe the crushing rent, along with your cash and facedown *previously mortgaged* deeds. The recipient must immediately pay the interest due, even if he elects not to unmortgage now.

3. Buildings may never be sold to another player. They may only be sold back to the bank for one-half their printed value. If, after doing so, you cannot raise the amount of your debt, you must go bankrupt as is.

4. Following bankruptcy, remove your token and retire from the game.

Going Bankrupt to the Bank

How is this possible? Let's say you have $85 in cash and all your deeds are mortgaged. You land on Luxury Tax and owe $100. You are $15 short of meeting the bank's tax demand. If you could raise this money by trading one or more mortgaged properties, well and good. If you can't, you must retire from the game. The bank takes in your $85 and your mortgaged deeds. The banker immediately conducts an auction for each such deed, from cheapest to most expensive. The auctions can begin at any price, even $1. Each property is sold to the highest bidder. Players may not make bids they cannot cover.

SECRET 21: **If you can afford to, bid at least the mortgage value of a property at auction, because after acquiring it you can raise**

Game 1 Round 15

rolls: 🎲🎲🏃
Shoe: 6,2+🏃
Top Hat:6,6+2
5,2+🚗
Racecar:6,4+1
Scotty:5,2+1

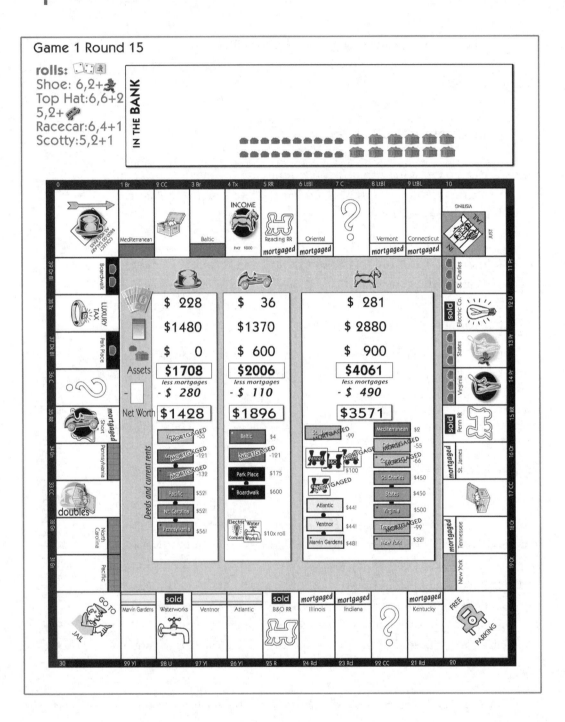

this amount by mortgaging the deed. Note: you must have the means to pay for a high bid in advance. You can't use a deed's mortgage value after acquiring it to help pay for it.

Although you don't often get the chance to buy distressed property in real life, this same principle can be applied. If you can buy something of value, which you know you can sell for more than your "bid," it is worthy of consideration. Many a successful entrepreneur has bought a broken, poorly managed company, cleaned it up, restored it to profitability, and sold it for many times his or her investment. By contrast, buying a "fixer-upper" and investing in its repair because you know someone who made a big gain doing likewise is insufficient reason to put money at risk. What is the state of the local market? Is it flat? It there an oversupply of homes? If so, your risk/reward is likely poor.

The Top Hat rolls a double (6,6) plus 2. She lands on Community Chest, where she is assessed for building repairs. Having none, she suffers no penalty. She next rolls a 5,2 and the Bus. She decides to move the sum of seven spaces, leaps over the Dark Blues, and lands on GO.

The Racecar rolls an 11 and lands on Short Line, which is mortgaged. No rent is due.

You roll an 8 and land on Income Tax. The $200 earned for passing GO is negated.

ROUND SIXTEEN—THE CALM BEFORE THE STORM

Now we have a three-player game. Your Purple group looks formidable, but you remain low on cash. The Racecar still has a chance, especially if he can afford to build a second house on Park Place (and, even more hopefully, a third house on Boardwalk). The Top Hat is in a tough position and knows it. She needs a minor miracle to gain enough cash to rebuild houses on the Greens. They are so darn expensive! Before she can consider building even one, she needs to successfully run the gauntlet of your Purples.

The Top Hat rolls a 7 and lands on Chance, where she pays a speeding fine of $15.

The Racecar rolls an 8 and lands on Baltic (his own property). He also collects $200 for passing GO and is therefore tempted to buy another house for Park Place, but your houses on the Purples loom up ahead. He holds on to his cash.

You roll an 8 as well (4,2+2), land on the Electric Company, and pay the Racecar $80 in rent. It stings. You only build one more house—after which you have four on St. Charles (rent: $625), three on States (rent: $450), and three on Virginia (rent: $500). Then, as if driven by a premonition, you build one more on Virginia (rent now $700). While you have a mere $1 in cash left—a very risky position—the Top Hat and the Racecar will roll before you but you do have borrowing power: the Yellows plus two other deeds.

What about those Yellows? You obtained them intact from the Shoe. Shouldn't you have put a house or two on them instead, perhaps by mortgaging New York and Mediterranean?

To Spread or to Concentrate?

Even great players sometimes falter when faced with the tempting prospect of developing two monopolies. Isn't it better to have a couple of houses on six properties than, say, four on the three properties of one color group?

You'll remember the key Secret 18: build a color group to the three-house level as soon as you can. This principle helps to decide the issue, modified by this one as well:

> **SECRET 22:** **When deciding to add to one color group or another, place a building where it will cause the greater increase in rent adjusted for the likelihood of landing on the property (its "frequency").** In Monopoly, each investment decision should be made to maximize your return, and that usually requires furthering an existing investment, not developing another.
>
> *Likewise, it is usually unwise to "weight" your investments equally. It is usually best to add new funds to those performing the best. I have known several bright businessmen who started successful new firms in the toy and game business. But the lure of maintaining a high rate of growth compelled them to add new products at a dizzying rate, expanding into categories in which they had no experience (such as action figures or dolls). Growth has a voracious appetite for cash. If it pauses, it will consume*

Game 1 Round 16

rolls: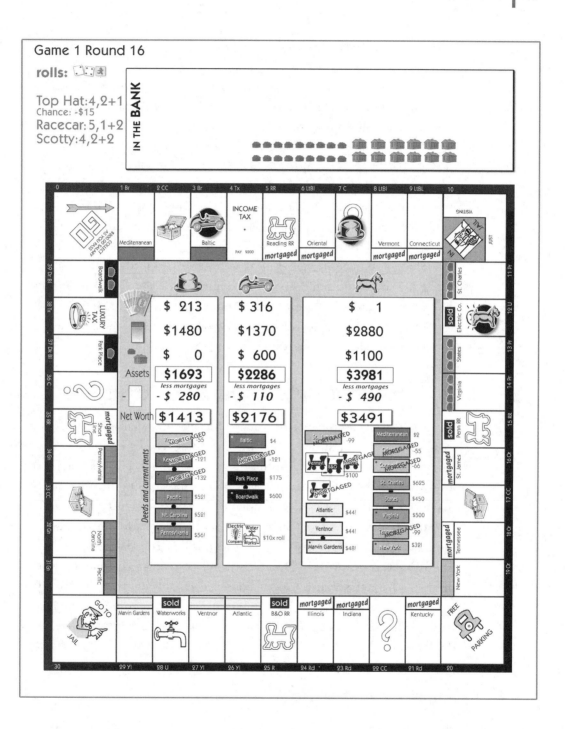

Top Hat: 4,2+1
Chance: -$15
Racecar: 5,1+2
Scotty: 4,2+2

IN THE BANK

Top Hat
$ 213
$1480
$ 0
$1693
less mortgages
- $ 280
$1413

Racecar
$ 316
$1370
$ 600
$2286
less mortgages
- $ 110
$2176

Scotty
$ 1
$2880
$1100
$3981
less mortgages
- $ 490
$3491

Assets
Net Worth

Deeds and current rents

Top Hat		Racecar		Scotty	
MORTGAGED	-55	Baltic	$4	St. MORTGAGED	-99
Ke MORTGAGED	-121	MORTGAGED	-121	Pennsy B&O	$100
Il MORTGAGED	-132	Park Place	$175	MORTGAGED	
Pacific	$52!	Boardwalk	$600	St. Charles	$625
Nt. Carolina	$52!			States	$450
Pennsylvania	$56!	Electric Water Co. Works	$10x roll	Virginia	$500
		Atlantic	$44!	Te MORTGAGED	-99
		Ventnor	$44!	New York	$32!
		Marvin Gardens	$48!		

Mediterranean	$2		
MORTGAGED	-55		
MORTGAGED	-66		

the undercapitalized. Their firms soon disappeared; most have personally recovered, but their lessons were learned harshly.

Frequency is a topic that plays an important role in Game Two, so for now let's be brief and just assume that the Purples and the Yellows have the same likelihood of being landed upon. A fourth house on Virginia raises its rent from $500 to $700—a $200 increase. By contrast, a first house on the Yellow's premium property—Marvin Gardens—calls for rent of $120. This simple comparison seals the deal and explains why you decided to further develop your Purples. But what about mortgaging the Yellows and building even more houses on the Purples? You can gain $400 by mortgaging all three Yellow properties, and with $400 you could build hotels. But doing so depletes your credit reserve, and landing on a high-rent space still might victimize you. True, more aggressive players would have taken the chance, but you're learning the value of prudent restraint, right?

ROUND SEVENTEEN—A DRAMATIC ENDING

The Top Hat shakes the dice for what seems like an eternity, beckons them to be kind, and then throws 7 plus Mr. Monopoly. The extra oomph did not pay off. The Top Hat reluctantly moves forward, first to Virginia, where she owes you a hefty $700. She can raise $460 by mortgaging the Greens, but that will only bring her cash total up to $676. She beseeches the Racecar to help out, perhaps by taking Vermont off her hands for $40. But the Racecar is worried about his own survival. He says no. The Top Hat is therefore finished. She turns over her $213 in cash and six deeds—as is—and removes her token from the board. You graciously accept, trying not to look too joyful, and proceed to pay interest on the three mortgaged deeds you inherited ($28). You decided not to flip any of these deeds, as you don't want to deplete your cash.

A Double Rent Thanks to Mr. Monopoly

What are the consequences of having to pay two rents in succession, due to rolling Mr. Monopoly? If both can be paid in full, the roller remains in the

Game 1 Round 17

rolls: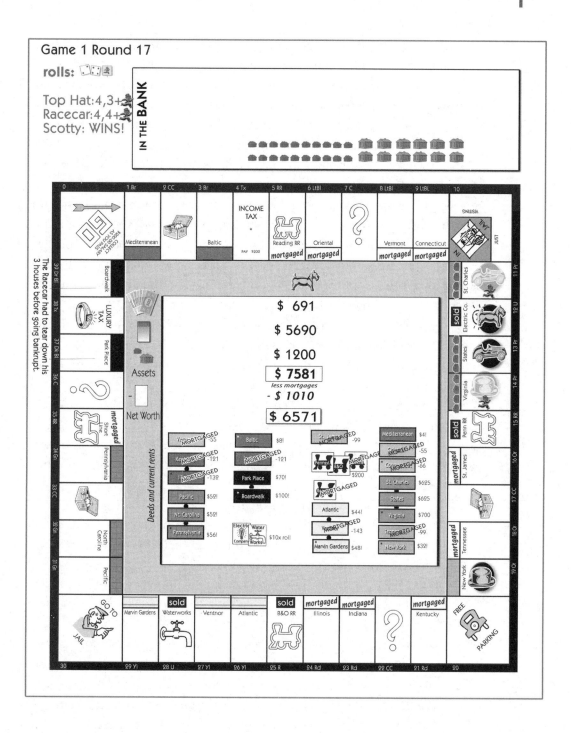

Top Hat: 4,3+💀
Racecar: 4,4+💀
Scotty: WINS!

The Racecar had to tear down his 3 houses before going bankrupt.

IN THE **BANK**

$ 691
$ 5690
$ 1200
$ 7581
less mortgages
- $ 1010
$ 6571

Assets

−

Net Worth

Deeds and current rents

Ye... MORTGAGED	−55
Ke... MORTGAGED	−121
Il... MORTGAGED	−132
Pacific	$52!
Nt. Carolina	$52!
Pennsylvania	$56!

Baltic	$8!
MORTGAGED	−121
Park Place	$70!
Boardwalk	$100!

Electric Company / Water Works $10x roll

St... MORTGAGED	−99
Pennsyl. B&O MORTGAGED	$200
V... MORTGAGED	
Atlantic	$44!
V... MORTGAGED	−143
Marvin Gardens	$48!

Mediterranean	$4!
C... MORTGAGED	−55
C... MORTGAGED	−66
St. Charles	$625
States	$625
Virginia	$700
Tennessee MORTGAGED	−99
New York	$32!

Board spaces:
0 · 1 Br Mediterranean · 2 CC · 3 Br Baltic · 4 Tx INCOME TAX + PAY $200 · 5 RR Reading RR *mortgaged* · 6 LtBl Oriental *mortgaged* · 7 C · 8 LtBl Vermont *mortgaged* · 9 LtBL Connecticut *mortgaged* · 10 JUST VISITING / IN JAIL

Left side:
39 Dr Bl Boardwalk · 38 Tx LUXURY TAX · 37 Dr Bl Park Place · 36 C · 35 RR Short Line *mortgaged* · 34 Grn Pennsylvania · 33 CC · 32 Grn North Carolina · 31 Grn Pacific · 30 GO TO JAIL

Right side:
11 Pr St. Charles · 12 U Electric Co. *sold* · 13 Pr States · 14 Pr Virginia · 15 RR Penn RR *sold* · 16 Or St. James *mortgaged* · 17 CC · 18 Or Tennessee *mortgaged* · 19 Or New York · 20 FREE PARKING

Bottom:
29 Yl Marvin Gardens · 28 U Waterworks *sold* · 27 Yl Ventnor · 26 Yl Atlantic · 25 R B&O RR *sold* · 24 Rd Illinois *mortgaged* · 23 Rd Indiana *mortgaged* · 22 CC · 21 Rd Kentucky *mortgaged*

game. If only the first can be paid in full, the outcome depends on a question: are both rents owed to the same player or to two different players?

Let's start with both rents being owed to the same player. For a moment, suppose the Top Hat had an extra $25. That would boost her total to $701 after mortgaging her Greens for $460. That's enough to pay for the $700 rent on Virginia, but not enough to also cover the $32 rent on New York (where Mr. Monopoly will take her). New York is also owned by the same player, namely you. In such a case, both rents are calculated in advance of paying either. Now, if the roller can raise enough cash to pay both rents, he or she remains in the game. But the roller goes bankrupt if it is clear that insufficient means exist to raise both rents. Now back to our example. The $701 raised by the Top Hat isn't enough to pay the $700 due you for Virginia and the $32 due on New York. So the Top Hat would go bankrupt, handing over her $213 in cash and deeds as is.

However, if the Top Hat began her turn with $273 or more in cash, she could raise $733 total via mortgaging. That would be enough to pay both rents to you. In this event, the Top Hat would stay in the game by mortgaging her Greens after paying you $732 in full.

If Mr. M brings about a rent to each of two players, the first rent is tested. If it can't be met, the roller goes bankrupt to the first player as is. If it can be met, the debt is paid and the roller's token is advanced to the second rent, where it is again tested. If it can't be met, the roller goes bankrupt to the second player.

You now build a fourth house on States.

The Racecar rolls 4,4 plus Mr. M. The rents he incurs on St. Charles and States are more than he can bear. He concedes. **Game over.** Your real estate empire is complete. You own the board!

Your final cash total is $691 after paying the interest due on Kentucky, and your final net worth is $6571! That's a 338 percent gain over your starting $1500.

To the uninitiated, it may appear that a whirlwind of casual financial transactions had taken place throughout the game and that luck ultimately smiled on you. In reality, you faced up to the "wall of uncertainty" and prevailed because, at each decision point, you calculated your risk/reward, applied the appropriate game secret, and by so doing maximized your chances. You made your own luck.

In much the same way, if you pay attention to your nest egg "turn by turn," do your homework before making any investment decision, and steadily salt money away, you'll greatly improve the odds of reaching your goal—perhaps ahead of schedule.

WHAT ELSE DID THIS GAME TEACH US?

Diversification

Let's do a little investigating. All 28 properties were purchased in this game, but did all 28 return money to their owners? What do you think? Chances are you correctly said no, because you noticed some deeds were mortgaged early in the game to raise money (to pay rents or erect buildings) and didn't earn a dime. But would you be surprised if I told you that 10 of the properties returned *zero* on their investments? That's right. Only the remaining 18 properties earned back some or all of their owner's investment capital. Further only 3 (States, Virginia, and the Electric Company) earned *more* than what was sunk into them. Mediterranean and Baltic earned paltry 3 percent and 7 percent returns, respectively, while the Pennsylvania Railroad and B&O Railroad earned a more acceptable 50 percent.

There's a lesson is these facts: *not everything you buy performs according to expectation, or hope.* That's why investment advisors consistently advocate that you spread your risk when allocating your savings. Diversification is fundamental to investment success. In Monopoly, the Orange group usually returns the most money. But it didn't in this game. So even the best bet in the game sometimes doesn't pay off.

You may shrug and gnash your teeth when diversifying because you are sure one class of assets is red-hot and bound to rise in value (perhaps tech stocks, or commodities, or bonds). But, truth be told, you can't foretell the future. Diversification may dampen short-term returns, but in the long term it can make you look and feel like a financial genius. You'll weather unexpected storms by cushioning losses and recover quickly with the next uptrend.

This raises a good question: Is Secret 2 (buy every property you land on) really ironclad? The answer: it is ironclad if you are not yet an accomplished Monopoly player.

Even though not everything you buy will pay off, if you spread your risk by owning a variety of properties, you'll also gain trading options. Think of the alternative: if you don't buy all the properties you land on, your opponents will buy them at auction and strengthen their holdings at your expense.

This secret is only reduced to a guideline when you are very accomplished and can competently evaluate every strategic situation. Savvy players will come to discern when it is better to preserve cash and let a property go to auction (typically because it will not harm them in the hands of an opponent). For example, you own at least one of each of the eight color groups—a so-called Rainbow Monopoly (see Chapter 12). In this situation, it doesn't matter if an opponent purchases that third Red property. The Red group will not be formed into a group unless you participate and approve a trade for the Reds. Cases like this one are uncommon. But you'll come to spot them (and even bring them about) the more you play and absorb the consequences.

Likewise, you may become so adept at investing that you'll learn how to concentrate your investment holdings, temporarily, to ride a trend for which you have a special understanding.

Cash Management

In this game, you may have noticed that the players who became cash poor could neither take advantage of opportunity nor withstand a financial blow. Cash management is both an art and a science in this game, much as in the world at large. If you sit on too much cash, you dampen your return and significantly hamper your ability for a timely win. In contrast, if you invest to the hilt (and can't easily extract your cash without penalty), you'll fall prey to every financial setback that befalls you.

Speaking of which, did you notice that each player endured his or her share of adversity? Some recovered nicely, at least for a while. Life throws us curves; how we handle them enables us either to recover and go forward or fall further behind. Think of the many real-life billionaires who stumbled and recovered. (Do Steve Jobs and Donald Trump come to mind?) How many do you know who sailed through life? We all have to deal with misfortune. That's another truism underpinning Monopoly.

5

THE TOKENS

WHO ARE YOU ANYWAY?
PERHAPS A RACECAR?

AND WHY DOES IT MATTER?

Your favorite token says a lot about you and how you are perceived when playing the game.

Hammy the Squirrel: Can I be the car?

Bucky: I wanna be the car!

Spike: I'm the car. You be the shoe.

Bucky: The shoe is lame.

Lou: Why don't you be that snazzy-looking iron there?

RJ: Hey! It's not important. Besides, I'm the car. I'm always the car.

—FROM THE MOVIE *OVER THE HEDGE*, 2006

Monopoly tokens possess a fascination beyond those found in other games. Many players stick with one token throughout their game-playing years. These shiny metal objects have iconic status; they are talismans, even avatars. Your choice of token reinforces the adage, "You are as others perceive you." Your choice of token is the first step to understanding the importance of "self" in the game and in real life—especially your inner self, the mechanism that either compels you forward or holds you back.

Truth be told, I harbor an innate instinct to avoid confrontation. But through years of experience I've learned that this tendency is often more formidable than my most worthy opponent. It resists good financial sense and holds back my assertiveness in negotiations. So I learned how to deal with it—by being true to myself, not being overly nice or witty or clever, and being consistently *assertive* (see Chapter 11). I saw these "virtues" in action, time and again, by watching the most effective Monopoly players in their dealings. Thank you.

During my long years of Monopoly adjudicating, I began to wonder: Is there a special "personality" and "character" associated with each token? I sensed there was. To find out, polls were conducted among players on the Facebook Monopoly fan page, members of a Monopoly association, students and teachers who use Monopoly in the classroom, and gamers in general. Here are the results. Do you see yourself?

The Racecar's Rush

- Nearly one out of four players prefer the Racecar as their favorite token. It is clearly number one in rank.

- The Racecar is perceived as the most appropriate icon to be traveling around the game's streets.

- Racecars tend to be outgoing, friendly, and versatile. They adapt well and want to be liked.

- Racecars claim their token and let others demand it (acceding to a roll-off if need be). They would settle for the Battleship or Scotty, but dislike being the Iron or Thimble.

- They regard themselves as realists and are not superstitious or overly hopeful. They prefer to build on the board's expensive side (Greens/Dark Blues) but will develop any group. They believe they are seen as fun and intelligent.

- Racecars tend to be male players.

The Battleship's Maneuver

- The Battleship is preferred by one out of ten Monopoly players. It symbolizes rugged determinism.

- Battleships tend to be more cutthroat than other players and have a bit of artistic flair. They are eager to play to win.

- Battleships like to rely on math, not circumstance, to calculate the merits of any investment. They believe others see them as intelligent and formidable.

- Battleships would settle for the Racecar if need be, but the Thimble is beneath their dignity.

- Battleships prefer to build on the Purple/Orange side, and when they build they do so with much consideration.

- More than any token, Battleships tend to calculate moves in their heads, then jump to the space landed upon.

- Battleships are mostly male players.

The Cannon's Roar

the
CANNON

- The Cannon was a standard token for many years. Many of the game's devotees continue to prefer it.

- Cannons are assertive and like to dominate.

- Cannons size up their prospective competition before agreeing to a game. When they play, they play to win, not just to have fun. They are somewhat superstitious.

- Cannons prefer the Purple/Orange side of the board, but they carefully develop whichever group falls their way.

- Cannons consider themselves to possess strategic vision; they believe others see them as both fun to play with and formidable.

- Cannons consider knowing the game's math to be vital.

- Cannons, more than any other token, prefer to play top-notch players.

- Cannons are mostly male players.

The Iron's Will

the
IRON

- One player out of twenty prefers the Iron.

- The Iron symbolizes toughness and agility.

- Irons tend to be pluggers who persist against long odds, and often prevail. They respond well to adversity.

- Irons would settle for the Thimble or Shoe tokens if need be, but would not want to be the Cannon or Racecar.

- Irons play for fun, but not too frequently. They are keen observers; little goes unnoticed in their games.

- They are neither superstitious nor impulsive. They calculate the merits of their investment decisions.

- Irons are more likely to create housing shortages than any other token.

- Irons are almost evenly divided between male and female players.

The Moneybag's Jingle

- This token was included from 1999 to 2008.

- One out of twelve players prefer the Moneybag.

- The Moneybag represents the fun side of greed and wealth. Moneybags want to be very rich in real life.

- Moneybags have fun while playing, and like to win, but not at all costs.

- Moneybags prefer the expensive side of the board.

- They build as many houses as they can as soon as possible.

- They rely more on luck favoring them than other tokens, but are not superstitious.

- They believe others see them as fun and intelligent.

- Moneybag players tend to be young (eighteen or under).

- Males and females equally prefer this token.

The Scotty's Trick

- Nearly one in five players prefer the Scotty, making it the second most favored token.

- Scotties consider themselves trustworthy, loyal, and eager to please. But they are also mentally agile and keen to win.

- Scotties would settle for the Racecar or Horse (animal lovers?), but would not want to be the Iron or Thimble.

- Scotties like the expensive side of the board and tend to develop properties opportunistically, while keeping some cash in reserve.

- Scotties believe others see them as fun-loving, while they regard themselves as mild risk takers and careful players.

- Scotties are always eager to play and are not superstitious.

- Scotties are more often female than male players.

The Shoe That Fits

- Shoes are discriminating players; only one out of sixteen prefer the Shoe token (the "Boot" to some).

- Shoes are generous, but can be easily riled. They have long memories if not dealt with honorably. (Watch out!)

- The Shoe would settle for the Top Hat or Scotty if need be, but would not want to be the Iron or Wheelbarrow.

- Shoes also prefer the expensive side of the board and use care when buying or mortgaging, as opposed to reacting impulsively.

- Shoes enjoy playing often and believe others see them as fun to play with.

- The Shoes are the least likely to create a housing shortage.

- Shoes are more often female than male players.

The Trusty Thimble

- One player out of twenty prefers the Thimble token.

- Thimbles consider themselves practical and sensitive, and many are introverts. They are also creative.

- The Thimble is the game's "stealth" token; it is often overlooked (free rent!).

- Thimbles would settle to be the Racecar or Scotty, but most dislike being the Battleship or Cannon. They are more possessive about their favorite token than any other.

- Thimbles prefer either the Brown/Light Blue or the Purple/Orange sides of the board.

- Thimbles play strategically and calculate the odds. They tend to keep track of each card played. They may play slowly.

- They feel others lack a clear impression of them.

- Thimbles are mainly female players.

The Top Hat's Tip

- The Top Hat (the third most popular token) is preferred by one out of seven players.
- The Top Hat has a sense of elegance (haughtiness?), even if it doesn't show. Top Hats don't mind drawing attention or being controversial. They might be introverted in real life, but in the game they show off their mojo.
- The Top Hat would accept the Moneybags or Racecar, but dislikes being the Iron and Thimble.
- Top Hats accept luck as inevitable. They are a little superstitious.
- Top Hats are organizers and try to get a game going often.
- They calculate the odds and play strategically.
- Top Hats like groups on the board's second or third sides.
- Top Hats are mainly male players.

The Wheelbarrow's Haul

- The token with narrowest appeal. Only 3 percent of Monopoly players prefer the Wheelbarrow.
- The Wheelbarrows are the game's heavy lifters. They expect a tough go and fierce competition. They are up for it, relying heavily on their math skills to win.
- They would take any other token if need be, especially the Shoe, but dislike being the Moneybags or Scotty.
- They have no preference for a board side; any group is fine. They lift what comes their way, good or bad. They feel that luck dominates the game.
- More Wheelbarrows play reactively (as opposed to proactively) than any other token, and they love to play, often organizing games.
- They feel others view them with dread and respect.
- Most Wheelbarrows are male players.

The Horse's Sense

- Even though the Horse (or "Horse and Rider") is no longer included in the basic Monopoly game, it remains the favorite of one player out of fourteen.

- The Horse is a lover of nature and down-to-earth humor. It plays fast and furious and loves adventure and the challenge of the game.

- Horses would take the Scotty if need be, but dislike being the Thimble.

- They prefer the Purple/Orange side of the board and build logically, holding cash in reserve.

- They feel others see them as intelligent and they regard themselves as mentally very competent and agile. Knowledge of the game's math is paramount to them.

- Horses play when the mood strikes, not on call.

- More females than males prefer the Horse.

Is there a strategy to selecting a token? The short answer is: only if you don't care which one you get. Most of us are attached to our favorite and play at our best when it represents us on the board. But if you don't care, here's a tip for you.

SECRET 23: **A small, innocuous token sometimes goes unnoticed on the game board.** A modest token (Thimble, Iron, Shoe) may benefit from missed rents or might fail to attract an opponent's attention when he or she makes investment decisions.

If you allow your ego to draw undue attention to yourself, you needlessly promote adversaries. Most career-minded individuals learn this adage early in the game. Yes, it can feel good to boast or put others in their place. Our sense of superiority does enjoy stroking! But do this repeatedly and you will close the door on many an opportunity and, even more significantly, engender a burning desire in others to see you fall from grace. Conversely, goodwill from those around you will improve your ability to find new sources of income. My advice: encourage this potential. (More in Chapters 6 and 11.)

SURVEY SAYS . . .

Taken as a whole, the respondents to these surveys had the following to say about 20 topics intimately associated with the game and its components: here are the collective opinions of all who responded to the survey.

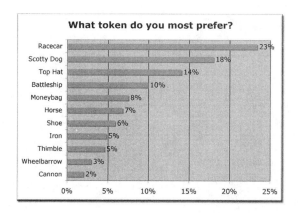

Over half prefer either the Racecar, Scotty, or Top Hat token.

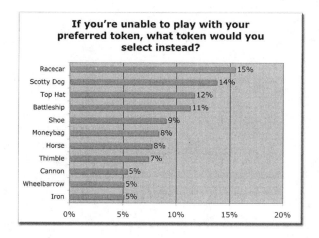

Not surprisingly, if unable to get their favorite token, 41 percent would like to be one of those three.

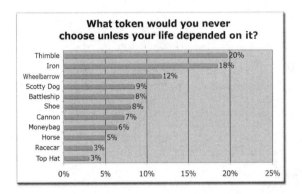

The Thimble and the Iron are least liked.

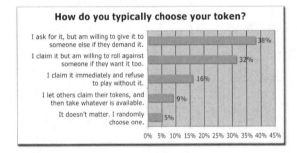

Most players either claim or ask for their favorite token, but they are willing to roll for it if there is another player interested in the same token. (Sportsmanship!)

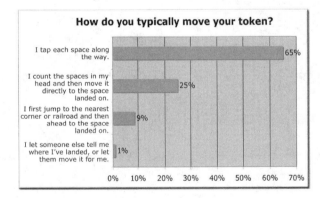

Most players tap each space as they move, but about one in four count the spaces in their heads and leap directly to the space landed upon.

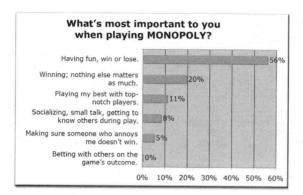

Over half believe that having fun is most important. Twenty percent feel it's "winning."

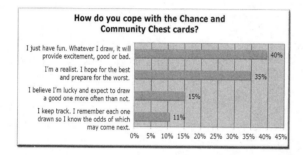

Drawing a Chance or Community Chest card evokes either excitement or preparation for the worst (while hoping for the best).

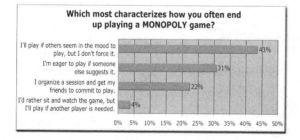

Over 40 percent of Monopoly players will play if others are in the mood, while a further 30 percent are eager to play if someone suggests it. Another 20 percent are the "organizers" who twist arms to get a game going.

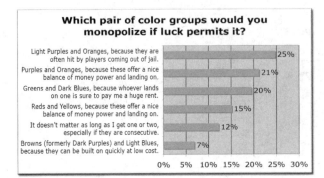

Which pair of color groups would you monopolize if luck permits it?

Light Purples and Oranges, because they are often hit by players coming out of jail.	25%
Purples and Oranges, because these offer a nice balance of money power and landing on.	21%
Greens and Dark Blues, because whoever lands on one is sure to pay me a huge rent.	20%
Reds and Yellows, because these offer a nice balance of money power and landing on.	15%
It doesn't matter as long as I get one or two, especially if they are consecutive.	12%
Browns (formerly Dark Purples) and Light Blues, because they can be built on quickly at low cost.	7%

0% 5% 10% 15% 20% 25% 30%

More players would prefer to own the Purple/Orange side, but the Red/Yellow and Green/Dark Blue sides are preferred by nearly as many. The inexpensive Brown/Light Blue side is little preferred.

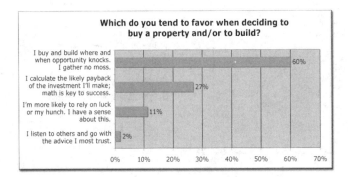

Which do you tend to favor when deciding to buy a property and/or to build?

I buy and build where and when opportunity knocks. I gather no moss.	60%
I calculate the likely payback of the investment I'll make; math is key to success.	27%
I'm more likely to rely on luck or my hunch. I have a sense about this.	11%
I listen to others and go with the advice I most trust.	2%

0% 10% 20% 30% 40% 50% 60% 70%

Half of all Monopoly players prefer to build carefully and keep some cash on hand.

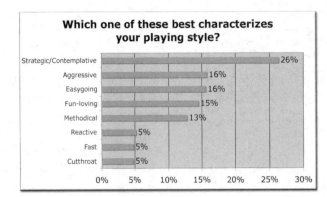

Which one of these best characterizes your playing style?

Strategic/Contemplative	26%
Aggressive	16%
Easygoing	16%
Fun-loving	15%
Methodical	13%
Reactive	5%
Fast	5%
Cutthroat	5%

0% 5% 10% 15% 20% 25% 30%

One in four players feel that they are "strategic/contemplative" in their playing style, while about one in six think they play aggressively; the same number feel they are relaxed.

When it's your turn to roll, which situation is most typical?

I pick up the dice, look at the board, and count to see which spaces would be good spots to land on. I wish for those numbers when I toss the dice. **36%**

I pay attention intently; I know when it's my turn. I roll the dice, move, complete the action, and pass the dice even if others don't know it was your turn. **32%**

Since I can't control the luck of the dice anyways, I simply toss them, move, and complete the action fate has willed me. **19%**

I chant out loud whatever number I want to roll. If the dice comply, I usually let out a joyful scream and evoke a good laugh. **8%**

Someone else usually tells me it's time to roll. I'm just having fun. **5%**

0% 5% 10% 15% 20% 25% 30% 35% 40%

When it's time to roll the dice, about a third will count to see which spaces would be good or bad to land upon before shaking the cubes.

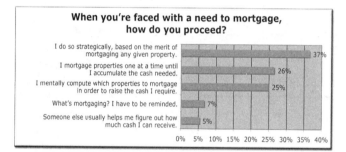

When you're faced with a need to mortgage, how do you proceed?

I do so strategically, based on the merit of mortgaging any given property. **37%**

I mortgage properties one at a time until I accumulate the cash needed. **26%**

I mentally compute which properties to mortgage in order to raise the cash I require. **25%**

What's mortgaging? I have to be reminded. **7%**

Someone else usually helps me figure out how much cash I can receive. **5%**

0% 5% 10% 15% 20% 25% 30% 35% 40%

About one out of three carefully mortgage properties when the need arises.

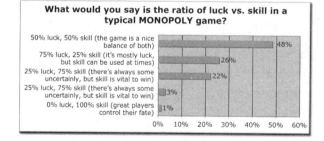

What would you say is the ratio of luck vs. skill in a typical MONOPOLY game?

50% luck, 50% skill (the game is a nice balance of both) **48%**

75% luck, 25% skill (it's mostly luck, but skill can be used at times) **26%**

25% luck, 75% skill (there's always some uncertainly, but skill is vital to win) **22%**

25% luck, 75% skill (there's always some uncertainly, but skill is vital to win) **3%**

0% luck, 100% skill (great players control their fate) **1%**

0% 10% 20% 30% 40% 50% 60%

Most players believe that skill and luck are equally balanced in Monopoly. (Interestingly, about the same number feel it is either 75 percent luck or 75 percent skill.)

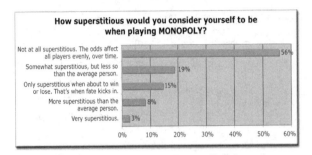

How superstitious would you consider yourself to be when playing MONOPOLY?

Most players are not superstitious and feel that luck is equally dished out. Some are only superstitious when about to win or lose.

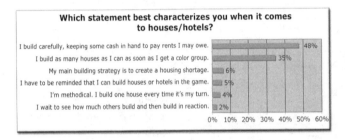

Which statement best characterizes you when it comes to houses/hotels?

Almost half of all players feel it best to buy and build carefully, while a bit more than one out of three build to the limit as soon as possible.

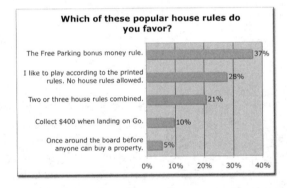

Which of these popular house rules do you favor?

Among house rules, the Free Parking bonus rule is the clear favorite, while about one in four prefer to play strictly by the written rules.

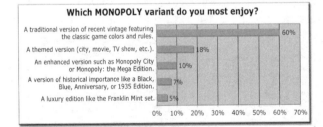

Which MONOPOLY variant do you most enjoy?

Most Monopoly players would prefer to play a classic or vintage edition; about one in five like themed versions.

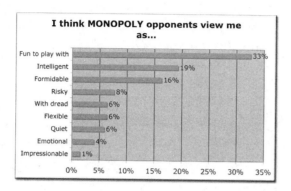

One in three Monopoly players feel their opponents view them as fun to play with. One out of five feel they are viewed as "intelligent." One out of six say "formidable."

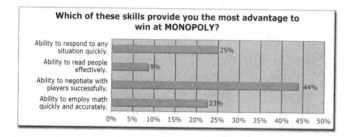

Nearly half of all Monopoly players feel that the most crucial skill needed to win the game is the ability to negotiate successfully with other players.

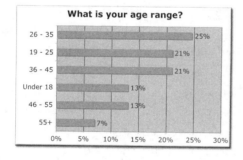

Monopoly players appear to be youthful.

WHO YOU ARE—
YOUR STRENGTHS AND WEAKNESSES

As noted at the beginning of this chapter, you *are* as others perceive you. In a game of constant interaction and frequent negotiation like Monopoly, it is essential that you know something about yourself—your strengths, your weaknesses, your tendencies—in order to know how others will react to you.

If you know yourself well, you'll be able to accurately judge your opponents. A piece of you is in everyone you must deal with.

Games that are not socially interactive (chess comes to mind) require little of your personality or character. You just need to know everything about the game's strategies to prevail over your opponent. There is a very significant concept called *game theory* that helps participants in a strategic "game" make optimal risk/reward decisions. Aspects of game theory can be applied to decision making in Monopoly (we'll come to them), but the multiplayer, luck-influenced, interactive dynamic of Monopoly requires even more. In addition to knowing the game's tactics and strategy, you need to interject your *self* into its play. In this sense, Monopoly is richer and more akin to real life than abstract games like chess or checkers.

It's fair to say that most of us become energized and more open when we engage in gameplay. One of the virtues of playing games is the opportunity to feel safe and let down one's emotional guard. It's therapeutic to be released from the rules of daily routine, especially those that determine how we should interact with family, friends, coworkers, and superiors.

For this reason, it's your *game persona* that matters most—how you approach the game (over a board or buying a car) and how you interact during negotiations. The art of negotiating is such an important topic that an entire chapter is devoted to it later. But here we want to stick with *who* you are when you *interact* in financial dealings.

Some of us are naturally assertive and confident. Some wait for others to take the lead and then attempt to turn the tables to their advantage. Some are willing to engage and respond to offers, while others are taciturn and choose to reveal as little as possible about what they are thinking. Some of us are instinctively emotional and ride the roller coaster of thrills and chills with every roll of the dice. Others are controlled and seem made of ice or stone.

Having observed Monopoly players for many a year, I believe each player, including you, can be measured while interacting according to *confidence, expressiveness, self-control,* and *affability.*

Look through the following and see which qualities ring a bell on behalf of your game persona. Each of us exhibits some measure of all four qualities. It is the *proportion* of each that makes you unique. Prepare to assess yourself.

Confidence

Are you a go-getter who sets the pace and tone and is willing to take big risks? Are you a born decision maker possessed of a confident air? Do you merely tolerate the ideas of others and respect those who share your views? Do you tend to be blunt? Do you use your power to roll over others who are in your way? Do others accuse you of sometimes being overbearing or unemotional?

Expressiveness

Do you like to turn on the charm, to engage and become the life of the party (and the game)? Do you try to be diplomatic and inspiring to others? Do you come across as carefree and reckless? Do others sometimes accuse you of being irrational, or too flippant . . . perhaps too in love with yourself and your views? Do you relish praise and attempt to defuse opposition?

Self-Control

Do you focus on the rational side of every decision, avoiding emotional considerations? Are you courteous but not easily swayed by emotional appeals? Would others say you are determined, neat (your money and deeds are always precisely ordered when playing Monopoly), and calculating? Do you tend to wait for offers to come to you before engaging in negotiations? Do you prefer to keep your own counsel?

Affability

Do you value trust and want others to regard you as highly trustworthy? Do you like to be perceived as reliable, consistent, dedicated? Do you keep working to find a solution to an impasse after others throw their hands up? Do you therefore find it tough to make up your mind or take a big risk? Do you try to address the needs of others when settling on what you need? Do you like to enlist aid (partners) to help you persuade others of your point of view? Do others sometimes think of you as passive?

Does each token tend to reflect one of the four qualities more than the other three? Yes, according to our survey. The dominant quality associated with each token is as follows:

The blend of confidence, expressiveness, control, and affability you display during gameplay sets the tone for your manner of decision making. And while you are likely conscious of the need to suppress the extremes of these qualities in your everyday life, they are ever-present (perhaps eager to burst through to the surface). They frequently influence your ability to engage others and gain an edge in financial transactions.

Think about your persona as you read how the players engage each other during the next two Monopoly games (Chapters 9 and 13). If you understand their motivations and actions, you'll benefit all the more when you read the important chapter on negotiation.

Speaking of which, one of the best negotiators of the twentieth century was a consummate Monopoly player: former president Dwight D. Eisenhower. In particular, when he was the commander in chief of Allied forces in Europe, he had to contend with, cajole, and unify the outsized egos of military and political leaders from several countries. He succeeded. And what did he do the night before a major battle or invasion? He played Monopoly.

Dwight Eisenhower's favorite token was the Iron.

News Flash: On February 6, 2013, as a result of an energized online campaign organized by Hasbro, the owners of Monopoly, the Iron token was retired from the game's standard edition (sorry, Dwight) and replaced by a Cat token.

6

THE DICE

ROLL WITH THEM

Nothing is certain. The dice see to that. But knowing they are capricious is certain to give you an edge when contending with them.

Life is a board game, and you hold the dice in your hands,
controlling the next move. . . .
Wherever you wind up, may the odds be in your favor.
—Anonymous

There's more than one way to skin a cat . . . and six ways to roll a 7. For all the skill and strategy you may bring to bear in Monopoly, there's always a good deal of luck to contend with. And often it leads to adversity at the worst of times. But before you throw your hands up and lament, "How can I hope to win if that's the case?," the answer is: "Because you know it's coming, and you'll learn how to contend with this fickle lady."

It's true you can't control the roll of the dice, and sometimes you may be at the mercy of your opponents. But in this regard is Monopoly any different from real life? No. We all take some lumps. Look around you—at your friends, neighbors, and coworkers. How many always seem to rally and get past any setback? How many are thwarted by bad luck and struggle to come back? How many ride a winning streak by engaging in foolish risk-taking ("I feel lucky") and then lose it all?

Luck can also be kind. But even when financial events seem to be breaking one's way, and making money on investments seems effortless ("stock market up again today"), vigilance is essential (as you'll see in Game Three). Why? We live in an era of dramatic fluctuations in the economy. Good times don't last as long. But the folks who recover first from the current round of setbacks move farther ahead during the next boom. What's their secret? Anticipation, realistic expectations, and the foresight to buy an umbrella for rainy days. Just as important, they seem to know when sunshine will return before the clouds begin to break.

With this bit of philosophical advice, let's return to Monopoly and the role of luck in the game.

As you'll recall from Game One, every outcome on the dice has an associated odds of occurring. Rolling a 2 or a 12 with two dice are the least likely outcomes. A 7 is the most likely. Yet 7 only appears on 6 rolls out of 36 (about 17 percent of the time). In contrast, the odds of rolling a 5, 6, 7, 8, or 9 total up to 24 out of 36 rolls. That's a whopping 67 percent, and an important concept. While you can't expect to roll a 7 on any given turn, the odds are great you'll roll a number between 5 and 9. If you own the Orange group, and an opponent is sitting on St. Charles, he will land on a space in your group if he rolls a 5 (hitting St. James Place), a 6 (landing on Tennessee), or an 8 (coming to a halt on New York). The odds of rolling these three numbers are 14 out of 36, or nearly 40 percent. In comparison, if the same opponent began his turn on Virginia Avenue, the rolls that would land him on your group would be a 2, 3, or 5. Their odds are only 7 out of 36. (Technically, they are a little higher in each example because doubles might have been thrown, resulting in another toss.) Let's say you have cash to build houses but are worried about incurring a big rent by virtue of your next roll. Fortunately, your opponent rolls before you do. Should your decision be influenced by this fact and where your opponent's token is resting? Absolutely. You have a much better chance of a quick return if he or she is on St. Charles than if on Virginia. The risk/reward of building houses is compelling if on the former, but may be too great if on the latter.

Let's dig deeper into the odds of throwing any number (including doubles and therefore moving farther than 12 spaces on a turn). To do so, we need to take the Speed Die into account. And it opens *many* more possibilities.

THE SPEED DIE—ROLL WITH IT!

The addition of the Speed Die enhances the dynamics of the game's movement probabilities. Whereas a  move of seven spaces is most common when two dice are rolled, the addition of the Speed Die changes the average likelihood to nine.

Rather than there being 36 possible dice rolls, there are now 216 (of which 72 include Mr. Monopoly and 36 include the Bus). Here are the 216 possible rolls. (You don't need to study the following table now, but it may provide a valuable reference while you're playing the game.)

Speed Die Odds and Outcomes

(The "&" symbol means "also move ahead to another space")

SPEED DIE'S OUTCOME					
White Dice	**+1**	**+2**	**+3**	**Bus (choices)**	**+Mr. M (×2)**
1,1	TRIPLES!	move 4	move 5	move 1, 2	move 2 &
1,2 2,1	move 4	move 5	move 6	move 1, 2, 3	move 3 &

(continues)

SPEED DIE'S OUTCOME (continued)				
White Dice	**+1**	**+2**	**+3**	**Bus (choices)**	**+Mr. M (×2)**
1,3 3,1	move 5	move 6	move 7	move 1, 3, 4	move 4 &
1,4 4,1	move 6	move 7	move 8	move 1, 4, 5	move 5 &
1,5 5,1	move 7	move 8	move 9	move 1, 5, 6	move 6 &
1,6 6,1	move 8	move 9	move 10	move 1, 6, 7	move 7 &
2,2	move 5	TRIPLES	move 7	move 2, 4	move 4 &
2,3 3,2	move 6	move 7	move 8	move 2, 3, 5	move 5 &
2,4 4,2	move 7	move 8	move 9	move 2, 4, 6	move 6 &
2,5 5,2	move 8	move 9	move 10	move 2, 5, 7	move 7 &
2,6 6,2	move 9	move 10	move 11	move 2, 6, 8	move 8 &
3,3	move 7	move 8	TRIPLES	move 3, 6	move 6 &
3,4 4,3	move 8	move 9	move 10	move 3, 4, 7	move 7 &
3,5 5,3	move 9	move 10	move 11	move 3, 5, 8	move 8 &
3,6 6,3	move 10	move 11	move 12	move 3, 6, 9	move 9 &
4,4	move 9	move 10	move 11	move 4, 8	move 8 &
4,5 5,4	move 10	move 11	move 12	move 4, 5, 9	move 9 &
4,6 6,4	move 11	move 12	move 13	move 4, 6, 10	move 10 &
5,5	move 11	move 12	move 13	move 5, 10	move 10 &
5,6 6,5	move 12	move 13	move 14	move 5, 6, 11	move 11 &
6,6	move 13	move 14	move 15	move 6, 12	move 12 &

Mr. Monopoly on the Speed Die does not change the move dictated by the white dice. Rather, he adds a bonus move according to the circumstances at the time he's rolled: you either move ahead to the next unowned property (if any remain) or move ahead to the next rent owed (if all properties are in play). **The Bus** offers a choice: you can move ahead according to either of the white dice, or both (as usual). This provides a very nice tactical advantage, especially late in the game.

The three numbered sides of the Speed Die do affect the basic roll: if one is rolled, its amount is added to the total showing on the white dice. For example, if the white dice show a 4 and a 6 and the Speed Die shows a 3, you would move ahead 13 spaces. Infrequently, a triple is rolled (1,1+1, 2,2+2, or 3,3+3). Triples permit you a jump to any space. You do not roll again after rolling triples.

Taking all of this into account, here are the odds of rolling any number when the Speed Die is included in play. Note how the Bus boosts the total possibilities up to 246.

Percentage Chance of Moving 1 to 15 Spaces on One Throw, with the Speed Die

roll:	White dice	& Mr. M	& Bus	& Speed Die 1, 2, or 3	Total throws	Odds per roll
1	0	0	11	0	11	5.09%
2	2.78%	2	11	0	13	6.02%
3	5.56%	4	11	(1 Triple) 1	16	7.41%
4	8.33%	6	11	3	20	9.26%
5	11.11%	8	11	6	25	11.57%
6	13.89%	10	11	(1 Triple) 9	30	13.89%
7	16.67%	12	0	12	24	11.11%
8	13.89%	10	0	15	25	11.57%
9	11.11%	8	0	(1 Triple) 16	24	11.11%
10	8.33%	6	0	15	21	9.72%
11	5.56%	4	0	12	16	7.41%
12	2.78%	2	0	9	11	5.09%
13	0.00%	0	0	6	6	2.78%
14	0.00%	0	0	3	3	1.39%
15	0.00%	0	0	1	1	0.46%
Total:	100.00%	72	66	108	246	~114%

Technically, the sum of the divisions of a whole needs to equal 100 percent. So why does this chart sum to 114 percent? It's because the Speed Die presents multiple choices. If you rolled, say, a 3,1 plus Bus, you would pick one of three outcomes (move 1, move 3, or move 4), not all three. Factor out the unused choices and the results add up to 100 percent.

SECRET 24: The most likely total you'll roll with two dice is 7. With the Speed Die added, the most likely total rises to 9.

MONOPOLY Speed Die Probabilities

NON-CHOICE				CHOICE		
Roll	Probability	Frequency	>	Bus	Bus+Trips	Roll
1	0.0%	0	83.3%	5.1%	6.5%	1
2	0.9%	2	82.4%	5.6%	7.9%	2
3	1.9%	4	80.6%	6.0%	9.3%	3
4	4.2%	9	76.4%	6.5%	12.0%	4
5	6.5%	14	69.9%	6.9%	14.8%	5
6	8.3%	18	61.6%	7.4%	17.1%	6
7	11.1%	24	50.5%	2.8%	15.3%	7
8	11.6%	25	38.9%	2.3%	15.3%	8
9	10.6%	23	28.2%	1.9%	13.9%	9
10	9.7%	21	18.5%	1.4%	12.5%	10
11	7.4%	16	11.1%	0.9%	9.7%	11
12	5.1%	11	6.0%	0.5%	6.9%	12
13	2.8%	6	3.2%			
14	1.4%	3	1.9%			
15	0.5%	1	1.4%			
Bus	16.7%	36				
Triples	1.4%	3				
Total	100.0%	216				

SECRET 25: The Speed Die opens up many possible moves and real strategic choices. The Bus creates moves of 1 to 12 spaces. The numbered sides of the Speed Die permit moves up to 15 spaces! Mr. Monopoly provides a bonus move of 1 to 40 spaces! And triples give you the choice of moving to any space you want.

In many ways, the Speed Die makes luck more akin to real life. The Bus offers a choice; fate often presents one with clear alternatives. Likewise, Mr. Monopoly's dual role is analogous to gaining a good opportunity

and exploiting its benefit, then later contending with a trapdoor open-
ing up beneath your feet due to a losing proposition. In a grander sense,
the Speed Die accurately reflects the faster pace of our age. When life was
slower, there were fewer options available for entertainment and infor-
mation gathering. The increased pace of modern life, along with instan-
taneous communications, compels finishing activities faster. Playing
Monopoly quicker, with its tedious middle game compressed, is just right
for our times. Likewise, your real investments also move faster nowadays
because trends are compressed. You can make money quicker than at any
time in history (or lose it quicker if you become complacent).

DEALING WITH LUCK

Monopoly is akin to real life; uncertainty plays a significant role in each.
Our surveys reinforce most people's belief that luck plays a major role in
its outcome.

But you are not prostrate before the Fates. Savvy Monopoly players shift
the odds by buying and building where favorable rents are likely to be collected, and by socking away cash for those turns when the dice inevitably
roll adversely.

There are other techniques you can employ to better your chances to
minimize the impact of the dice; these apply to the real world as well.

1. **Develop good rapport with your fellow players.** In his book *The Luck*
   Factor, Max Gunther talks about how a spider catches her meal—
   by constructing a big web. The bigger the web, the more surface to
   catch the fly. Likewise, Gunther advocates a big web of friendly con-
   tacts who can steer opportunities to you. In a game of Monopoly, your
   "web" is limited to your fellow players. The key is to gain their respect,
   perhaps even their compassion. This is possible if you treat them with
   regard and consideration. I have long observed that those players the
   opponents don't mind losing to get more interest when making deals
   (either to gain a good color group or to stave off bankruptcy). If you
   have, let's say, three opponents in a game of Monopoly, it's ideal if
   all three are part of your web of trust and respect. And whether it is
   on the job, in your community, or just among your friends, you'll be

amazed by the unexpected benefit from actions by those who think well of you. Instinctively, they will direct opportunities your way, not toward someone they hold in lesser regard.

2. **Rely on instinct and gauge what is really important within a split second's time.** Malcolm Gladwell highlights this innate ability in *Blink: The Power of Thinking Without Thinking.* Spontaneous decisions, honed by experience, are often better than highly deliberated ones. Don't ignore what you "know you know." The key here is enough experience. If you've played many Monopoly games, you know what the likely outcome will be when a particular color group gets developed, or if you run low on cash, or if you are left high and dry after a key negotiation consummates. Don't be afraid to play your hunch when your inner voice of experience shouts its advice. The same advice applies to real life.

3. **Be audacious when faced with adversity.** The old Latin aphorism, "Fortune favors the bold," remains sound. Notice it doesn't read, "Fortune forgives the reckless." There is a difference between being bold and being reckless. Risk management favors the former. If you study the lives of most successful people, you will learn that while they were struggling on the road to success, a bold, well-thought-out decision overcame that struggle and led to victory. The same applies to Monopoly. You can't be cautious and hope to win. A daring decision and exercise of initiative often lead to shaking up the game and putting your opponents on edge. You thereby gain a leadership position. Your opponents begin to react, not act. It's been said that adversity engenders the most creative solutions that your brain can muster. Rely on that the next time it rains.

4. **Not every decision you make works to perfection.** Seemingly lucky people are those who know how to stem a loss before it wipes out their entire gain. They tend to bounce back quicker after a losing venture. In Monopoly, this knack can be as subtle as mortgaging or unmortgaging a property to better direct the effect of Mr. Monopoly on the Speed Die. Or it can mean abandoning a color group under

development because a better group becomes available. Case in point: I once played a game where one crafty opponent sank all of his money into the Greens with two houses on each. But after he bailed out an opponent who needed cash to pay a rent to me, he ended up owning the Light Blue group. After a short deliberation, he tore down his houses on the Greens, mortgaged all three of its deeds, and erected hotels on the Light Blues. I had just built two houses on Park Place and three more on Boardwalk. I was certain a few rolls separated me from victory. But I twice hit those red hotels on the Light Blues and had to tear down my expensive houses. While I could have weathered a two-house rent on the Greens, the rent for a hotel on a Light Blue was too much. My opponent's apparent step backward had instead propelled him into the lead.

5. **Successful people, while usually fun to be with, are not unduly optimistic.** They are lucky because they have learned to keep their feet on the ground and be realistic. There's an admittedly tired saying, "If something can go wrong, it will," attributed to a mythical Professor Murphy. In Monopoly, this should be read as, "Always assume the dice are unfriendly." You're likely to be clobbered if you base your decisions on the alternative. You need to be ready for a setback or two by holding assets in reserve. There is one vital exception to this guideline. If the game is on the line, and the only way you can hope to win is to develop your best group to the limit of your finances, you must do so and hope for the best. Defeat is otherwise inevitable. But when the outcome is still in doubt, remember to be a bit pessimistic about good fortune shining on the dice when you toss them. Likewise, in real life always think about what could go wrong and have a plan to deal with contingencies. I once worked with a sales executive who would spend the evening before a key sales presentation thinking about every doubt the buyer might voice that could scuttle a big purchase. The preparation seemed like overkill, but then I realized that by going through this grueling exercise he had a plausible response on the tip of his tongue to be uttered the moment any possible objection was voiced. Consequently, he seldom came away without that all-important order.

SECRET 26: **Don't rely entirely on luck to help you gain an advantage over your opponents or lead you to victory, unless you are desperate.** Make your own luck by fostering added opportunities. Engender more choices, find more people to root for you, hone (through experience) your instinct to make sharp, reliable decisions, and avoid falling on your sword when it's obvious you've made a bad choice. Accept, adjust, and then advance once more.

Game Changer 3—
Capitalizing on Good Luck

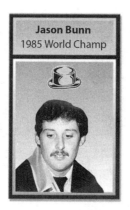

Jason Bunn
1985 World Champ

Motivational author Robert Collier once opined, "All of us have bad luck and good luck. The man who persists through the bad luck—who keeps right on going—is the man who is there when the good luck comes and is ready to receive it." Jason Bunn was ready and primed to take advantage of his good luck in the 1985 World Monopoly Championship and soon claimed victory.

Bunn: "I endured several tough, adversity-filled preliminary games to reach the 1985 World Finals. So when I had the good fortune of landing on the three Purple properties in successive trips around the board, I didn't look this gift horse in the mouth. I raised as much cash as I could and eventually had hotels on each Purple. My opponents did not react in time by trading and building competing color groups. I was able to turn my luck into an insurmountable advantage and won the game by bankrupting each in turn."

How does Jason apply his Monopoly savvy in real life?

Bunn: "For one thing, I don't feel bad if I get a break. I try to build on it. For another, I

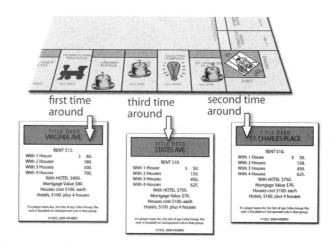

know I can't improve my lot without interacting with other humans. While I didn't need to negotiate in this game, when I do, my style is to be affable. And quietly firm. Same in life. Whether I am buying a new car or a household, I've learned that few people enjoy dealing with someone who comes across as arrogant or as a bully. Oh, one other tip—don't think you need to achieve an overwhelming advantage in your first deal. It may prove strategically sound if all it does is better position you for a bigger deal down the road."

7

THE DEEDS

CONVERTING CASH WITH THE AIM OF GROWTH

> Deeds represent what's tangible in the game. You give up money to get them because they promise more in return.

No [one] acquires property without acquiring with it a little arithmetic also.

—RALPH WALDO EMERSON, ESSAYIST AND POET

I t's been said that every piece of property is worth something, even if it is just to permit passage to the next property. Mankind has always been fascinated with the concept of land ownership. Most desire it; some despise it. In our capitalistic society, everyone has a chance to get rich through acquiring property. In real life, any *asset* you own is a "property." Perhaps you own a car and a house and a bit of land. Hopefully, you own a bank account, a variety of mutual funds, plus a retirement plan. Perhaps you are also fascinated by real estate and buy other plots of land and erect buildings on them. Monopoly is patterned after the latter means of getting rich: real estate investment.

The lessons of this singular focus are universal. As in real life, you must first dig a riverbed before water (in our instance, a flowing stream of money) can flow your way. Many fail to perceive this powerful two-step process.

In the real world, this is the equivalent of starting and growing a business, or initiating and steadily adding to one's investment portfolio. If you do either or both intelligently, diligently, and successfully, you won't need to work as hard once you begin to age. In fact, you'll be able to work much less but gain far more. (Don't feel guilty!) It bears repeating: wealthy people are wealthy because their money is working for them. People who aren't wealthy are working hard for their money. For example, if you manage to set aside $100,000 over 10 years, it will be earning for you when you sleep, while you're reading a book, or hiking in the Adirondacks. But if you spend that money instead, you bear the full opportunity cost by earning nothing when you take time off to enjoy life. Believe me, it is far more satisfying to know that money is working for you while you play.

Property of any kind has both price and value. Often, price is equated to value, but truth be told, this is mainly an illusion. Knowing the value of a property helps determine if the asking price is too dear or a true bargain. As in real life, the so-called best properties on the Monopoly board have the highest prices. Sometimes their value is worth it, sometimes not so. And unless you have a serious run of good luck via the cards and dice, you're not going to amass enough money to buy and develop an expensive group. Even if you could, would it be worth your while? Circumstances dictate this because value is dynamic.

You've seen how owning many deeds in Monopoly improves the odds of winning the game. But which properties, and how many?

THE PROPERTIES

Twenty-two deeds represent developable properties, each offering seven different levels of rent. Six more deeds can't be developed; their rents vary with the degree of ownership. You have many choices. Which ones would you own if you could have your pick? The most expensive? Maybe the ones with the highest rents? The ones with the highest ROIs? Maybe just the ones most landed upon? Or given your modest $1500 starting capital, the ones you can afford to erect hotels upon?

Let's apply the technique of risk management with this easy-to-grasp chart:

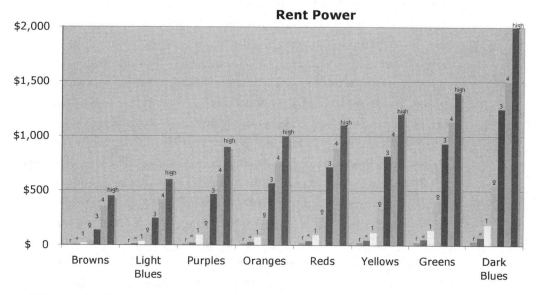

The vertical bars on this chart reveal the dramatic increase in rent among the investment levels within each color group. On the extreme left of each is the rent due for an ungrouped property, and on its far right is the rent due for a hotel on its premier property. In between are rents for one, two, three, or four houses on all spaces in this group. The range of possible rents in a group is rather vast. For example, you might collect as little as $35 on the Dark Blues or as much as $2000.

What counts, however, is not what is possible, but what is real. A fundamental goal of Monopoly is to have the most "rent power" at any particular moment in the game. If you do, you stand to collect more per rent than any opponent. For example, the Browns with hotels result in a taller rent power bar than many others on this chart. You can earn as much as $450 with a hotel on Baltic. That's higher than a pricier group with two houses on each of its properties. Of course, this advantage is wiped out the moment any one of several groups reaches its third-house level of development.

Let's now look at the Reds with four houses each. Of the 56 different rents depicted on this chart, only six bars exceed the height of the rent power bar representing the Reds with four houses each.

Another observation: by developing a group from the Purples onward to its three-house level (prior to any other player developing a competing group), you should drain enough cash from your opponents to prevent them from ever developing against you. (Remember in Game One how the Shoe couldn't muster the funds to develop his potentially powerful Greens?)

As in Monopoly, any real investment you contemplate will have a yield (a dividend or rate on interest) and an expected rate of growth in principal. Backing these up are lots of investment "facts" to support the anticipated payoff. You should absorb these carefully before deciding to buy. But "facts" are just the starting point, as Monopoly proves. What good is rent power if a property doesn't get landed upon, or if a real investment doesn't live up to its promise? Rent rates are, after all, merely *potentials*. They become meaningful only when opponents land on these chunks of real estate.

This is where a second factor—frequency—enters the equation. Frequency is the likelihood of a property being landed upon. Picture it this way: far more people visit Times Square each day than visit the Times Building. Both are located in Manhattan, and they are only a few blocks apart. But one is a transportation hub and tourist attraction, while the other is a business center. Each is appropriate for the traffic it expects. Yet when head count is used to keep score, Times Square wins hands down. And so it is in Monopoly. B&O gets more riders than the Short Line. St. Charles Place gets more visitors than nearby States Avenue. Remember the four reasons for these discrepancies (cards, Jail, Go to Jail, Speed Die)? A golden rule to apply when developing commercial real estate is to build where there is high traffic. The investment equivalent is to invest where smart money is entering, not where it is exiting ("undergoing distribution," in the parlance of technical analysts). And this is what you need to do in Monopoly, given a choice: develop where players are most likely to land.

Let's revisit the diagram of a Monopoly game board where each of its 40 spaces (41 including Just Visiting) is either stretched or squeezed to represent its likelihood of being landed upon.

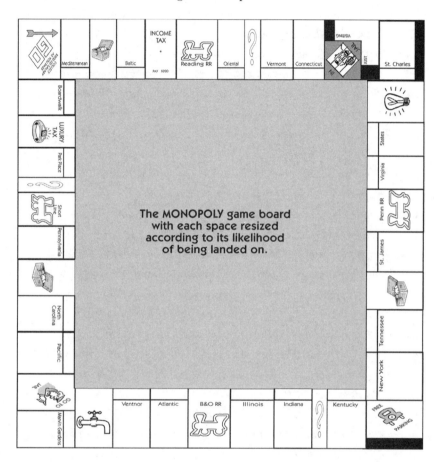

The MONOPOLY game board with each space resized according to its likelihood of being landed on.

You'll notice that the spaces on the board's first side have compressed. In fact, St. Charles Place moves around the corner, along with Jail,* to fill in the lost ground. Meanwhile, the second side maintains its original size with only nine of its spaces! The third side grows as well, with Marvin Gardens pushing Go to Jail around the corner to the fourth side. This final side needs Marvin and Go to Jail because it has shrunk accordingly. All of this stretching and compacting demonstrates a very simple secret:

---

*Just Visiting has black bands around it to show that it gets landed on much less than In Jail itself.

SECRET 27: **The properties on the second and third sides of the board get landed on more often than the properties on the first and fourth sides.**

*As we know from experience, some investments have a higher likelihood of growing their dividends and increasing in value. Are energy prices rising? If so, energy stocks, mutual funds, and ETFs (exchange-traded funds—you buy and sell them like stocks) would be smart investments. Some groups come into favor because their long-term prospects suddenly appear bright. "Group rotation" is a common fact of investment life. Is unemployment going down? Then retail stocks, durable goods makers (cars, refrigerators, TVs), and vacation providers, among others, come back into vogue, while defensive stocks (utilities, pharmaceuticals, food companies) are seen as less exciting to own. This demonstrates another risk concept—the difference between **risk on** and **risk off**. When investors feel good about the future for a type of assets, they are willing to pay more to own it; their demand causes its prices to rise. This gain emboldens their confidence further, bolstered by the pride of knowing they were wise. This dynamic is risk on. By contrast, if demand for something is reported to be set for a drop, investors will not be willing to pay current prices for its makers. While some bargain hunters will buy in if prices drop, the majority will be selling and prices will drop. That's risk off in action. You don't want to be on the wrong side of risk off, because the odds of losing money are too high. The world's economy is likewise driven by risk on and risk off. Currencies, commodities of all types, precious metals, global companies, and trading partners all suffer or blossom based on the outlook for growth forecasts globally, by region, and by country.*

Monopoly has risk built in. Let's reprise the more jarring way of viewing the board by reordering the 40 spaces according to their landing frequency, from the most likely (in the position normally occupied by GO) to the least likely (in the position Boardwalk typically occupies).

Wow! Jail has displaced GO, while Illinois, New York, Tennessee, and three of the railroads have moved to side one, along with Free Parking. Sides two and three are mainly populated by "out of place" properties, while side four is crammed with the 13 remaining spaces.

The MONOPOLY game board with its spaces reordered from the most to the least landed upon.

No matter how odd, this representation of the board makes a vital point: the six most landed-upon properties are Illinois, New York, Tennessee, and three of the Railroads. Furthermore, since Kentucky, St. James, and Indiana are among the first four properties on side two, all the Orange and Red properties are more likely to be landed on than the properties among the other six color groups. Pretty important when deciding where to buy and build, given a choice. And through this depiction you can easily see how frequently the Railroads are landed upon (especially the three seen on side one.)

Here's one final, very useful visual. Let's align the squeezed and stretched-out property spaces according to group. This will reveal the relative likelihood of each being landed on.

Now the probability of landing on any group can be visually compared to that of the Railroads (whose index value is arbitrarily set at 100), the

RAILROADS Index: 100	Reading RR	Penn RR	B&O RR	Short Line
ORANGES Index: 78	St. James	Tennessee	New York	
REDS Index: 77	Kentucky	Indiana	Illinois	
YELLOWS Index: 71	Ventnor	Ventnor	Marvin Gardens	
GREENS Index: 69	Pacific	North Carolina	Pennsylvania	
PURPLES Index: 67	St. Charles	States	Virginia	
LIGHT BLUES Index: 61	Oriental	Vermont	Connecticut	
UTILITIES Index: 48	WATERWORKS	ELECTRIC CO.		
DARK BLUES Index: 42	Park Place	Boardwalk		
BROWNS Index: 37	Mediterranean	Baltic		

most landed-upon group. This makes it easy to see how frequently any group is landed on by comparison. For example, the Dark Blues and the Utilities *combined* are not landed on as much as the four Railroads (48 + 42 = 90). The best color group, the Oranges, is landed on 78 percent as often. Yet that's more than twice as often as the Browns.

In real life, Monopoly's concept of landing frequency can be equated to demand or *trend*. If demand for an asset class is rising (risk on), its trend is up and money can be more likely made than if the inverse were true (risk off). I used energy previously as an example, but as you read this, what types of assets are actually on the rise? Stocks? Bonds? Commodities, precious metals, real estate? Something more exotic? Just as important, why? How long is the uptrend anticipated to last? Is it early in the trend, or is the trend long in the tooth? It is good homework to investigate and reach conclusions about such trends before investing. Follow the action for a while and see if your perception is accurate. If so, you can be more confident about investing real dollars.

Game Changer 4—
Turning Weakness into a (Fleeting) Strength

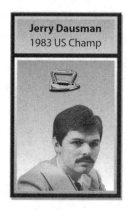

Jerry Dausman
1983 US Champ

Sometimes our greatest strength is derived from an apparent weakness. The key is knowing that the right moment to invest is at hand, and more important, that it may not last. Jerry Dausman, recognizing his poor position, turned his weakness into a game-winning trade on his way to winning the 1982 United States Championship.

Dausman: "One of my opponents came to own one deed in each of seven color groups. He essentially controlled the game. I only had Baltic, Kentucky, Waterworks, and two Rails. There was no likelihood I could acquire the other two Reds in a deal, so my strategy became to hold on as long as possible and wait for a break. It came when another opponent was pressuring this player to make a deal. I simply leaned over and said, "So he's demanding four of your deeds for $1600? I'll give you $1600 for just three of them!" I didn't mention how the other deal would have killed me if it went through. And just like that, it was rejected. You see, I had built a little trust and now became the focus of my opponent's deal-making. With his attention gained, I withdrew my original offer and suggested trading my Red for his Mediterranean, a Rail, and a bit of cash. He jumped at it. Normally, no player wants the lowly Browns [they were dark purple in color back then], and no player wants to face an opponent with developed Reds, but there wasn't a lot of cash in the game and I had enough to build hotels on Baltic and Med. Sure enough, my modest investment drained the opponent I had traded with. After he went bankrupt to me, I ended up with the Reds and the Rails. I couldn't lose."

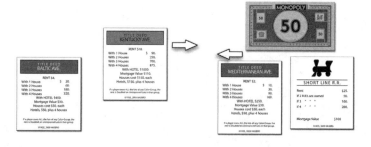

(continues)

(continued)

So how does Monopoly influence Jerry's everyday money habits?

Dausman: "By forcing me to pay attention to what's hot and what's not. Just like the lowly Browns paid off and provided the means for me to win this game, I know I'm better off investing in what's in favor than hoping some prior favorite of mine will make a comeback. I once loved financial stocks, but if I stuck with them I would have lost all my gains and then some. You can't bank affection."

8

THE BUILDINGS

UPPING YOUR RETURN

Life is like building a house or hotel. Build it in the wrong place or at the wrong time and you'll end up wrong.

You are the architect and builder of your own life, fortune, destiny.
—ALFRED MONTAPERT, MOTIVATIONAL AUTHOR

Adding buildings to your color groups is an application of a vital financial discipline: *delayed gratification*. This means exercising patience and waiting for something big to happen at the expense of enjoying yourself in the present. Save (invest) rather than spend. You can't win Monopoly if you don't embrace delayed gratification. It's also pretty tough to get far in life if you spend all you make. You may continue to work hard and earn, but money won't be working for you as well.

WHY YOU MUST INVEST AND DEVELOP

Let's begin with a simple question. If the Railroads get landed on the most, why not own only them? The Rails may be money machines, given their hit percentage, but they can't win the game for you by themselves. To come out on top, you need to own and develop a color group. A powerfully developed color group stands to collect big rents.

As noted, these rents have the added merit of denying funds for your opponents to develop their groups. Your mission is to try your darnedest to own and develop the best group at the moment. It is seldom essential to own the most expensive group, or have the most houses or hotels.

SECRET 28: There is often a *big* difference between the apparent rent-earning power of a group (based on its printed rent values) and its real income-producing potential.

Let's use the Orange group as our example. Here's what the board might look like as the Orange group nears its ultimate development.

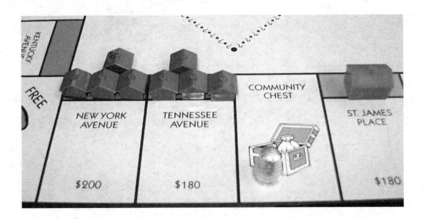

You'll notice how nicely the group is built up: four houses each on two of its properties, a hotel on the third. Now look at the chart below. It illustrates the Orange group's *apparent* return on investment. It quantifies the average rent earned by a property in this group, according to its level of development. For example, if each of the three Orange properties had but one house, each would earn an average of $73. This represents an 8 percent return on your investment (the number in the attic of the "1 house each" symbol). Thus it would

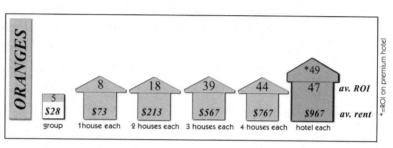

Note: the "*49" is the ROI for a hotel on the group's premium property.

take 12 such rents to recoup your entire investment. But once you build three houses per property, your ROI would rise to 39 percent, an average of $567 per rent. Only two and a half such rents would recoup your outlay. However (and this is the catch for every color group), straightforward analysis like this is incomplete. It requires adjustment for the likelihood of the group being hit. Frequency, my friend.

The next chart tells all. It depicts the *real* return on investment for the Orange group. As before, each level of development is illustrated, but this time each level's improvement in ROI is dramatized by stretching its building's symbol according to the odds of landing on the group, coupled with its absolute dollar increase.

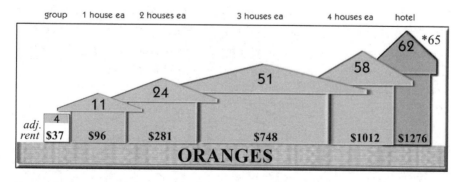

Note: the "*65" is the ROI for a hotel on the group's premium property.

We can now see how significantly a third house on each Orange property contributes to the group's overall income potential. Note how the rent and ROI numbers differ from those in the first chart. At the three-house level, the ROI becomes a "real" 51 percent versus an apparent 39 percent in the prior chart. The rent at this level is adjusted upwards to $748 from $567. So how did these improved numbers come about?

The first chart ("apparent" ROI) is based on what an average property earns when a rent is due. That rent is divided by the investment required to reach this level of development (the purchased price of all its deeds and the added cost of buying houses on each). This initial chart is also based on the assumption that at least one property in the group will be landed upon during the time your opponents circle the board (it assumes there are three opposing players).

Now let's assume a property has a 2.5 percent chance of being landed on per player turn, and five such turns (with the Speed Die) are typically required for a player to circle the board. There is therefore a 12.5 percent chance that this property will be landed on during one opponent's circuit of the board. However, since there are three properties in most groups, the odds of one of these three being hit is actually 37.5 percent. And when you consider that three opponents are circuiting the board, there is a 112.5 percent chance of at least one of the group's properties being landed upon once during the time all circle the board. That's great odds.

When adjusted for actual frequency of landing on St. James, Tennessee, and New York, the "real" ROI chart for the Oranges reveals the group's superiority. An increased frequency also improves its average rent and ROI. Having demonstrated the great expected return for the Oranges, you will want to know how it stacks up against the other seven color groups. Check out the next chart. On the left you'll see the eight color groups stacked according to apparent ROI potential. Meanwhile, on the right, you'll observe each group's real ROI. Which groups would you like to own?

APPARENT ROI vs. REAL ROI ©PEO

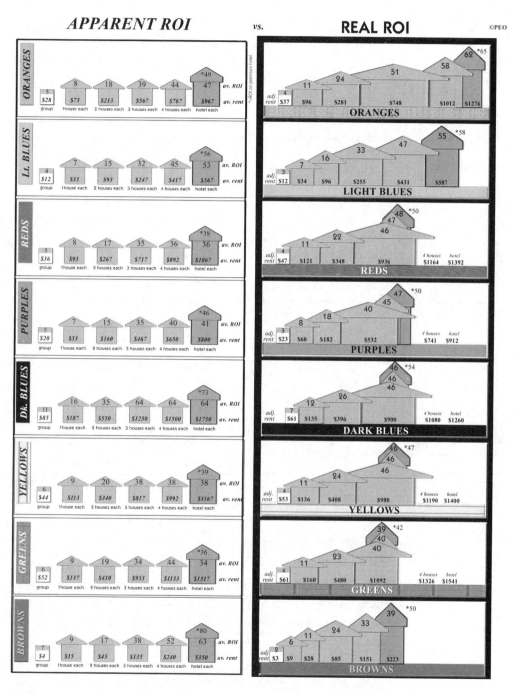

Note: the numbers beside the "*" indicate the ROI for a hotel on the group's premium property.

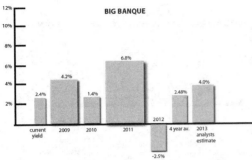

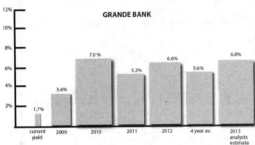

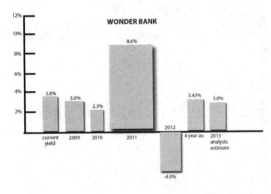

Why do some buildings appear behind others, such as the fourth house and hotel in the Dark Blues' real ROI chart? It's because no growth in ROI occurs for investing in these buildings (their absolute rent increases only in line with, or less than, their actual cost).

Let's "get real" for a moment. Your real-life investment decisions might be easier to visualize if you create a comparison among the alternative investments under consideration. Here's an example. The following charts represent three different (imaginary) banks. Vertical bars represent each bank's current yield (dividend) and the total return of the bank's stock during each of the past four years (this return includes its dividend). The four-year average bar comes next, followed by the expected return during 2013 (according to the consensus of stock analysts who follow the stock). Note: if the return in any year is lower than the stock's dividend, its stock price has declined during that year. Okay. Take a look at Big Banque, Grande Bank, and Wonder Bank. Which one seems to be the most reliable investment?

Back to the game. There may be no more important secret in this book than this one:

SECRET 29: **Not all groups provide increased returns when investing in a fourth house and/or hotel on each of its properties.** These produce subpar returns (although the bankrupting power of their increased rents should not be ignored when aiming for a knockout blow).

Likewise, not every real-life investment justifies further capital. This is a frequent point in this book, because it is essential to nurture your gains given the likelihood of losses due to bad events. As a rule of thumb, when adding to your investments, add to the investment class that is generating the most growth in your principal. The primary classes are equities (stocks), fixed income (mainly bonds and CDs), and cash (which includes money market funds). Commodities, real estate, and precious metals are often considered to be primary classes as well. You have investment choices, just as you do in Monopoly. If equities are barely growing in value, but bonds are rebounding, placing your new money into bonds should gain you a better return.

The real ROI for the color groups underscores another truism. Some people know the price of everything and the value of nothing. Without realizing it, they are prone to throw good money after bad. As comedienne Lily Tomlin once said, "The road to success is always under construction." The Monopoly board is much the same. The game is dynamic and the relative value of each group is based on the level of development of every other group, along with the current location of each token.

Alas, investments don't always pay off. In fact, it is not uncommon to absorb many small losses in pursuit of one significant gain. Monopoly is much the same. So what happens if you have to pay a substantial rent and you're short of cash? Answer: you need to mortgage.

MORTGAGING

Which of your properties should go belly up? The answer is in accordance with Secret 17, found in Chapter 4. Namely, it is usually wise to mortgage in reverse order of the group "size" depicted on this chart. For example, if you needed to raise $100 and you own Illinois and Pacific, you're better off mortgaging Pacific because Illinois collects rent more frequently than Pacific. This leads to the next two secrets.

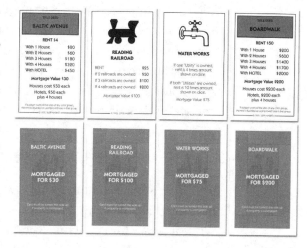

SECRET 30: **If you need to mortgage one of two color groups, pick the one with the lower ROI.**

SECRET 31: **The never-mortgage-unless-you-must properties are those most frequently landed on, especially Illinois, New York, and the Railroads.** Boardwalk also earns a high rent and can be included in this list, if you can afford to keep it face up. The remaining properties are top candidates to mortgage *after* these priorities.

Likewise, if you have to sell an investment, it is often better to sell the one(s) that is underperforming. Ironically, it is human nature to do the opposite: to take a profit by selling one's best-performing investment while holding on to the "dogs" in the hopes they will return to glory and recoup their losses. (I admit to wrestling with this desire, even though I know better.)

THE SPEED DIE'S EFFECT ON MORTGAGING

The above needs to be modified by one important consideration. The time comes when the Speed Die advances players to the next property where they must pay rent. Let's say that several properties are mortgaged immediately before St. James with a hotel. St. James and that hotel are going to get a lot of visitors. Let's say you own Virginia Avenue. Keeping it active means Mr. Monopoly will cause opposing tokens to stop here and not slide forward onto St. James. Your rent might be modest, but you will hinder the owner of the St. James hotel from earning many big rents.

Conversely, let's say you own the Orange color group with hotels. Should you also own the Electric Company, States, and Virginia, it behooves you to mortgage them all, so that Mr. Monopoly can do his job and advance opponents to St. James, thereby delivering your top rent.

THE HOUSES AND HOTELS

Yes, there is math behind these as well because of their scarcity. There are precisely 32 houses and 12 hotels in the official game, no more and no less. While it is rare to see a game wherein all 12 hotels enter play, it is far more likely that you will find yourself engaged in a game where all or most of the houses get erected.

Keeping tabs of how many houses remain in the bank can be crucial. For example, if 11 or fewer remain, and you've just acquired a three-property color group, there is no way you're going to build hotels. This is because you need four houses on each property before you are permitted to move up to hotels. The only way around this dilemma is if one more house is returned to the bank, via bankruptcy or sale. And you will typically need to compete for it at auction, because your opponents will want to block your goal.

> **SECRET 32:** **Do not exchange four houses for a hotel unless your opponents cannot afford to buy them! Maintain a housing shortage if you can.** *(There's a real-life parallel; be patient.)*

By now, the merits of creating a housing shortage are obvious. Let's say you own a two-property group and a three-property group and have built each to four houses. That means you own (control) over half the game's supply of houses (20 out of 32). And here's another fact: if the remaining 12 houses are split between two players, you likely won't be worried about hotels appearing (unless one player already has four houses on each of the other two-property groups). So the tactic of owning a lot of homes is very sound for both offensive and defensive reasons. In fact, it is only wise to give up on your houses and advance to hotels when your opponents either cannot afford to buy them or no opposing color group endangers your cash via a high rent.

> **SECRET 33:** **Houses not only earn you rent, they also drain your opponents of the opportunity to fund their own purchases and cause you harm.**

You should watch the supply of hotels if you are cash rich and can afford to buy some. Let's say 10 are already on the board; only two remain in the bank. Sorry, there's no way you can purchase a hotel for all three of your Red properties, only two of them. Timing is essential in Monopoly as well as in real life. Opportunity is seldom convenient to your preferred timing.

Here's another example: suppose there are only six houses in the bank. What good does it do you to acquire the Reds, knowing you'll only be able to build two houses on each? This shortage means you won't be able to earn the big rents needed to bring down your opponents. Thus the status of the bank's building supply may significantly impact your investment strategy. To ignore this reality is to commit an avoidable mistake.

Back to real life. If you chase hot investments that are rapidly rising in value (because they are in vogue), you risk overpaying. One day they defy all the optimistic predictions of their eternal rise and suddenly crash. Such "blow-offs" are easy to see with the benefit of hindsight. (Remember the Internet bubble in the late 1990s/early 2000s?) However, even as such investments are approaching their bursting points, many sound minds continue to rationalize how scarcity caused by overwhelming demand justifies their stratospheric prices.

While it is easy to get caught up in the excitement of a stock that never falls in price, it takes real courage to buck a downtrend and buy into a rapidly declining asset. Fear and convictions of doom lead to excessively low prices—and opportunity—especially in cyclical types of assets (those that rise and fall in value in line with the ebb and flow of the business cycle). I recall, in early 2009, a reputable analyst proclaiming that the real value of GE's stock was $2 a share. GE is among the world's leading industrial companies, but at the time its financial arm was viewed as "cancerous." It needed to be "cut off." The stock's price had fallen from a high above $40 to a low of $7. What happened next? It went no lower, and as of February 2013, GE is around $23, more than triple its nadir.

Game Changer 5—
The Importance of Timing

Jim Forbes
1985 US Champ

Mark Twain one said, "I was seldom able to see an opportunity until it had ceased to be one."

Jim Forbes, on his way to the 1985 United States Championship, seized his moment and didn't let go.

Forbes: "It came down to a trade between Jerry Dausman, the previous U.S. champ, and myself. I had two Oranges, plus Park Place, and Jerry had Boardwalk and the third Orange. I talked him out of the Oranges and offered him the chance to get the Dark Blues. We traded [as shown below]. I then waited until most of the players were approaching my Oranges and mortgaged all my nonessential properties and invested all my cash in houses. I then had two each on Tennessee and St. James and three on New York, which immediately paid off. My advantage grew with each successive turn and I won this big game."

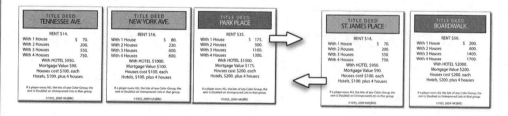

Jim is a CPA and investment advisor in real life. How does he apply his Monopoly skills?

Forbes: "Timing is very significant in real life. Invest when the market is shaky, and it could take a long time to get even. Cash flow analysis is equally important. If you don't have the means, and have expended your credit, you can't seize the moment. My trade and investment into those five Monopoly houses came at the moment of greatest opportunity. I had the means, but if I waited even one more turn, I would have lost my advantage. One more thing: you can't wait to have perfect information in real life or the window of opportunity will close while you're still doing the math. Experience is a time-saver. You'll be able to act wisely with only a few essential facts at hand."

9

GAME TWO

2009 UNITED STATES CHAMPIONSHIP

On Tax Day, 2009, four finalists confronted each other across a table in the expansive foyer of Union Station in Washington, D.C. At stake was the title for the nation's Monopoly champion. The four had prevailed over dozens of other players during two days of preliminary games. They were:

- Richard Marinaccio of New York (Thimble)

- Kenneth "Brandon" Baker of Alabama (Racecar)

- Dale Crabtree of Indiana (Battleship)

- Tim Vandenberg of California (Iron)

These four young men came from diverse backgrounds: attorney (Marinaccio), student (Baker), communications coordinator (Crabtree), and teacher (Vandenberg). Vandenberg's story, in particular, was intriguing. He employed the Monopoly game to impart a broad range of mathematical topics to his sixth-grade students in Southern California. To do so, he meticulously superimposed a wealth of numbers onto Monopoly game boards for use in his classroom (including the kind of numerical analysis found on the pages of this book, and then some). Guess what? His students rocketed to the top in California math competition and Vandenberg was able to use his intimate knowledge of Monopoly's numbers to win a place among the competitors in Washington, D.C., and ultimately qualified for the championship game.

The game he competed in took 22 rounds and one hour and 15 minutes to play. Color groups were first formed in round 12, and each player had his share of opportunities, ups and downs, and moments of truth in the rounds that followed.

The vast property holdings of the Iron (Vandenberg) at the start of round 12 highlighted a financial dilemma called *overdiversification*. You'll remember the key financial lesson from Game One—the need to diversify. You may ask, is it possible to overdiversify? There's a saying in financial circles that goes something like this: "Owning too many stocks is like a sheik with too many women in his harem. He never gets to know them all." In

Monopoly, it's good to own a variety of properties to improve the chances of collecting rents and to have trading options. The downside is: where to focus? If one owns too many properties, one is typically cash poor. In order to exploit one group, mortgaging properties and/or selling some off (which could prove dangerous) is therefore essential.

Faced with such a need, how would you pick among your properties and decide which to keep and develop, and which to sacrifice? The most trusted method is akin to what you'd employ to focus real financial holdings should they become unwieldy: you'd conduct a risk management analysis. The aim, as always, would be to hold on to the properties (investments in real life) that offer the best chance for maximum gain versus downside risk. Doing so tests your objectivity. One of the twentieth century's brightest financial minds, Benjamin Graham, put it this way: "The investor's chief problem—and even his worst enemy—is likely to be himself." It's human nature to favor one investment over another for purely emotional reasons (maybe you like its name, or you treasure the firm's products). In Monopoly, I've observed countless players covet a favored group simply based on its color, not its numbers.

So, as this game progresses, observe how the Iron contends with his dilemma and how his opponents react.

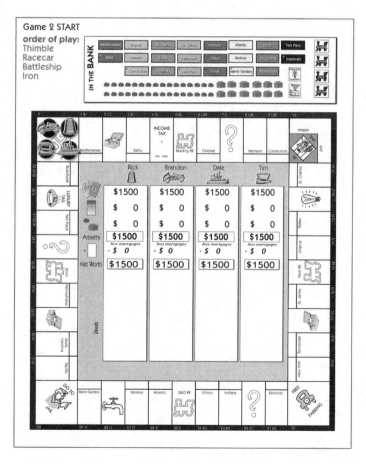

ROUNDS ONE TO FIVE

Routine decisions marked the first five rounds. The Thimble (Marinaccio) purchased Baltic and North Carolina. The Racecar (Baker) acquired Connecticut, St. James, Kentucky, and Waterworks. The Battleship (Crabtree) picked up Oriental, States, Tennessee, and the Pennsylvania Railroad. The Iron (Vandenberg) purchased Mediterranean, Atlantic, Electric Company, and two Rails—the Reading and Short Line.

Game 2 Round 5

order of play:
Thimble
Racecar
Battleship
Iron

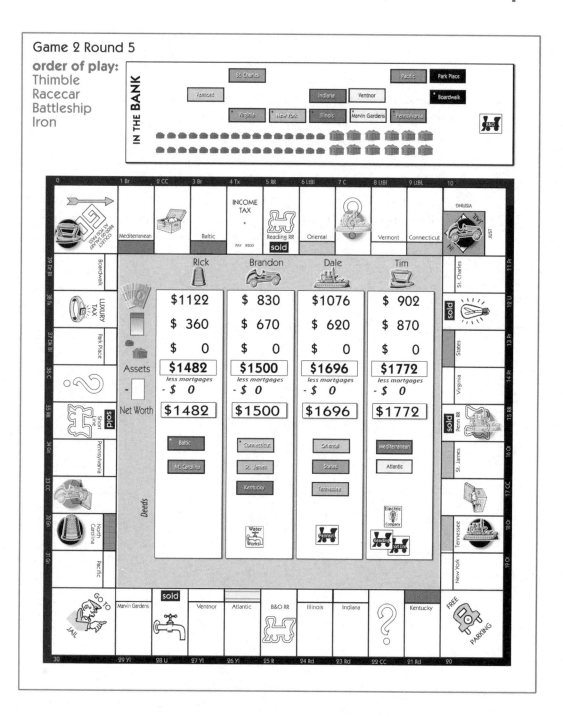

ROUNDS SIX TO TWELVE
(PRIOR TO THE START OF TRADING)

Nominal rents and card penalties/rewards occurred during these rounds. By round 12, all properties were owned aside from Ventnor Avenue: five by the Thimble, five by the Racecar, seven by the Battleship, and a hefty ten by the Iron.

While no player had gained a "natural" monopoly, three players each owned two properties of a three-property group. Meanwhile, the Iron had a grip on three Rails. The Battleship controlled the fate of six color groups, by virtue of his ownership of one deed in each.

Game 2 Round 12 - pre trade

order of play:
Thimble
Racecar
Battleship
Iron

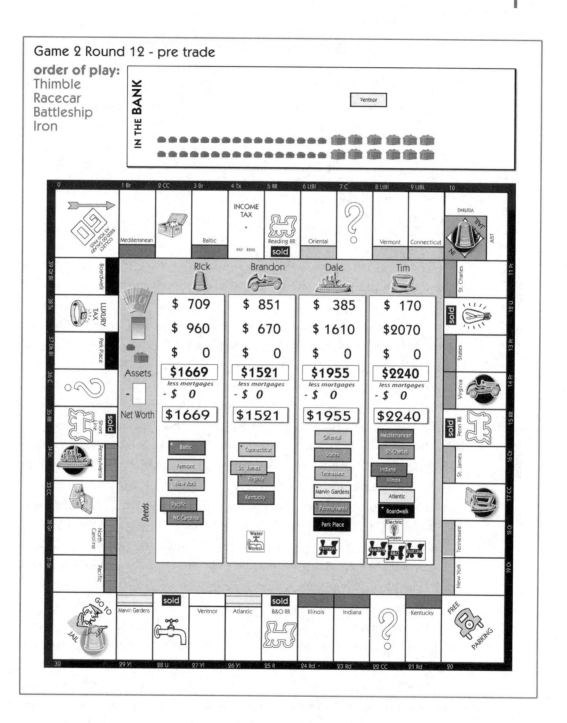

ROUND TWELVE—THE FIRST TRADE

After 11 rounds of play, $1435 had been infused into the game courtesy of the bank. This money had been gained unevenly, as would be expected:

The Thimble: +$169

The Racecar: +$21

The Battleship: +$455

The Iron: +$740

The Racecar had not collected a single rent during these early rounds. The Iron, given his big increase in assets, was clearly in the most favorable position. But his accumulation of deeds left him cash poor—a paltry $170.

And herein lies a key lesson. Too much cash tied up in long-term investments reduces flexibility. You may not be pleased with the interest rate on your short-term cash (like bank savings or certificates of deposits), but they are readily converted into cash to provide you with the ability to react to both opportunities and setbacks.

At the start of round 12, the Thimble landed on Go to Jail and proceeded to the opposite corner. *Clang!* Next, the Racecar rolled 2,4 plus the Bus. He decided to move two spaces to Virginia Avenue and buy it for $160. Trade talk suddenly heated up, with the Racecar offering St. James for States; the Battleship readily agreed. Done deal. Not to be outdone, the Thimble offered Vermont and New York to the Battleship in return for Marvin Gardens and Pennsylvania Avenue. In theory, this offer was lopsided—two heavyweight properties in return for two middleweight properties—but the Battleship would gain the Oranges and he could not resist the possibility of quickly developing them to drain his opponents of their development funds. He said yes.

The Thimble now owned the Greens and the Battleship the Oranges. Without a blink, a house went up on New York. Pressure was mounting for the Racecar and Iron to make a deal or be bled by hefty rents.

The Battleship rolled a 7 plus Mr. Monopoly. He received $200 for passing GO and moved to Ventnor, which he purchased for $260. All 28 properties were now in play. Henceforth, rolling Mr. Monopoly would result in a

Game 2 Round 12 - post trade

order of play:
Thimble
Racecar
Battleship
Iron

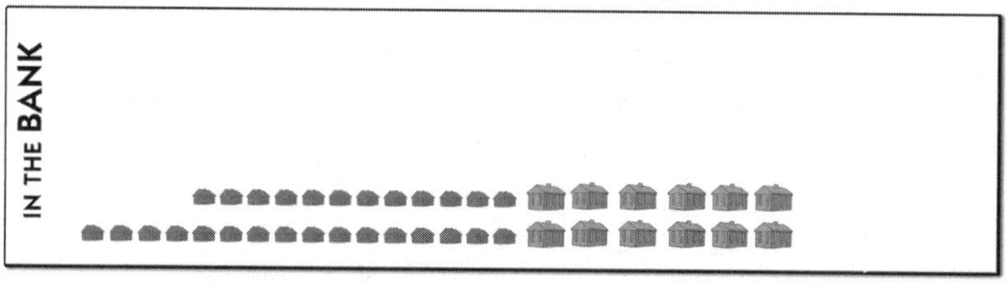

IN THE **BANK**

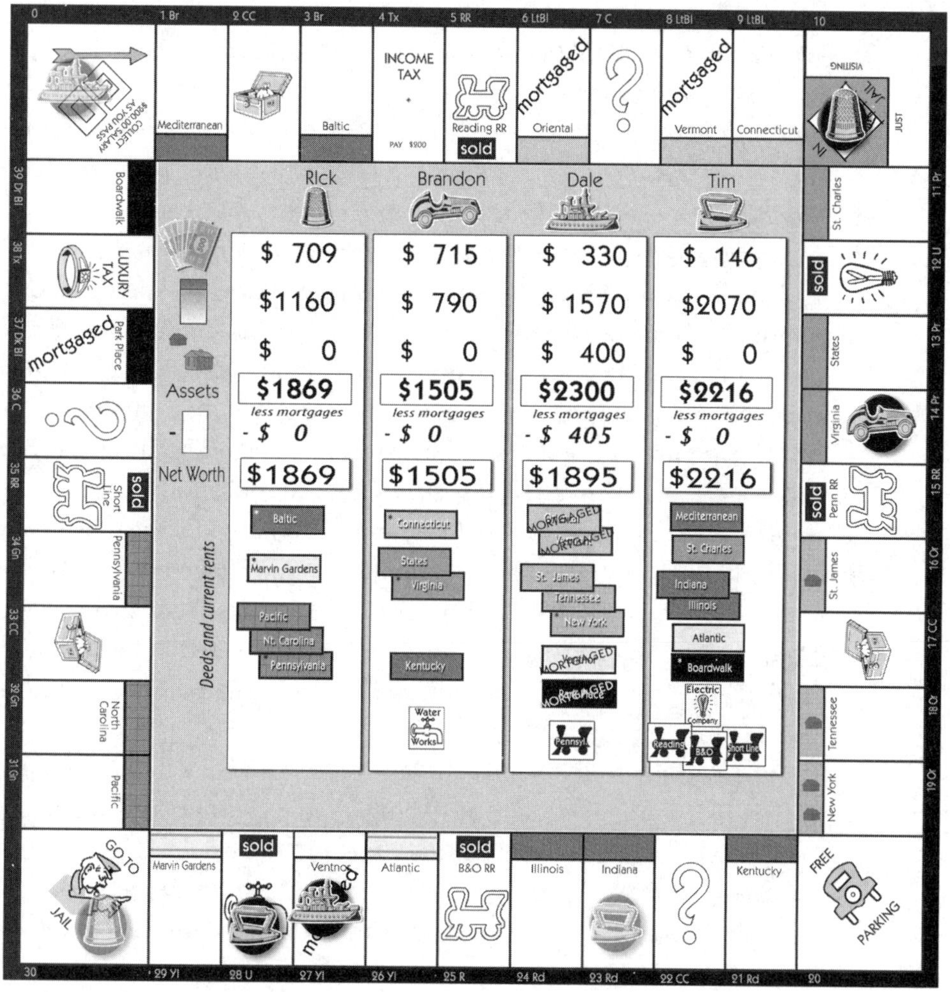

	Rick	Brandon	Dale	Tim
	$ 709	$ 715	$ 330	$ 146
	$1160	$ 790	$ 1570	$2070
	$ 0	$ 0	$ 400	$ 0
Assets	$1869	$1505	$2300	$2216
	less mortgages	*less mortgages*	*less mortgages*	*less mortgages*
	- $ 0	- $ 0	- $ 405	- $ 0
Net Worth	$1869	$1505	$1895	$2216

Deeds and current rents

rent (likely a big one). Not yet finished, the Battleship decided to mortgage Oriental, Vermont, Ventnor, and Park Place for $405. He used much of the proceeds to purchase three more houses on the Oranges.

The Iron rolled a 6 plus Mr. Monopoly. He landed on Indiana, which he owned, then advanced to Waterworks, paying the Racecar $24 in rent.

ROUND THIRTEEN

The Thimble's roll of 11 kept him locked in Jail. While he languished, trade discussions intensified.

Notice how the Thimble's cash enabled him to maneuver and increase his net worth, to the point that he was now within striking distance of the Iron's worth. Spreading your assets sensibly is a sound principle; it protects you against the nagging impulse to concentrate when your confidence is running too high.

The Racecar and Iron—both expert, agile players—knew that the circumstances demanded action. They concluded a trade that gained a color group for each. The Racecar acquired St. Charles, completing his Purples, while the Iron acquired Kentucky, which completed his Reds. Eight houses rapidly rose up on the Purples. The Iron mortgaged Atlantic and Boardwalk for $430 and invested this sum plus $20 more to buy three houses among the Reds. Meanwhile, the Thimble depleted his cash by investing in four houses on the Greens. The Battleship mortgaged the Pennsylvania Railroad and added two more houses to his Oranges (each property in the group now having two each). The Thimble mortgaged Baltic and Marvin Gardens, the Racecar Connecticut, and the Iron belatedly decided to mortgage Mediterranean.

The Racecar rolled 8 plus Mr. Monopoly. Chance directed him to the Boardwalk (mortgaged), and Mr. M took him past GO to the Reading Railroad. He collected $200 and paid $100 rent to the Iron.

The Battleship rolled an 8 and landed on the Short Line, forking over $100 to the Iron. The Iron then rolled a 9 and landed on Park Place, which was mortgaged.

Game 2 Round 13

order of play:
Thimble
Racecar
Battleship
Iron

ROUND FOURTEEN

The Thimble remained comfortably in Jail after rolling a 3. The Iron un-mortgaged Waterworks before the Racecar rolled. The big trade of Round Thirteen now backfired on both players involved. The Racecar rolled double 2s plus Mr. Monopoly. He advanced to Connecticut (which he owned), and then Mr. M carried him to St. James. To pay his $200 rent, he was compelled to sell two houses on his Purples, yielding $100 cash. He then persuaded the Battleship to accept $100 and Connecticut (mortgaged) to satisfy his rent. He had to roll again and this time rolled an unfortunate 5,3 plus the Bus. Every possibility—moving three, five, or eight spaces—required him to pay a rent. He elected to move to Illinois and paid $100, financed by re-moving two more houses from his Purples. The Battleship passed GO, col-lected $200, and came to rest on Oriental. The Iron then rolled a 9 plus Mr. M. He collected $200 for passing GO, landed on Oriental (mortgaged), and advanced to St. Charles, where he was obliged to pay another rent—$150—to the Racecar. The Battleship built two houses on the Oranges; he now owned eight in all on this coveted group. The Battleship was beginning to stretch. Was he taking on too much risk?

Taking a look at the players' balance sheets, you can see that the Thimble, at this time, had become cash poor. He had mortgaged both of his non-grouped properties. One more significant rent and he'd be compelled to tear down all his houses, crippling his chances. The Racecar had raised cash by trading Connecticut, mortgaged, to the Battleship. But as a result, he had no borrowing power left, short of tearing down houses on his Pur-ples. The Battleship was in a slightly better position. While all of his prop-erties, save his Oranges, were mortgaged, he had nearly $300 in cash after adding two more houses on his Oranges (eight in all), entitling him to pow-erful third-house rents on Tennessee and New York. He anticipated the Thimble being crushed by one of them after he exited Jail. The Iron also seemed cash rich, with a wad of bills totaling $373. Also, his cash-producing Railroads were still operating. On the surface, he seemed to be in the lead.

Game 2 Round 14

order of play:
Thimble
Racecar
Battleship
Iron

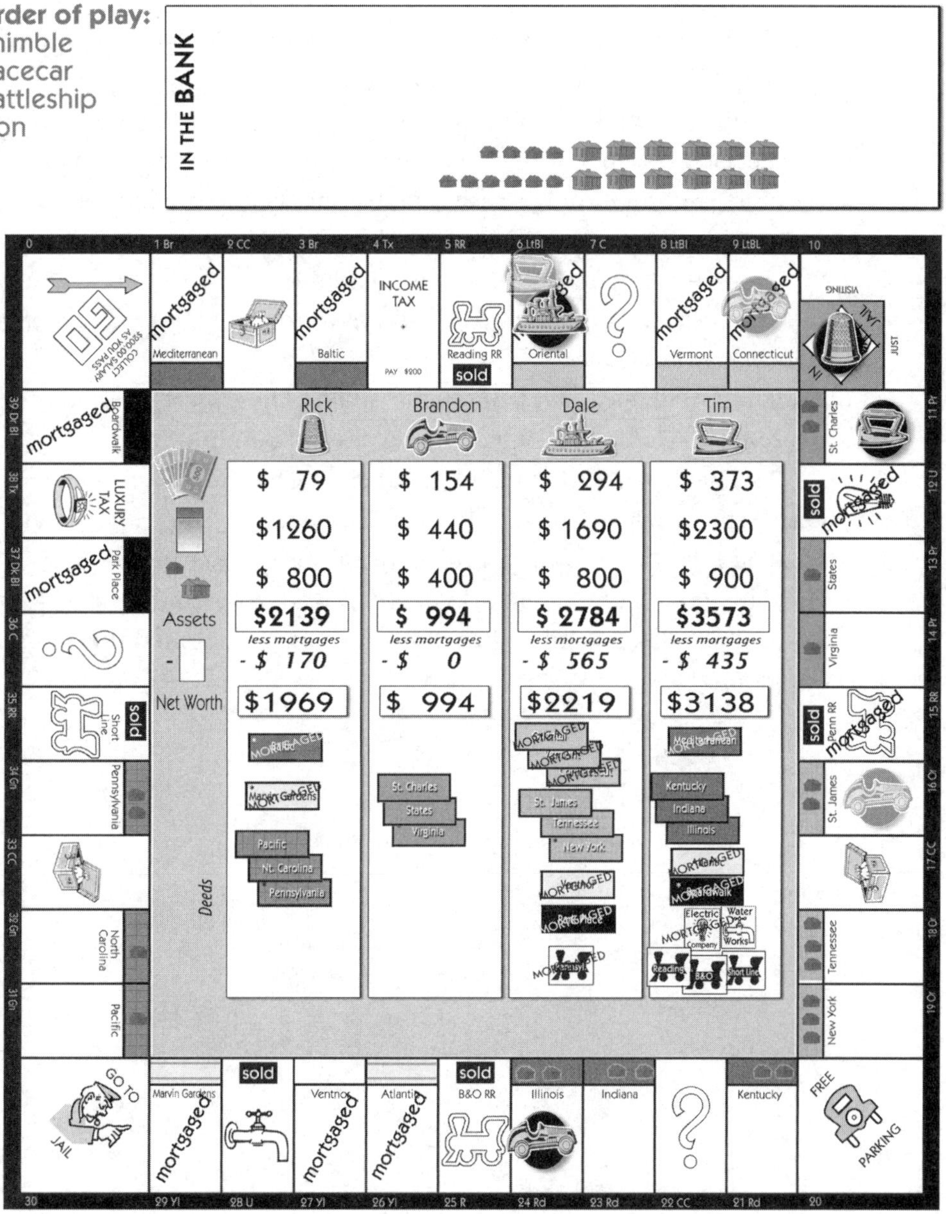

IN THE **BANK**

	Rick	Brandon	Dale	Tim
	$ 79	$ 154	$ 294	$ 373
	$1260	$ 440	$ 1690	$2300
	$ 800	$ 400	$ 800	$ 900
Assets	**$2139**	**$ 994**	**$ 2784**	**$3573**
	less mortgages	*less mortgages*	*less mortgages*	*less mortgages*
-	- $ 170	- $ 0	- $ 565	- $ 435
Net Worth	**$1969**	**$ 994**	**$2219**	**$3138**

Deeds

Board spaces and labels:

0 / GO / COLLECT $200 SALARY AS YOU PASS
1 Br Mediterranean — mortgaged
2 CC
3 Br Baltic — mortgaged
4 Tx INCOME TAX · PAY $200
5 RR Reading RR — sold
6 LtBl Oriental
7 C
8 LtBl Vermont — mortgaged
9 LtBl Connecticut — mortgaged
10 VISITING / JAIL / JUST / IN

11 Pr St. Charles
12 U — sold / mortgaged
13 Pr States
14 Pr Virginia
15 RR Penn RR — sold / mortgaged
16 Or St. James
17 CC
18 Or Tennessee
19 Or New York
20 FREE PARKING

21 Rd Kentucky
22 CC
23 Rd Indiana
24 Rd Illinois
25 R B&O RR — sold
26 Yl Atlantic — mortgaged
27 Yl Ventnor — mortgaged
28 U — sold
29 Yl Marvin Gardens — mortgaged
30 GO TO JAIL

31 Gn Pacific
32 Gn North Carolina
33 CC
34 Gn Pennsylvania
35 RR Short Line — sold
36 C
37 Dk Bl Park Place — mortgaged
38 Tx LUXURY TAX
39 Dk Bl Boardwalk — mortgaged

Rick's deeds: MORTGAGED, Marvin Gardens MORTGAGED, Pacific, Nt. Carolina, Pennsylvania

Brandon's deeds: St. Charles, States, Virginia

Dale's deeds: MORTGAGED, MORTGAGED, MORTGAGED, St. James, Tennessee, New York, MORTGAGED, MORTGAGED, MORTGAGED

Tim's deeds: Mediterranean, Kentucky, Indiana, Illinois, MORTGAGED Boardwalk, Electric Company MORTGAGED, Water Works, Reading, B&O, Short Line

ROUND FIFTEEN

The Thimble escaped from Jail with a roll of 5,5 and landed safely on Free Parking, having leapt over the rent nightmare posed by the Oranges; the Battleship shook his head in disbelief. But now it was the Racecar's turn and he had no such luck. His roll of 8 plus Mr. M landed him first on North Carolina, and then on Pennsylvania Avenue. His combined rent due was greater than his assets of $774 after selling back to the bank his remaining four houses. He went bankrupt to the Thimble.

Would you have managed your cash any differently? Where do you think the Racecar went astray?

The Thimble gained a new lease on life. His assets consisted of more than $400 in cash and $2500 in properties and buildings.

The Battleship rolled a 7 and landed on Chance, where he incurred a nasty $200 penalty.

The Iron came to rest on his own property—Kentucky—and he decided to remortgage Waterworks in order to add another house on Illinois. It was a calculated gamble, because ahead of him loomed the Thimble's dangerous Greens.

Game 2 Round 15

order of play:
Thimble
Racecar
Battleship
Iron

IN THE **BANK**

0 | 1 Br | 2 CC | 3 Br | 4 Tx | 5 RR | 6 LtBl | 7 C | 8 LtBl | 9 LtBl | 10

GO | mortgaged Mediterranean | Baltic | mortgaged | INCOME TAX * PAY $200 | Reading RR sold | mortgaged Oriental | | mortgaged Vermont | mortgaged Connecticut | JUST VISITING / IN JAIL

mortgaged Boardwalk | LUXURY TAX | mortgaged Park Place | Short Line sold | Pennsylvania BANKRUPT! | CC | North Carolina | Pacific

GO TO JAIL | Marvin Gardens | sold mortgaged | Ventnor mortgaged | Atlantic mortgaged | B&O RR sold | Illinois | Indiana | CC | Kentucky | FREE PARKING

St. Charles | mortgaged sold U | States | Virginia | Penn RR sold mortgaged | St. James | CC | Tennessee | New York

Rick

$ 433
$1700
$ 800
$2933
less mortgages
- $ 170
$2763

Assets
-
Net Worth
Deeds

MORTGAGED
St. Charles
States
Virginia
Market Gardens
Pacific
Nt. Carolina
Pennsylvania

Dale

$ 94
$ 1690
$ 800
$ 2784
less mortgages
- $ 565
$2019

MORTGAGED
St. James
Tennessee
New York
MORTGAGED

Tim

$ 298
$2300
$1050
$3648
less mortgages
- $ 510
$3138

Mediterranean
Kentucky
Indiana
Illinois
MORTGAGED Boardwalk
Electric Company | Water Works
Reading | B&O | Short Line

ROUND SIXTEEN

The Thimble mortgaged two of the Purples gained from the Racecar's bankruptcy and used the proceeds to help finance two more houses on the Greens. He rolled and moved to the Short Line, where he paid $100 to the Iron (who used the cash to help buy yet another house on Kentucky). The Battleship rolled 3,4 plus the Bus and elected to move to Free Parking and temporary safety.

The Iron's housing gambit did not pay off, because he rolled 5 plus Mr. M. He landed first on Atlantic (mortgaged) and then on Pacific, where a $390 rent awaited him. He had to mortgage two of his rails (B&O and Short Line) to pay the bill. But he did avoid the need to tear down houses.

The Iron still had the highest net worth, but do you think his investments had enough immediate rent power to offset his low-cash position?

The Thimble decided to mortgage the last operating Railroad, the Reading. Thus all the trains lay dormant, their rent power gone for the moment.

Game 2 Round 16

order of play:
Thimble
Racecar
Battleship
Iron

IN THE **BANK**

Rick — $ 463 / $1700 / $1200 / **$3363** / *less mortgages* / - $ 310 / **$3053**

Dale — $ 94 / $ 1690 / $ 800 / **$ 2584** / *less mortgages* / - $ 565 / **$2019**

Tim — $ 158 / $2300 / $1050 / **$3508** / *less mortgages* / - $ 810 / **$2698**

Assets

- Net Worth

Deeds and current rents

ROUNDS SEVENTEEN TO NINETEEN

At this moment, the game was in flux; it could tilt in favor of any of its three remaining players. These three rounds were played quickly, and with impact.

The Thimble collected $200 for passing GO, paid a rent of $200 on St. James to the Battleship (who lamented not having a third house on its Orange band), drew a Get Out of Jail Free card (to the delight of the audience), passed GO again (+$200), and paid another $70 rent on St. James.

The Battleship landed on New York (his own property), but on the next round Mr. Monopoly took him to Pacific and a $390 rent. He gritted his teeth and was forced to sell three houses from his precious Oranges and watch helplessly as the Thimble added a house on Pacific with the money he handed over. On his next turn he passed GO and collected $200.

The Iron began by passing GO (+$200), added a house on Illinois, and unmortgaged the B&O. On the next round, a double 4s plus 3 on the Speed Die landed him on mortgaged St. Charles. A roll of 4 took him to St. James, where the Battleship once more collected $70. The Iron reluctantly mortgaged B&O once again. On his next turn he rolled 4 once more and came to rest on Free Parking.

Game 2 Round 19

order of play:
Thimble
Battleship
Iron

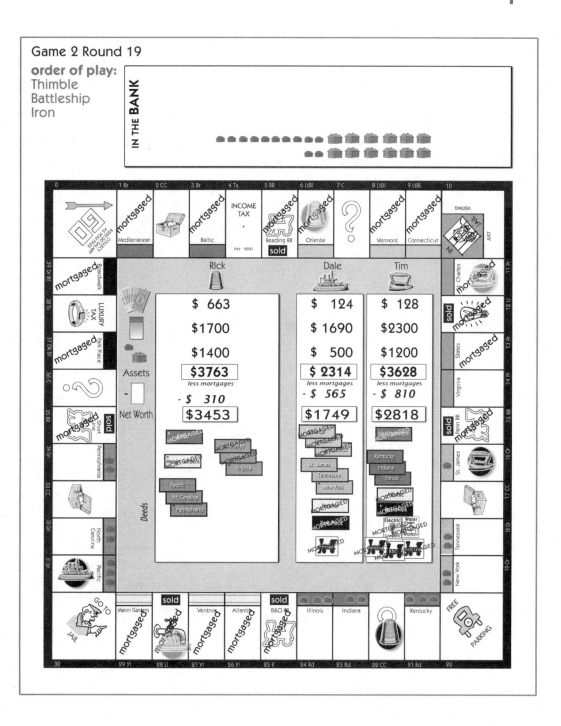

ROUND TWENTY

The Thimble rolled 4,5 plus the Bus and moved to (mortgaged) B&O. He calmly purchased two more houses on his Greens and awaited his opponents' next moves.

The Battleship rolled 7 plus Mr. M. This took him first to the Pennsylvania Railroad (mortgaged), then to Kentucky, where he had to pay a $700 rent to the Iron. With minimal cash on hand, he had to sell all five remaining houses from his Oranges and mortgage both St. James and Tennessee.

The Iron rolled an 11 and landed on Pacific, where a $900 rent claimed his cash, along with two houses on his Reds.

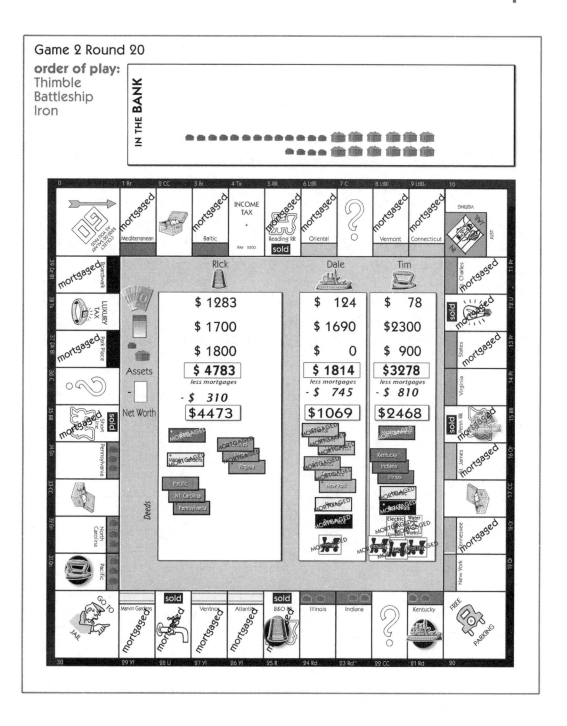

Game 2 Round 20

order of play:
Thimble
Battleship
Iron

ROUND TWENTY-ONE

The Thimble began by unmortgaging St. Charles and States for $154. He rolled 8, landed on Community Chest, and received $10 for services rendered.

The Battleship, who was one fortunate throw from taking control of the game, instead found himself destitute. His unlucky roll of 10 plus Mr. M landed him on both Pacific and North Carolina. He couldn't even cover the debt on Pacific and was forced to go bankrupt to the Thimble, transferring his $124 in cash and $945 in properties. The Thimble, after paying the interest on the mortgaged properties he gained, mortgaged New York and bought another house on Pacific.

The Iron rolled a 6, easily skirting danger, and landed on mortgaged Park Place. He was momentarily safe, but faced a formidable road ahead. He desperately needed the Thimble to incur a big rent on one of his Reds in order to restore a semblance of parity, before the Greens could decimate his finances.

Game 2 Round 21

order of play:
Thimble
Battleship
Iron

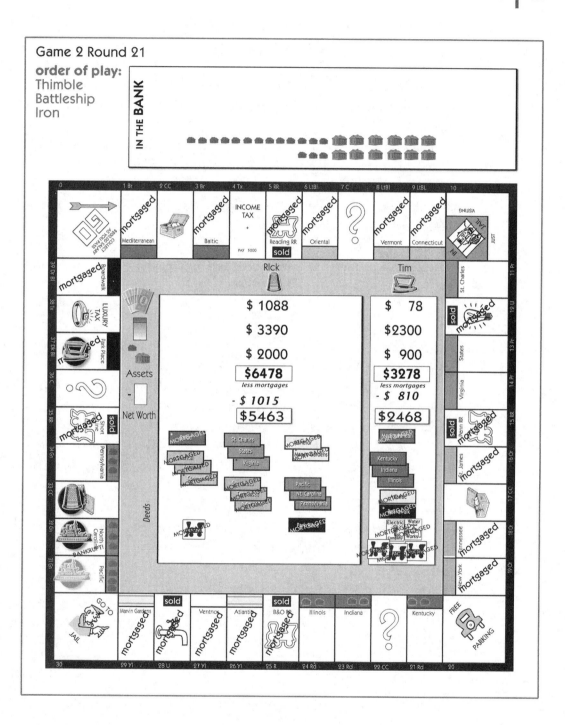

ROUND TWENTY-TWO

The Thimble rolled a 9, landed on Community Chest, collected $200 for passing GO, and collected another $100 from the bank thanks to the card drawn.

The Iron's hope ended quickly when he rolled an 8 plus Mr. M, which carried him to Pacific and North Carolina, revisiting the Battleship's prior road to ruin. He graciously conceded the game and went bankrupt to the Thimble. And so the dilemma of overdiversification resolved itself unfavorably for the Iron.

Rick Marinaccio, who possessed a handsome $7610 in net worth at game's end, defeated Tim Vandenberg and became the 2009 United States Monopoly champion.

Let's go back to your real-world holdings. It is a good idea to spread your investments across a variety of asset classes with low correlation to each other. This is because different types of investments tend to move up and down at different rates and at different times. Diversified holdings usually do not march in unison. Mixing things up in your portfolio cushions against sudden drops. (Haven't we experienced more than our fair share in the last few years?) Your total net return should be better as a result. It may not be the best, but it won't be the worst and, more important, will likely be positive. However, if you keep buying stocks or assets similar to what you already own (another bank, another energy fund, another REIT, another precious metals ETF), you won't be helping yourself to cushion a potential blow. This is because by so investing, you will mimic the ups and downs of your current holdings. I suggest you do yourself a favor and keep it simple. After diversifying sensibly, continue to add to what you have, according to principles we've discussed previously.

Game 2 Round 22

order of play:
Thimble
Iron

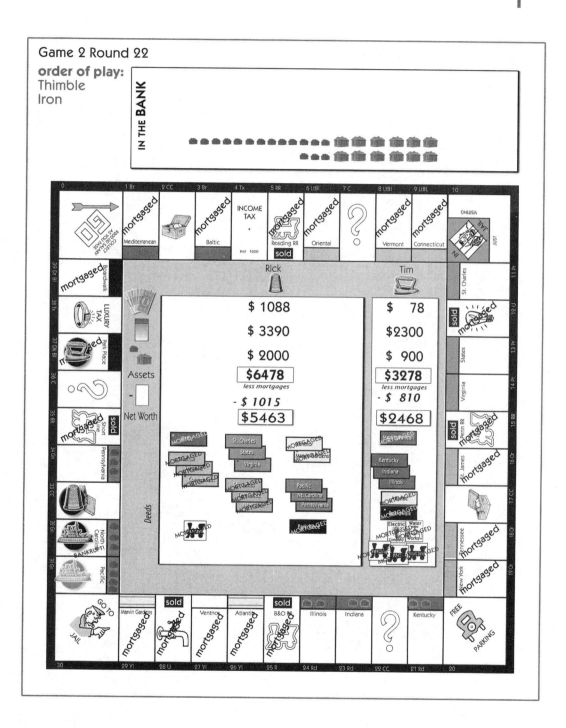

Game 2 Round 22 - game's end

order of play:
Thimble
Iron

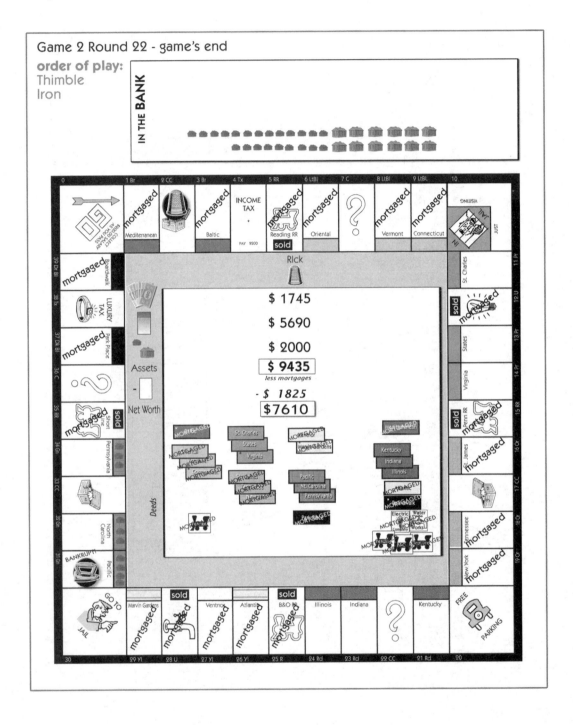

10

THE CARDS

EXPECTING THE EXPECTED

The cards give and take. You can't control that. But you'll cope better if you know what to expect...and when.

They believed Daimler was a fortune hunter, but when he picked "Bank Error in Your Favor—Collect Two Hundred Dollars," he used the capital to start an Internet company, for which he was offered six billion dollars, although he refused to sell unless the buyer threw in at least one "Get Out of Jail Free" card.

—WOODY ALLEN, COMEDIAN AND AUTHOR, *NEW YORKER*, JANUARY 24, 2011

While the likely outcome of each roll of the dice is a probability, there is also a category of random game events that provide certainty, much like the inevitability of death and taxes. I'm referring, of course, to the card decks and their messages. There are 16 such cards in the Chance deck and the same number in the Community Chest deck. All 32 of them will enter play if the Chance and Community Chest spaces are landed on often enough. And since the decks are not shuffled, the sequence will repeat thereafter.

It's been said that one who claims never to have had a chance never took a chance. Well, it's pretty certain you'll get your share of Chance (and Community Chest) while playing Monopoly. They are to be expected.

"Expecting the expected" is the philosophy applicable to contending with these cards in the game and, more important, preparing for the inevitable in real life. The likelihood of a particular *certain* event in life increases with each passing day. Likewise, the odds of a particular card being drawn increases the longer it remains in the deck. Just ask Dana Terman (see the sidebar in this chapter), who knew he had won the game even before his opponent moved to Chance from Jail.

Preparing for the expected events in your personal life requires both thought and anticipation. Each phase of your adult life brings about new certainties and potential uncertainty. For example, once you have children you'll need more space, will incur added monthly expenses, and will confront the need to establish an educational fund. When the kids grow up and leave the nest, you may need less space and be able to divert more of your income into investments, accelerating progress toward your retirement goal (retirement being another inevitable for most of us).

In addition to major life passages and interim goals, any number of certainties occur throughout our lives. The Chance and Community Chest decks actually offer pithy reminders of these. Let's take a closer look at these cards and their parallels.

Game message

Life message

STOCK DIVIDEND
When you invest in income-producing stock, you earn a dividend, typically every three months.

CHAIRMAN OF THE BOARD
The role of board chairman is somewhat ceremonial in many companies. The chief executive officer (or president) is responsible to the board to execute the firm's annual business plan. Take on a community leadership position and you must commit your time to satisfy our obligation.

BUILDING & LOAN
B&Ls take in savings and invest in residential mortgages. By contrast, S&Ls (savings and loans) typically invest in commercial loans. Investing in CDs is a modern parallel. When one matures you get your principal back plus interest.

BEAUTY CONTEST WINNER
You might win a raffle, or hold a winning ticket for something. That's the real-life equivalent. (Entering real beauty contests can be an expensive proposition.)

Game message

Life message

STOCK SALE
No stock should be purchased without an expectation to sell when opportune. "Buy and hold" may be an outdated strategy.

A similar card appears in the Chance deck.

GO TO JAIL
This is the equivalent to a major setback in life (but hopefully not because you committed a crime). The lesson is to prepare (for example: carry insurance, anticipate what might break down—do preventive maintenance, avoid great physical risk, don't gamble).

A similar card appears in the Chance deck.

GET OUT OF JAIL
Escaping without harm from a setback happens, but you shouldn't count on it.

Assessment (a similar card) is in the Community Chest deck.

REPAIRS/ASSESSMENT
It is inevitable that if you own a home (or a housing development), you're going to have to maintain it and pay taxes on it.

Game message

Life message

LIFE INSURANCE
Forgoing life insurance is as risky as walking a tightrope. "Whole" life insurance pays you back upon maturity, but "term" life insurance is cheaper and frees more of your money to be invested, in the expectation of a better return.

CONSULTANCY FEE
If you are working part-time or are retired, consulting in your area of expertise can be a nice source of extra income.

INHERITANCE
It happens; someone leaves you some money unexpectedly. Best advice: invest it.

BIRTHDAY GIFT
Your friends should brighten your day! Cash is always welcome.

Game message	Life message

HOSPITAL BILL
You gotta have insurance. Medical bills can be immense and will quickly drain your savings if you are not covered.

DOCTOR'S FEE
Same as above.

SCHOOL FEE
If you are in school, or supporting someone who is, you know how modest this fee is in the game. If need be, plan in advance and set aside money for expected school expenses.

TAX REFUND
If you overpay, you are due money back. But is it wise to "loan" the government your money and not earn any interest during the period of the loan?

Game message

Life message

HOLIDAY FUND
Depositing funds weekly in a holiday fund is a
sound practice; it prevents a sudden drain on
your savings account.

If you take a moment and think about it, you can likely make a list of the expected events that lie ahead in your life, including those far ahead. It's a worthy exercise. Your list comprises your own "card deck." Once you envision the cards that remain to be drawn, you'll become more confident of handling their impact when they do appear. In this regard, there's a related Monopoly game secret:

SECRET 34: **Memorize all the possible results on the game's 32 cards. Keep track of which have entered play. Know which loom in your future, and when the deck will recycle.**

Think through the annual events affecting your finances that you need to anticipate. For example, do you have a big insurance premium due in June? Have you set money aside to cover it? For homeowners, how about your quarterly property tax bill? Do you need to do routine maintenance (painting or roof repair) in order to avoid a bigger bill due to neglect next year? Are you likely to earn an annual bonus? If so, have you figured out how much you can and will invest, and where? Perhaps you'll finish paying off an installment debt, such as a car payment. If so, how much of this amount will be freed up to invest?

Returning to Monopoly, here's a convenient summary of all the cards in the game, to help you memorize them (any monetary influence is shown first).

Chance cards	Community Chest cards
+$200, by moving to GO	+$200, by moving to GO
+$150, your building and loan matures	+$200, bank error in your favor
+$50, dividend paid to you	+$100, from inheritance
−$15, pay for speeding	+$100, your life insurance matures

(continues)

Chance cards *(continued)*	Community Chest cards *(continued)*
–$25 per house, –$100 per hotel (repairs)	+$100, from holiday fund
–$50, pay to each player (you're elected chairman of the board)	+$50, from sale of stock
Move to Illinois ($200 possible)	+$25, for consultancy
Move to Reading ($200 possible)	+$20, tax refund
Advance to St. Charles ($200 possible)	+$10, from each player for your birthday
Move to nearest Railroad	+$10, beauty contest prize
Move to nearest Railroad	–$40 per house, –$115 per hotel (repairs)
Move to Boardwalk	–$50, pay school fee
Move to nearest Utility, might pay dice roll × $10	–$50, pay doctor's fee
Go back three spaces	–$100, pay hospital fee
Go to Jail	Go to Jail
Get Out of Jail Free	Get Out of Jail Free

Here's a reminder of two easy-to-remember facts:

A Chance card will likely send you to another space.

A Community Chest card will most likely gain you money.

We've all been there in the game—Jail. You're suddenly on the sidelines. What if you need to be moving on the board to stay competitive? Either you're lucky enough to have a Get Out of Jail Free card, or you hope to roll a double during the next three turns, or else you must part with $50. You know Jail is a place you'll visit at least a few times during the game.

But are you equally prepared for a visit by a setback in real life? Sadly, lots of people deal with a sudden financial setback by hoping for the real-life equivalent of a Get Out of Jail Free card (and one is rarely forthcoming). The lesson from Monopoly is straightforward: anticipate and prepare for obstacles before they occur. If your first thought about how to "get out of jail"—that is, recover from a layoff, pay for a major car repair, or rebuild your checking account after overspending—occurs when you are in jail (translation: trapped due to lack of a financial reserve), you're too late to avoid unnecessary pain.

Some folks seem to endure a long unlucky streak. Just how bad can an unlucky streak be in the game? Here's one example. Assuming you were to land on three Chance spaces and two Community Chest spaces on your first circuit of the game board, you could end up losing a total of $300 if you have three opponents, become chairman of the board, and go to Jail. That's pretty bad: a loss of 20 percent of your starting net worth and a big delay before you attain a payday. But what if your luck is running hot? How good can it be? Draw five different cards and you could earn a total of $500 and fly past GO for another $200. And you might keep going all the way to Illinois Avenue (setting you up for another quick payday). This $700 total represents a whopping 46 percent gain on your starting net worth. What a difference luck can make—from down 20 percent to up 46 percent in your assets during one circuit of the board, at least in our example.

If you live on the edge, with no savings, no insurance, and "invest" heavily in lottery tickets, you're in for a similar ride. What likely things will go wrong in real life? Is your job in jeopardy? Might the roof start leaking, or might some unscrupulous character abscond with your identity? Are you running the risk of major engine damage by not changing your car's oil? Expose yourself to dangers like these and the "cards" representing such setbacks are bound to land on your lap. On the plus side, you might learn that a stock you own has raised its dividend or has received a juicy takeover offer. And instead of being worried about job security, perhaps your hard work has garnered attention and a potential promotion. "Good" cards are equally likely to be drawn in return for positive effort. Life is more a function of your own decisions than not.

And that brings us to another core topic: maximizing the outcome of any decision you make—that is, keeping losses to a minimum when you must lose, and gaining as much as prudent when the Fates are kind. Believe it or not, the relevant technique can be reduced to a formula if competition is not present (for example, the risk of not servicing your auto when it needs oil). But when you are competing against one or more real opponents, and each has a similar goal (that job promotion perhaps), it's not only your decision that counts; it's each of theirs as well. Is there any way to improve the chances of a "win"? Indeed. There's a science entitled game theory that offers valued insights. Let's warm to it by playing an illuminating game.

THE HI-LO GAME

Many years ago when calculators became programmable, one of the first games to enter the digital era was the classic "Hi-Lo" game. You likely know it.

The machine secretly picks a number at random, from 1 to 100, and challenges you to guess it. You make a series of guesses. After each of your guesses, the machine replies "higher" or "lower." Sooner or later you pinpoint its secret number. The challenge is to do so in as few guesses as possible.

Against a machine, the guessing procedure adheres to the tenets of game theory. Each guess you make halves the gap. For example, "50" is your best starting guess, since it is at the midpoint of the range of possible numbers. If the machine replies "higher," you know the secret number is between 51 and 100. If it replies "lower," the number is between 1 and 49. Your next guess halves the gap again—"75" or "25"—depending on the machine's first reply. This process continues until you guess the machine's number. Five guesses are typically required.

A machine generating a random number is one thing. But when you play against a human, the secret number is (generally) carefully chosen, not at random. You can wager to make the game more interesting (and closer in spirit to Monopoly). Let's say your opponent is willing to pay you $5 if you guess his secret number on the first try, $4 on the second, $3 on the third, $2 on the fourth, or $1 on the fifth. Sounds good, right? The rub is, if you don't succeed by the fifth try, he takes a five-dollar bill from you.

Since your opponent knows you are likely to "halve the gaps" when making your guesses, he or she will avoid picking a "gap" number, like 50, 75, or 25. A machine generating a random number might do so. You'd beat the machine on an early guess every now and then. So what number might your human opponent select? Perhaps a 4, knowing you are likely to guess "50," "25," "12," "6," and then "3," thereby losing your $5.

How does this relate to Monopoly? Simply put, when structuring a trade, your Monopoly opponents want to best you, just as they would in Hi-Lo. All the books and tables of advice on how to mathematically determine the merits of a fair trade are outweighed by the need to gain an edge. So if the trade you propose has an obvious edge for you, a savvy opponent will say no. This means you need to see beyond a trade with undeniable numerical benefits in order to propose one with a subtle edge. As in real life, you're not competing against a machine, you're competing against humans. Perhaps a little persuasion might help. There is art in deal-making. Stay tuned.

Game Changer 6—
When the Unexpected Is a Sure Thing

Dana Terman
1979 US Champ

Henry David Thoreau said, "I have learned, that if one advances confidently in the direction of his dreams . . . he will meet with a success unexpected." The gasp from the crowd indicated how unexpected was Dana Terman's victory in the 1979 United States Championship (he was also champ in 1977), but he knew he had won even before the Chance deck was consulted.

Terman: "Key to me having a chance to win was persuading an opponent to accept $1100 for two Green deeds. I told him I wouldn't repeat the offer; he bowed to my demand. I used $1000 to build five houses on the Dark Blues. This led to my only chance to win, as I was facing hotels on the Purples and their owner was safely in Jail. But he threw a 6,6, and the moment he did, I knew I had won. Double 6s is the only throw in Jail that forces you out and onto Chance. I knew my opponent would draw the sixteenth card in the deck, the only one that had not entered play: Advance to Boardwalk. Knowing this card was waiting to be drawn, I had placed my fifth house on Boardwalk, not Park Place. Down came his hotels on the Purples to pay the $1400 rent ($800 greater than if I had just two houses on the space)."

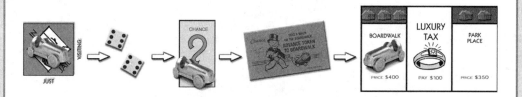

How does Terman apply his Monopoly skills to his job?

Terman: "To win on the job, or over a game board, you need to capitalize on all the knowledge at your disposal. Knowing what cards remain in the Monopoly decks may seem trivial, but it is exactly the kind of special knowledge that can provide an edge. In real life, many people overlook the need to do their homework as well. Advantage: you."

11

THE PLAYERS

WHO ARE YOU UP AGAINST?

Listen to your opponents to learn what makes them tick. Never interrupt one when he or she is making a mistake.

"Go directly to jail. Do not pass go. But I wasn't read my rights."

The healthiest competition occurs when average people win by putting [forth] above-average effort.

— COLIN POWELL, RETIRED GENERAL AND STATESMAN

What about the competition? Who and what stand in your path? What makes them tick?

As 2003 U.S. champ Matt McNally says, "One of the greatest skills that someone can glean from Monopoly is the knack of how to read people. What drives them? What makes them tick? How do they reach a conclusion? Is there a method to their thinking? The answers are the key to effectively negotiating and succeeding in the game. Monopoly teaches you how to forge relationships with individuals. It encourages you to gather information, apply knowledge to make sense of that information, and thereafter develop a plan. You then execute, evaluate, and revise your plan as needed to accomplish your goal. Successful people do this every day, instinctively, in business and in their personal lives."

Having watched the best Monopoly players in action, like Matt, I can tell you that another key skill honed via deal-making in Monopoly is learning when to say no. This means developing a knack for giving up on an opportunity rather than saying yes out of ignorance, as a product of emotion, or as part of an irresistible desire to just make something happen.

Games are won or lost on deals you make or don't make. I've seen deals fall through for something as trivial as not including a Get Out of Jail Free card. Shrewd Monopoly players are on the lookout for deals that even slightly strengthen their positions or barely weaken opponents. The most consistent winners make the right deals at the right time, and aren't afraid to say, "No, maybe later," to avoid bad deals at the wrong time.

BE ASSERTIVE, NOT AGGRESSIVE

This is a life secret that many of us fail to grasp. I was fortunate to learn it early in my career, thanks to a training seminar. Assertiveness is easily confused with aggressiveness. But they are quite different. The former is a negotiating positive; the latter is not.

Assertiveness is employed to communicate clearly and confidently your needs, feelings, desires, or goals. You do so without attacking the other individuals. You respect their right to be heard, their feelings, and their needs, but you leave no uncertainty about what you expect as a result of a transaction. And you express a willingness to consider compromise. Aggressive behavior, by contrast, is emotionally driven, based on threats—implied or otherwise—to force someone to give you what you want "or else." Even if such intimidation should work for the moment, it engenders a desire for revenge later and increases the likelihood of future setbacks. As a result, your chances of, say, getting a raise are far greater if you are willing to forthrightly state your case and negotiate for it by being assertive.

The same behavior can knock a few thousand dollars off the price of a new car or home. An added benefit for assertiveness is respect rather than dislike. Assertive behavior brings about the prospect of achieving a satisfying financial outcome, rather than meekly accepting the status quo or what's "on the table." And to this end we come to game theory and how it can lay a sound foundation upon which to build a trade.

GAME THEORY

Game theory is the science of decision making, typically economic decision making. Despite its name, it is not a hypothesis of how to design, analyze, or evaluate board games. Rather, it is a decision-making method to aid judgments in gamelike situations.

In this era when "gamification" is gaining widespread acceptance, game theory has gained added luster. Gamification (to divert just for a moment) is the use of game design techniques to improve nongame applications. What does this mean? Put simply, we humans like gaming and we enjoy engaging in it. So why not add an element of gaming to make a boring activity more interesting? What if the IRS offered you a bonus for filling out your taxes accurately and submitting them a month in advance of the due date? What if you could gain "points" after reading an article on insurance options and then passing a short test, which you could spend on a travel award? What if your company rewarded you with a day off if you came up with an idea to reduce paper waste?

These are examples of how applying game rewards—gamification—can achieve results in real life. Speaking for myself, it works. I like games, I like winning, and I respond well to gamification.

Game theory is a basis for judging the effectiveness of gamification. But it has far broader applications. For example, the Monopoly game, which is very much an economic conflict, can be used to teach the use of risk versus reward.

Here's a simple Monopoly-inspired game to demonstrate game theory. You and I each wager $50 in Monopoly money, so a total of $100 is up for grabs. We each have four cards in hand: the Ace, 2, 3, and 4 of a suit. Secretly, we each pick one card from our hands and lay them facedown on the table. We turn them over simultaneously and determine the outcome according to the table below. For example, if I play my 2 and you play your Ace, I take $40 of the $100 wagered and you take $60. We continue until one of us runs out of money or a fixed number of plays occurs (perhaps 10).

I pick: **You pick:**	*Ace*	*2*	*3*	*4*
Ace	I win $100	I win $40 You win $60	I win $20 You win $80	I win $80 You win $20
2	I win $30 You win $70	We each win $50	I win $75 You win $25	I win $40 You win $60
3	I win $75 You win $25	I win $60 You win $40	I win $10 You win $90	I win $50 You win $50
4	I win $60 You win $40	We each win $50	I win $60 You win $40	You win $100

Hmm. Is one of your cards better than any other? Does one card give you a better chance to consistently make money? Let's investigate.

If we sum up the results for *each one of my cards* played in turn against each of your four cards, we find:

Ace: I win $265, you win $135. *Net +$130 for me.*

2: I win $200, you win $200. *Net $0.*

3: I win $165, you win $235. *Net +$70 for you.*

4: I win $170, you win $230. *Net +$60 for you.*

Here are results for *each one of your cards*, if played against each of mine in turn:

Your Ace: You win $160, I win $240. *Net +$80 for me.*

Your 2: You win $205, I win $195. *Net +$10 for you.*

Your 3: You win $205, I win $195. *Net +$10 for you.*

Your 4: You win $230, I win $170. *Net +$60 for you.*

You might notice that my gains and losses total zero, and so do yours. Thus this game is known as a *zero-sum* game (my losses are your gains, and vice versa).

Monopoly would be a zero-sum game if no added cash entered after play began, or if all players periodically received exactly the same amount of new money. But the infusion of money is disproportionate over time because of Chance and Community Chest cards, tax spaces, and GO salaries. Monopoly may not be a zero-sum game, but it can be considered so during trade sessions conducted with a single opponent. And that's why your thought process in the above game exercise is instructive and applicable.

Now back to the big question: is there one card that is a better choice to play most or all of the time? If not, are you better off just randomly playing a card, and shouldn't I do likewise? Will either of us come out ahead?

Game theory helps you figure the answers to these questions, according to the *minimax* rule. This rule has a simple objective: achieve an outcome that will cause the least amount of regret if the worst happens, but provide a reasonable chance of achieving a gain (even if it isn't the greatest gain possible). This sounds like the idea behind risk management, doesn't it?

I'll begin with me and ask, "Which is my best card?" The Ace, right? It nets me $130. Meanwhile, your 4 looks like your best because it nets you $60 over time. So why would I ever *not* play my Ace, and why would you ever *not* play your 4?

Here's why. While my results net zero like yours, each of my cards produces different outcomes than do yours. Two of my cards (3 and 4) seem like losers, while only one of yours (Ace) seems like a loser. Our game therefore lacks symmetry. Your 4 does produce the best outcome for you (+$60) over time. By contrast, my worst card (the 3) is not as bad as your Ace. It loses $70 over time, while your Ace loses $80.

So, to maximize your gains, you will always play your 4 card, right? Hold on—I'm on to you. I will always play my best card (Ace) and cause you to consistently lose $20. Perhaps your 4 is not your best after all. In fact, if you begin to suspect that I will consistently play my Ace, why not switch to your

2 and take $40 from me every time? But if I suspect you're going to always play your 2, I can play my 2 as well and bring about a draw (or play my 3 and win $50 in the hope you don't switch back to your 3 and take $80 from me).

What to do? If your sense of intuition isn't sharp, or you just don't want to think too hard, your best bet is your 2, according to minimax, because it enables you to gain $10 over time without ever losing more than $50 on a play. Likewise, my 2 seems the safest for me because I can't lose more than $20 per play. And if we both play our 2 cards, the result is a push (draw).

The value of this exercise is fundamental: when you need to engage someone to make a business deal or a trade in our game, the outcome is usually a minimax decision. Without undue influence from persuasion or fatigue, each of you will negotiate until minimax is reached for both and a deal is struck.

RESTRAINT

One final piece of advice: avoid getting carried away, either in the game or in the business world at large. Don't insist on making a trade or closing a transaction because you crave the "action" and want something, anything, to shake up your status quo. You'll likely live to regret it.

Here's a telling example? Let's come back to game theory and play . . .

THE DOLLAR BILL GAME

This game is deceptively simple. Imagine yourself at a party where your host lays down a dollar bill on a table. She then conducts an auction. The player who bids the highest gets her dollar in return for his bid. Sound insipid? Well, not when you know the second and final rule. You see, while our host collects the highest bid in return for her dollar, the player with the *second* highest bid must also pay up to her. Let's say I bid 60 cents for the dollar, and you quit after a bid of 55 cents. Our host collects a total of $1.15 and in return gives me her dollar bill. She's made 15 cents, I made 40 cents, and you're out 55 cents. What? Aren't you outraged? Sure you are. Now, if we were playing at a real party and a couple of our friends had been lured into the auction, the bids would rise rapidly, and before you can say "sucker," one of us would bid and break the $1 barrier.

Once the dollar barrier is broken, our thinking changes sharply. We're no longer pondering a gain, but rather trying to minimize our loss.

Let's say the other two players bail out, leaving just you and me. If you bid $1.05, you're accepting a nickel loss to win the buck. But me, well, if I quit at my $1 bid, I'm going to lose a dollar and gain nothing in return. I can't be rational, and so I bid $1.10. You're in the same sinking boat, so you keep bidding as well. When the boat sinks, we both lose big, while our host is high and dry, smiling like the Cheshire Cat. Lucky her.

The moral: know when to quit a trade negotiation. Never pursue one beyond a point where your potential losses become too great. Restraint is a winning habit in the game, as well as when spending your hard-earned paycheck.

THE ART OF THE TRADE

You have to defeat a great player's aura more than his game.
—PAT RILEY, NBA COACH

I've learned that people will accomplish any task as long as you convince them it was their idea. (Ego, as noted earlier, can be an unnecessary opponent.) There is a mental side to trading, and you can get your opponents to trade with you (to your advantage) provided the deal seems advantageous to them (perhaps because they feel the deal is their idea.)

You will have to deal unless you gain a color group "naturally" (landing on each of its properties first). And even if you acquire a color group naturally, you may well need to transact other deeds to finance the group's development. Also, there are times when your only means to raise cash (in order to pay a stiff rent) is to trade one or more deeds, and you will want to get as much cash in return as possible.

> Good deal-making is a clash of armies without a drop of blood being spilled.

There is also an important defensive reason to trade: to block an opponent from acquiring a threatening color group. Think about this: every group in which you own at least one deed blocks its group from completion unless you consent to trade it.

I know that negotiating is not a comfortable skill for many of us in life. Most people don't enjoy bargaining, quibbling, or besting another human being via persuasive salesmanship. Of course, there are those who do, and who do it quite well. For them, banter and barter and barking come naturally. Can you hope to compete?

If you're not a born negotiator, the following is for you. (And if you happen to be one of those born to sell, rest assured, there are eye-opening lessons on the next several pages that hold rewards for you as well.)

SECRET 35: When you negotiate, be yourself. Stay on track. Agree to a trade only if it improves your chances of winning.

Negotiating is not scary if you abide by this secret. Be yourself; don't try to sell any harder, or any differently, than you do in normal life. Your down-to-earth technique improves the odds that you'll be perceived as credible, no matter what your style. I can't emphasize enough how essential building rapport is to concluding a successful negotiation. If others perceive you as worthy of trust (a person of integrity), you get your fair share more often than not. Admittedly, in the game everyone knows you'll be looking for an edge because you want to win, but in real life you want the party on the other side to look forward to a win-win transaction down the line. For example, build a rapport with a car dealer and you may find he won't sell as hard the next time. Rather, he will more likely lay out the facts and steer you into a sounder deal than you might anticipate. Why? Because he realizes that furtherng your loyalty improves the chance you'll come back again if you are satisfied once more. By contrast, if you or your trading partner pull a fast one and convince the other of facts later proven false, a bridge of partnership is quickly burned and negative recommendations will likely be sparked against you. ("Don't deal with Joe; he'll charm the shirt right off your back.")

You might be the kind who gets easily confused and talked into doing something you don't want to. Listen up. To trade successfully, you need to keep firmly in mind what you need in order to make a trade worth your while. The trade has to deliver the possibility of winning, or at the least curtail the likelihood of going bankrupt.

Now let's talk rules. First, a trade can only consist of assets you own *at this time*—namely, deeds, cash, and Get Out of Jail Free cards. That's it; nothing else. A trade may not include buildings. If any buildings are located on the properties involved in a trade, they must be sold back to the bank at half price before the trade is consummated. Further, a trade may not consist of future promises of rent relief, or contingencies, or any other kind of pledge. This rule is important and bears repeating: a trade may only consist of certain assets owned at the time of the trade.

This limitation makes negotiating in Monopoly much simpler than in real life, where you can always throw something else in or ask for an added promise of sorts. While much of the real world's negotiating advice applies restrictively to Monopoly, sound principles work in both realms. Improve your negotiating skill in Monopoly, and you'll likely feel more capable when negotiating deals in everyday exchanges. So what are these principles in common?

PROPOSITION AND PERSUASION

First, any trade you propose is a combination of a *proposition* (what's involved in the deal) and *persuasion* (how you present it). The offer is the sum of both, and for the sake of our lesson, the sum equals 100 percent.

It is possible to make an offer that's all proposition and no persuasion. For example, you could stare and with a blank face say in a monotone, "I will trade you Marvin Gardens . . . and $100 . . . for New York . . . and Virginia." If you do, the proposition is 100 percent of the offer.

More likely, you would couch the deal with a bit of encouragement, like, "I'm willing to offer you Marvin Gardens and $100 for New York and Virginia. This helps us both. What do you think?" This offer might be weighted as 75 percent proposition and 25 percent persuasion.

But if you have your selling cap on, you might make the offer with far more conviction. With fingers pointing to the deeds as if they were musicians awaiting a command from a conductor, and with your eyes lit up, you might exclaim, "Look, you have what it takes to get Ventnor from Mary, so I will offer you $100 and Marvin Gardens in return for New York and Virginia. Sure, I'll have all three Oranges, but the Yellows pay higher rents and Virginia gives you what you need to make Mary say yes. I'm willing to take this risk—having two color groups against me—in order to get this game moving. Let's have some fun and rev up the action!"

In this offer, your proposition is perhaps one-third of your offer and persuasion is fully two-thirds, because you're attempting to swing a *very* favorable deal. If it were consummated, you'd have a color group, while your trading partner would still have to swing a second deal before he gained one. If your persuasion works, the trade will instantly happen. More likely, your trading partner will engage Mary first to see if she will go along with a second deal. Even if she says no, you will learn a lot about her trading stance.

No matter how much persuasion you apply, be true to yourself (maintain credibility) and persuade in a manner befitting your sense of fairness. Be assertive in establishing your needs and desires in a trade, never be aggressive, and *never* bully if you can avoid doing so, because you run the risk of alienating your trading partner(s) now and forever. You may have noticed how the best real-life deal-makers avoid ruffling feathers unless it is absolutely critical to close a deal. They are in it for the long term and know they may be negotiating with the same party across a different table in the future. Be open to suggestions, be creative, and when the opportunity presents itself, don't be afraid to apply persuasion to improve the perceived value of your offer.

GENERAL NEGOTIATING TACTICS

Here's a quick summary of tactics that will stand you in good stead when negotiating over the game board.

1. Have goals in mind before you negotiate. Don't let others tell you what you want, and don't trade for the sake of trading.

2. Try to filter out persuasion in order to evaluate the true merits of a deal.

3. Ask yourself: How much influence can I exert to make this trade happen? If you are in a weak position, you will not have as much as

you'd like and will have to take the best among what is offered. Since the Monopoly game is in effect a finite world with finite resources, the influence you bring to bear in the game (namely, your assets) is "scientific." Everyone knows what you have; there are no cards up your sleeve. In real life, influence is often more art than science, as Donald Trump's book title *The Art of the Deal* and his bravado both suggest.

4. Maximize your influence (leverage) by identifying what you have that your opponent covets, or must get. Try to make its value appear greater than it may truly be, especially if your position is weak. (Sympathy plays a role in many trades; if you lack influence, ask for understanding. It works.)

5. Rapport with an opponent determines the ease with which you two can strike a deal. If rapport is lacking, any deal you propose will be seen with jaundiced eyes. I've long noticed that it is better to present yourself as someone your opponents wouldn't mind losing to rather than one they'd resent winning the game.

6. Ethical behavior works to your advantage in the game as well as in real life. What is ethical? Offering good value, especially if the same is not being offered by another opponent; being likable and liking others; maintaining an air of authority (not haughtiness); acting reasonably; being sociable; and being consistent. Ethical behavior begets trust.

7. Let the opponent make the first concrete offer. Rather than say, "I'll give you $400 for Pacific," ask the owner, "What will you take for Pacific?" He or she will now have to establish a ceiling price from which you can negotiate down.

You should assume that your opponent knows general negotiating tactics as well. So how to get an edge? It becomes crucial to identify the negotiating style of your worthy opponent. Doing so will help you handle the tactics each typically employs. This is not unfair; it is being astute. It is our next topic.

Game Changer 7—

No Price Is Too High If the Value Received Is a Game Winner

Yutaka Okada
2003 World Champ

If you think face value is the best determinate at evaluating a financial purchase or exchange, you will miss the opportunity for a game changer. Yutaka Okada knew face value was meaningless when he traded a bundle to get the Dark Blues. The result was victory in the 2003 World Monopoly Championship.

Okada: "I had a lot of deeds but no color group. They were impressive to look at, but worthless if I was going to win. I took a risk and offered an opponent eight cards for Park Place and Boardwalk. He said yes. The crowd gasped, as if I were a fool. I tried not to show my own unease. The Dark Blues don't have a high likelihood of being landed on and the Advance to Boardwalk card had already been drawn. However, no other player had acquired a color group as yet. And before they were able to swing decisive trades, they fortunately landed on my Dark Blues, with powerful rent-producing houses."

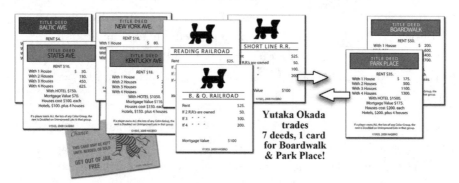

Yutaka Okada trades 7 deeds, 1 card for Boardwalk & Park Place!

What Monopoly-inspired tactic works for Okada in real life?

Okada: "I value the importance of timing in real life. Make a decision when the time is right; don't wait until it is too late to get the most out of it. I also realize there are always fresh obstacles on the path of success, every day. I look for creative ways around them. I don't give up. If something is important for me to achieve, I find a way."

10 COMMON NEGOTIATING STYLES

Here is a list of the 10 common negotiating styles I've observed, with advice on how to contend with each. They spill over into real life as well. I group the 10 common negotiating styles by the dominant trait in their game persona, starting with confidence.

Confident Negotiating Styles

1. *The Punisher.* This player presents an offer that is blatantly one-sided (in his favor, of course). And when you try to reason with him (or even politely say no), there is outrage, and the offer is changed. In fact, it becomes even worse for you! It is as if the Punisher is saying, "I was too generous, be satisfied with less." Of course, his motivation is to get you to accept the original offer, whereupon he will make you think you've done well to recoup.

    How do you deal with a Punisher? Best bet: ignore him. Let him vent and bully. By so doing, he will sow the seeds of distrust in the other players, while your calmness and insistence on a fair offer will make them more inclined to deal with you. Punishers generally disrupt games and the good spirit that accompanies the play of Monopoly. If a Punisher doesn't reform, best bet is not to play with this person again. That will be their ultimate punishment.

2. *"I'll Get You."* This is typically a female player (sorry, ladies) who becomes really upset with one opponent ("Player X," typically a male) and then finds great joy in ensuring that Player X doesn't win. This negotiator doesn't care if she wins so long as Player X doesn't either. This may well result in her making unbalanced "spite" trades.

    You might benefit from the tendency for revenge by "I'll Get You," especially if you can keep on her good side. On the other hand, if you allow yourself to become Player X, your best recourse is to appeal to the sympathy of the others. Note: men have been known to adopt this style too.

3. *"Boy, Do I Have a Deal for You."* This type of negotiator plays the ultimate confidence game. He or she paints a trade in glowing terms,

alerting you to the future possibilities. If only you had this deed, boy, would you be sitting pretty. Common sense may make you hesitate, but he or she won't waver. "Sure, you're hesitant, you think it's too good to be true." Of course, it is too good to be true, so don't be fooled into believing you're about to strike it rich if you say yes. And if you do make the trade and it backfires, "Boy, Do I Have a Deal for You" will shrug and tell you the dice were the culprit. It was a sweetheart deal that should have worked.

The way to deal with "Boy, Do I Have a Deal for You" is simply to listen for the magic words that suggest you can't lose if you pull the trigger on the deal. If you detect them, walk away immediately. Nothing good will come about if you say yes and shake hands.

Expressive Negotiating Styles

4. ***"Let's Be Fair."*** In stark contrast to the Punisher, "Let's Be Fair" wants the best for everyone. In fact, he (or she) will often suggest waiting until most of the properties are sold before any trade is made. (Mr. Fair might also be named "the Explainer.") Once the deeds are mostly owned, he'll suggest a giant trade among all players that will yield a color group or comparable goodies for each. Of course, if you look closely at Mr. Fair's offer, don't be surprised if he gets the upper hand, perhaps subtly. For example, by having more cash in hand after the deal, he can better develop his group, or perhaps the group he ends up with lies ideally in front of several players' tokens, so he will likely collect a big rent before anyone else.

    To deal with "Let's Be Fair," applaud his efforts and ask everyone to judge them; don't accept his expected biased opinion. Appeal to his sense of "group" by having everyone influence his "fairness."

5. ***Mr. or Ms. Urgency.*** This player wants action, and wants it now. He or she conveys a warning that it is "now or never" to close a proposed trade because of a perceived game-winning threat by another opponent. If one rattles you into action, chances are you will regret it once your emotion calms down. "Now or never" does arrive in most games. But this player tries to leverage fear before the threat is genuine and while you appear to be susceptible to the notion.

The best way to deal with Mr. or Mrs. Urgency is to objectively evaluate the board. If an opponent owns a powerful color group and you and the Urgent One have none, chances are you both must act. But if the board hasn't consolidated, or insufficient money is in play to permit building three houses on this color group, you can turn a deaf ear to Urgency and patiently strive for a more advantageous deal; make his or her anxiety work for you.

Self-Controlled Negotiating Styles

6. *"I Want My Favorite Color."* This player (who is rather common among younger people) wants his or her favorite color (be it Purples, Greens, or whatever) and is willing to trade almost anything to acquire it. As you might imagine, this player dreads parting company with even one deed from this group (even if it yields a color group in return).

   It is usually not difficult to conclude a good deal with "I Want My Favorite Color." Chances are this player will give up more than he or she should to secure the entire group.

7. *The Chameleon.* Watch out. The Chameleon is typically a top-level player who can smoothly adjust his or her negotiating style to fit the nature and situation of the game. This is usually a very effective skill. This player can read people quickly and adjust offers and strategies to appeal to their sensitivities. The Chameleon is flexible and complies with the mood and emotion of the moment. He or she is fully capable of transcending the advice offered earlier in this chapter to be one-self when negotiating. To be a good Chameleon, a player must learn the foibles and weaknesses of *all* other negotiating styles and contend with each accordingly.

   Dealing with Chameleons is easier if you recognize them on sight. Counter them by showing that you can see behind their mask. For example, reply to a proposition, "That offer doesn't sound like one you'd be comfortable with. I think you'd be more comfortable with trading for . . ." This often brings about an end to their act.

8. *Mr. or Ms. Scarcity.* This player tries to keep as many color groups broken for as long as possible, with the aim of eventually engineering

a very favorable trade. This is quite possible if Scarcity has a Rainbow Monopoly, or at the least one deed for each of the three-property groups. Mr. or Mrs. Scarcity often emerges by engineering seemingly innocuous trades that bring about a Rainbow Monopoly. Achieving this makes him or her kingmaker in any deal.

The only way to deal with Mr. or Mrs. Scarcity is to prevent the Rainbow Monopoly from falling into their hands. Once it has happened, it is often too late. Thereafter, you have to hope they make a poor trade or that luck runs against them. Hope more typically loses games than wins them.

Affable Negotiating Styles

9. *"I'm Your Best Friend."* We all know this player, because most of us like to be friendly and believe others should be friendly toward us. In fact, in our Monopoly survey most players think others view them as "fun and likable." But "I'm Your Best Friend" exploits this innate sense of goodness by making it seem like you're both against the "bad guys" sitting on the other sides of the table. If successful, "I'm Your Best Friend" will dissuade you from dealing with the "enemy" and compel you to trade within his limited palette of deeds.

It's difficult to contend with "I'm Your Best Friend" because to do so seems wrong, as if showing suspicion is unwarranted and unnecessarily rude, given his "trust." But—and this is a lesson for real life as well—everyone has self-interest, and this opponent is not looking out for yours as much as he claims. With this motivation in mind, you are perfectly right to be suspicious and keep trade options open with the "enemies." After all, if you can weaken them through deal-making, isn't that a good offense, rather than strictly playing defense?

10. *The Expert.* This player knows everything about the merits of each deed and cautions you when you're about to make a deal in which you haven't adequately considered the facts. He or she is usually very friendly and likes to be seen as a font of knowledge. ("No, you really don't want to do that. Let me tell you why that's a bad trade.") The Expert holds sway with facts and figures and is adept at thwarting a

trade that would mainly threaten his or her position. Strangely, an Expert remains quiet if the facts and figures favor his side of a deal.

The way to deal with an Expert is actually to use the secret of dealing effectively with any opponent: knowledge counters knowledge.

SECRET 36: **The best way to evaluate any deal, after filtering out negotiating style, is to rely on the numbers.** Will this deal (or any deal) gain you ROI, frequency, and rent power (meaning a better chance for a big return)? If it will, engage and continue. But what if the edge seems to lie with your competitor? Say no and push back.

Game Changer 8—
The Mental Side

Leon Vandendooren
2004 Canadian Champ

English philosopher John Locke once said, "We are like chameleons, we take our hue and the color of our moral character, from those who are around us." Leon Vandendooren demonstrated this talent to perfection on his way to winning the 2004 Canadian Monopoly Championship.

Vandendooren: "This game became intense when it got down to one opponent and myself. My competitor was quite tense; he was not liked by the other players, and I didn't sense the audience was on his side either. I leveraged myself in this situation by using humor to ease the tension and win the crowd. We kept exchanging big rents, tearing down and rebuilding houses. I soon realized the mental side would tip the scales. This gave me a feeling of power like I had the upper hand even though I was just psyching him up to become distracted by the mind game. I had to suspend my usual gentlemanly conduct, and I bordered on the unwritten law of player-to-player respect. Yes, I was cautioned for it. But he was too good and I needed to distract him. It worked. He made one more mistake than I did and I finally sent him packing. The Oranges won it for me."

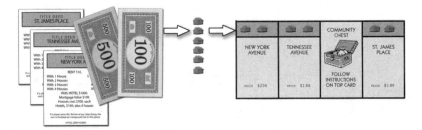

What's Leon's take on how Monopoly applies to real life?

Vandendooren: "It's a thousand little decisions that add up to the big picture. If you have a game plan and know where you want to be, you won't lose track of the big picture when you come to a fork and one of those decisions threatens to detour you."

12

THE CLOCK

YOUR GAME PLAN

The key is not just spending time playing the game, but profiting from the time you invest in its play.

Half the game is 90 percent mental.
—Yogi Berra

TIME MANAGEMENT AND
YOUR GAME PLAN

Time management is not a new concept. Ben Franklin offered wisdom about it over 200 years ago:

- "Time is money."

- "You delay, but time will not."

- "Time lost is never found again."

Think about the games of Monopoly you've played. Like the games illustrated in this book, they share a common flow of events during the ticking of the clock (buy 'em, build 'em, bankrupt 'em). Depending on how casually you play, this journey could take three hours or longer. But if you play completely focused, with a sense of urgency (as in tournaments), it could conclude in 90 minutes, or even less thanks to the Speed Die.

Regardless of the pace you keep, time in Monopoly remains relative: early game, midgame, endgame. The significance of these phases lies in the opportunities they present. Do you buy North Carolina even though it will deplete your cash early in the game? Do you build another house on New York or Atlantic in the midgame? Do you hold on to some cash or buy three more houses and go "all in" late in the game?

These kinds of strategic assessments are timely. Often, you don't get a second chance if you fail to grab an opportunity. When the moment arrives, you must contend with it, like it or not. To repeat Mark Twain, "I was seldom able to see an opportunity until it had ceased to be one."

That's the essence of time management in the game: choosing the right alternative the moment it presents itself. But the big lesson to be learned from sharpening your timing skills in Monopoly is to recognize that real life is the same. When fortune calls or a threat surfaces, you must maximize the outcome (be it enhancing your prospects for gain or minimizing your losses)—game theory again. Likewise, the rhythm of the game parallels real life. There's typically an opening, middle, and end phase of any endeavor, any project, be it at home or at work. It helps to know where you and your teammates stand within the time span of such endeavors. For example, how long should you watch a potential investment before you jump on board?

Once you invest, how long do you hold, especially if it goes down in value? Likewise, has a project at work progressed far enough given the money invested? Should you cut your losses now or keep going?

By now, you've encountered all the principles of smart play, and you know that time management is vital. But how do you put them all together in the big picture by devising a strategy to carry you through an entire game? In other words, how do you formulate a game plan, as referenced by Leon Vandendooren in the last chapter?

GAME PLANS

For every winner in Monopoly there are several losers. Yet everyone has an equal chance to win when the game begins; there is no handicap applied at the outset, other than the order of taking turns. Chances are the losers weren't fated to lose. They lost because they didn't execute their game plan well. (Not having a game plan is, by default, still a plan—usually a losing one.)

We repeatedly hear this term, "game plan," applied in sports. "We got knocked off our game plan, and that's why we lost"; or "We came out strong, kept to our game plan, and knocked them off of theirs"; or "I try to stay calm, follow the game plan, and see it through to the end." So how do you go about devising your own plan to enhance your chances of winning the Monopoly game?

The following pages provide you with alternatives. You might decide one approach feels most comfortable and stick with it time and again. Or you might elect to try a different one each time you play. The important thing is to stay focused, keep to your plan as long as possible, *and* try to figure out your opponents' plans in order to block them.

Believe it or not, there are really just three types of game plans you can employ. They are:

1. The Low Price Strategy

You set a goal to acquire a cheap color group early, develop it, and quickly reinvest the cash you earn. The beauty of this strategy is that, if worked well, it drains cash from players seeking to develop more expensive color groups, before they reach the killer three-house level.

Let's say you have the opportunity to acquire the Purples in a trade and have $800 or more in cash. You make the deal and immediately put up eight houses (St. Charles and Virginia get three houses each, and States gets two). An opponent who lands on St. Charles will owe you $450, on States $150, and on Virginia $500. Once you collect any of these rents, you bring States up to three houses. Depending on the cash level of your opponents, and the color groups aligned against you, you might decide to keep going up to four houses. If you collect $500 or more from the owner of the Red group, who already has two houses per property, you have denied him the ability to purchase three more houses against you. That's critical. If this strategy manages to drain all your opponents of their free cash, you take control of the game. Eventually, one goes bankrupt to you and you may well gain an expensive color group, perhaps the Yellows, in the process. Now you also have a killer group and may begin to build houses on it, hastening the demise of the remaining players.

That's how the Low Price Strategy can work. But it won't work if you hesitate or don't have the means to build quickly. If need be, mortgage and/or sell other deeds that won't immediately help your opponent. You have to build, baby, build.

A sly technique is to lure an opponent to accept expensive properties from you in return for, say, the Purple group and cash. You're much better off with the Purples and three houses each than with the Greens with one house each.

What groups can make this strategy a winning proposition? The Light Blues, Purples, and Oranges. (See Game Three for more proof.)

Forget the Brown group; its rents are nominal and it doesn't get landed on much. Surprisingly, the expensive Dark Blues can be used with this low-end strategy, because there are only two of them. It is cheaper to develop Boardwalk to the three-house level than Pennsylvania Avenue, for example.

What's the real-life equivalent? Focusing your investment capital in promising but lesser-valued firms, or mutual funds that specialize in such companies, and/or investments that are currently out of favor. (For example, housing stocks took a beating after the subprime crisis. At some point they became undervalued and stood a good chance of rebounding.)

2. The High Price Strategy

Your goal with this strategy is to get an expensive group early and build it over time, as cash becomes available to you. It's delayed gratification at its finest. While your opponents are happy to seek the cheap groups in trade, you zero in on the Yellows, Greens, or even the Reds.

The risk in this strategy is, of course, the need to grow your cash. Let's say you decide to go for the Greens. Buying them outright plus nine houses will cost you a cool $2720 ($920 in deeds and $1800 in houses). You started the game with $1500, so you need to earn $1250 more. Imposing. Of course, if you get the Greens in trade for properties you paid, say, $600 for, you may well be able to afford two houses each (yielding at least $390 per rent). Collect this amount a couple of times and you'll have the means to build each property up to three houses. (The Russian player Oleg Korestelov used this strategy to advance to the final game of the 2009 World Championship.)

Another approach is to get the Greens (or Yellows) in a trade and sit tight. Your opponents may begin to ignore the looming threat. Then, when you have the cash, and their tokens are approaching your group, buy eight or nine houses. If one of them hits you, you're golden.

The risk of a "patient" High Price Strategy becomes acute if an opponent develops a low-priced group to three houses. Your cash may disappear. One defense is to deny, as best you can, the ability of your opponents to acquire "bread and butter" groups. If you lack such ability, "high price spread" becomes highly dangerous.

What's the real-world parallel? Buying only top-quality blue-chip firms or mutual funds that specialize in their ownership, and/or buying only investment classes currently in vogue, because their demand is on the rise.

3. The Rainbow Strategy

Not every game engenders the formation of color groups and a quick entry into the midgame. Players may not be in a trading mood or the dice may have divided the properties so awkwardly that no one has a trading edge. If this sounds like the situation in your game, there is a strategy to contend with it. Nicknamed the Rainbow Strategy or the Rainbow Monopoly Strategy, this strategy is based on a simple idea: prevent your opponents from building a color group *unless* they come through you. Ideally, you gain one deed from each of the eight property groups. This creates a perfect Rainbow Monopoly. And although a Rainbow Monopoly can't be built upon, no opponent will ever obtain a color group unless you permit it, and why do so unless you gain more in return, right?

Let's say you own, among other properties, a Purple, an Orange, and a Red. No opponent owns more than one of the other two deeds from each group. Given the pressure to form a group and get going, you can likely swing a three-way deal that brings you whichever of these groups you want.

Another name for this strategy is the "Tortoise Maneuver," because restraint and discipline may be required to make the Rainbow Strategy work. You need to wait out your opponents until their desire for action becomes overwhelming. Then you become agreeable and without fanfare bring about the deal. You want to own the most powerful color group after the dust settles. This doesn't necessarily mean the most expensive group among those involved, but the one best positioned after development to bring down one's opponents. Let's say two or three of your opponents are coming up on the Purples and you have enough cash to build nine houses there. The Purples might wreck the aspirations of the players who end up with the Oranges, Reds, and/or Yellows.

Note: a Rainbow Strategy does not require ownership in the Browns. And if the Greens are scattered among three of your opponents, you can still apply this strategy (a bit less effectively, of course). By contrast, a valid Rainbow Monopoly must have a Purple, an Orange, a Red, and a Yellow (and hopefully a Light and Dark Blue).

The real-world analogy is: broad diversification. You decide to first acquire a large number of investments, placing a modest amount of cash in each, then sell those that don't perform in order to concentrate money on the proven winners.

But life is not always what we hope it will be. Just like the sports team that got knocked off its game plan, it is unwise to pursue your vision without taking into account what else is happening on the board. Here are five *tactics* to help you adjust.

1. The Bad Weather Gambit

The Bad Weather Gambit requires you to maintain enough cash and mortgage potential to pay the biggest rent you might incur. To do so, you must monitor the situation on the board and be willing to sublimate your strategy. Why? Because it becomes a losing proposition to invest in houses if they are likely to be quickly torn down. Of necessity, this will put a brake on your housing development, because for each $100 you invest in a house, you're only going to get $50 back from the bank (even less if you had to overpay to buy this house at an expensive auction).

Let's say there are three houses on Illinois and you are, unfortunately, seven spaces away on Community Chest. You have $900 in cash, have just acquired the Purples, and know you need to build three houses on each to reap the benefit. How many houses do you buy?

The Bad Weather Gambit dictates that you buy only one in order to preserve $800 cash for that potential rent. Meanwhile, the Low Price Strategy suggests you buy nine houses. What to do? Fortunately, the Bad Weather Gambit is circumstantial. All things being equal, you would hold on to the $800 until you roll again and learn if you've escaped the hangman's noose *except* if one or more opponents are approaching your Purples and roll before you. If so, your hefty wad of cash will do little good if one of them lands on Virginia. So in this circumstance, it would be foolish to sit on the cash. Admittedly, this situation is fraught with risk, but as you've learned, game theory teaches that you must make the best decision consistent with risk/reward. Here, you must take on added risk and buy the houses. Damn the weather.

2. The Cash Machine Stratagem

Delaying your strategy to pursue the Railroads first is the feature of this tactic. It's not worth it to own one, as it generates but $25 rent. Two is not great, because each earns only a modest $50. But if you can get three ($100 rent) or, better yet, four ($200 rent), you can implement the Cash Machine Stratagem. The average rent on a property with two houses is about $200—and you don't need to build a single house to get this return with four Railroads.

Let's say you do acquire all four Railroads. From now on, you can expect to earn more than $120 each time an opponent circles the board. If you have three opponents, that's a cool $360, which you can use to develop a color group. And, just as important, it depletes your opponents of the means to build aggressively against you.

You can't win outright with the Cash Machine Stratagem, but it solidly supports whatever strategy you implement. For example, if you gain the Purples, the Rails will typically provide enough cash for you to buy seven houses within the time it takes three opponents to circle the board twice.

It is wise to hold on to your Railroads until later in the game when property development peaks. Then the Railroads become good trading material, especially if you get enough cash for them to build a color group up to four houses or hotels. Time is money, and the more time your opponents remain in play, the longer they have to prosper, rejuvenate, and, worse still, bankrupt you.

It should be noted that the Utilities are not a candidate for the Cash Machine Stratagem. If you own both and an opponent lands on one (not even half as likely as landing on one of four Railroads), the opponent must roll and pay you 10 times the number showing on the dice. That's $120 maximum, or $70 on average. Your likely return is only $15 per opponent's trip around the board. There just isn't enough time in the early and midgame to generate the kind of cash you need to develop a color group.

Is there a moment when you would want to own the Utilities? Perhaps, such as if you get them in trade as a throw-in while also getting a color group or the Railroads. Owning them might also foster future trades (using the Utilities to grease the wheels).

3. The Housing Shortage Discipline

This one is obvious, based on advice in earlier pages, but it bears repeating here. The Monopoly game has a limited number of houses and hotels (32 and 12, respectively). It will do you little good to form a color group unless you can build upon it. If there are too few houses left in the bank, you can't. Case closed. Even more agonizing is if there are plenty of hotels in the bank and you are swimming in cash. But unless there are also 12 houses (between the bank and on your desired group) you can't buy those hotels.

The Housing Shortage Discipline becomes viable after you own a three-property color group (no matter its color). You build four houses on each property and resist the urge to trade them in for hotels. By so doing, you control nearly 40 percent of the game's supply of houses. Let's assume you have three opponents; this means that the remaining 20 houses will average out to six or seven per player—not enough to build a competing color group up to the three-house level across all three of its properties.

In similar fashion, if you had previously purchased hotels, you can break them back down to four houses per property to "back into" this tactic. This will work if the bank still has a lot of houses, because no housing auction will need to take place. (Note: in tournament play, building up takes precedence over breaking down. Those players who want to buy houses get first crack at them before the player who wishes to break down his hotels. This ruling makes it rather dangerous to move up to hotels and forgo one's houses.)

Take a look at the board and players' cash holdings before you decide to move up to hotels. Is the Housing Shortage Discipline to your advantage? If so, implement it and stand pat. But if there is no meaningful group competing with yours, or players have neither the cash nor groups to consume the bank's supply of houses, it is safe to advance to hotels.

4. The Damage Control Priority

Use this one when adversity strikes and you need to minimize the impact of your loss. Okay, you owe $1000 on Pennsylvania Avenue and only have $432 in cash. Where will the remaining $568 come from (assuming you can't interest your creditor in taking less by way of a trade)? Let's also assume an opponent is not willing to provide the $568 shortfall via trade. Fortunately, you have assets to convert into cash. The question therefore becomes, in what order do you convert them to cash? Think back to Secrets 30 and 31. Let's review.

- First, mortgage a single Utility, because its rent is trivial.

- Second, mortgage a single property (beginning with the cheapest that will help you reach your cash goal). You're giving up your cheapest rent first, etc.

- Third, mortgage a two-property holding. This is especially valid if the third member of this group is still in the bank.

- Fourth, mortgage a single Railroad. Short Line should be mortgaged first, because of its lower landing frequency.

Now it becomes more painful if you need to keep going:

- Fifth, mortgage a second, third, and fourth Railroad if absolutely necessary.

- Sixth, alas, mortgage an entire color group. In the event you own two groups, pick the one that's undeveloped or underdeveloped. Then, if still short of cash, tear down buildings on the more developed group.

Since a group without buildings won't win you the game, the most essential (golden) priority when raising cash is to preserve your "money pot": namely, a group with at least three houses per property.

5. The Pauper's Desperation

In the endgame, it often becomes clear who has the edge. In fact, it is not uncommon for one player to have such an edge that only a miracle can prevent his or her victory. Are you capable of such a miracle? Perhaps.

Let's say there are houses looming in the high-rent district. The Reds have four houses each, and this line of buildings offers so much green that it confuses them with the Greens, which have red hotels. The Yellows share 11 houses. Meanwhile, you're stuck with the Light Blues and seven houses between them, but somehow have gotten Boardwalk to go with Park Place, and now have one house on each. Inexplicably, the player owning the Reds turns in his 12 houses for hotels. The housing shortage abruptly ends. And the Yellow player can only buy one of those 12 houses.

Big decision: should you go for broke and dump the houses on your Light Blues, mortgage the three properties, and invest all you can into the Dark Blues, building each to three houses? No doubt. You're bound to lose if you don't, and just might pull off a miracle if you do. This is the Pauper's Desperation. It becomes possible when an opponent unblocks a housing shortage, as noted here. Miracles do occur, even in Monopoly.

There's another circumstance wherein you can try the Pauper's Desperation. In this one, you're truly desperate. Let's say you're in a hotly contested game (translation: there's bad blood around the table). Tragedy strikes; you land on Pacific with a hotel. You must pay $1275 rent. How in the world are you going to raise that kind of money? There may be a way: pitting one rich opponent against another.

It so happens that among your holdings are properties that one or more of your opponents would love to get their hands on. Perhaps they might realize the damage your creditor would do if he gained them and formed one or more new color groups. Well, be ruthless and pit them against each other in a bidding war!

You are not obligated to trade with the player who offers you the most; you can trade with any player(s) who enables you to pay your debt and who otherwise preserves your life in the game. Let's say you owe Tom the $1275. Joe offers to give you $1275 in return for all six of your properties (three of which are the Light Blues), but that would mean tearing down seven houses. Katie has a different proposition because she doesn't want Joe to build by virtue of trading with you. She will give you $1100 for the three properties apart from your Light Blues. If you accept Katie's offer, you keep your color group but lose your houses. Well, that's better than losing the color group. Meanwhile, Tom is watching and doesn't want either Joe or Katie to benefit, so he abruptly offers to take your three single properties in return for the rent. Wow! Tom is permitting you to keep your group and its houses. So which option is best? It's your decision, of course, as any one of these three options satisfies your debt. The important thing is that the Pauper's Desperation has kept you in the game, however long the odds against you.

WHAT'S THE MERIT OF THESE MONOPOLY STRATEGIES AND TACTICS?

It's this: employing a game plan is vital if you are to know how to pick among conflicting alternatives when adversity threatens. As President Dwight Eisenhower famously said, referring to his days as commander of Allied forces in Europe during World War II, "I have always found that plans are useless, but planning is indispensable."

Chances are your plans will not work out as expected and you'll need to adjust. You must be agile, not dogged. This is the approach advocated by game theory. Good plans take into account options to deal with obstacles that pop up, not to mention unexpected opportunities. When these occur, you need to change course and respond, hopefully successfully so you can quickly return to your game plan.

Circumstantial planning (tactics) prepares you for the changes that may occur because of competition, be it due to the choices made by your opponents in a game or the real world's ebb and flow of economic events.

Game Changer 9—
Capitalizing on Rapport and Influence

Matt McNally
2003 US Champ

John Hancock said, "The greatest ability in business is to get along with others and to [be able to] influence their actions." His advice was perfectly followed by Matt McNally decades later when he won the 2003 United States Monopoly Championship.

McNally: "I was fortunate enough to secure the Dark Blue color group [Park Place and Boardwalk] and invest in them by selling off nonessential Red and Green deeds. 'Nonessential' because they could not cause me immediate harm as the bank still held the third deed in each group. More important, I retained a deed in all the other significant groups. The opponent who took this trade soon went bankrupt to the bank and his properties went up for auction. It quickly dawned on me that the only deed I had to outbid my opponents for was St. James, as my owning it would prevent the coveted Orange group from being completed. I made one bold bid, $400, for this $180 property. This stunned my opponents and they let me have it (I would have bid even higher). I was left with my Dark Blues, $2 cash, and a bunch of mortgages. More important, I had a near Rainbow Monopoly and therefore absolute influence in the game. My opponents had to come through me to deal, and while I treated my opponents with respect, I held ultimate influence and was unwilling to let it go."

McNally: "Hindsight is always 20/20, and committing to a decision with no regrets in advance is hard to do. A principle that novice players often overlook is the need to maneuver and adapt, based upon the situation. It isn't calculated in dollars and cents, but rather in creativity. First, imagine every possible scenario. Second, think of a solution. Third, think

(continues)

(continued)

of a backup solution. Fourth, proceed without fear. Fifth, *act*, and do it fast before your opponents catch on.

"Monopoly offers so many lessons I apply in my daily life. Treating others with respect, exploring possibilities, then establishing commitments. Applying the elements of persuasion and argumentation, adapting to the moment, finding comfort in my environment and surroundings. Setting short-term and long-term goals, then acting to accomplish them. Just as important, having fun and enjoying the moment."

13

GAME THREE

2009 WORLD CHAMPIONSHIP

n late October 2009, four international finalists met across a table in a ballroom of the glamorous Caesars Palace resort in Las Vegas and matched wits over a Monopoly board. One was destined to be crowned World Monopoly Champion. Over 40 national champions had come to Vegas in hopes of reaching this position, but only these four made it:

- Bjorn Halvard Knappskog of Norway (Iron)

- Geoff Christopher of New Zealand (Battleship)

- Oleg Korostolev of Russia (Top Hat)

- Richard Marinaccio of the United States (Thimble)

Knappskog was a 19-year-old student who barely squeezed into the semifinals. Christopher (whose uniformed fan club accompanied him to Las Vegas) worked in risk management (good training, right?). Korostolev was a youthful businessman. You already know attorney Marinaccio as the U.S. champ from Game Two.

This game's 22 rounds flew by quickly (44 minutes). During round nine, all players traded for color groups and buildings popped up around the board. The first bankruptcy occurred in round thirteen. And when it was over, the player who had seemed most likely to go bankrupt was crowned the winner!

The key lesson driven home by this game is the danger of *complacency*—that is, not recognizing a threat to your finances until it becomes too late to avoid loss. We'll analyze these dangers when they become alarmingly clear in round nine.

Game 3 START

order of play:
Iron
Battleship
Top Hat
Thimble

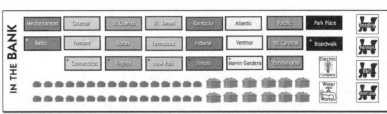

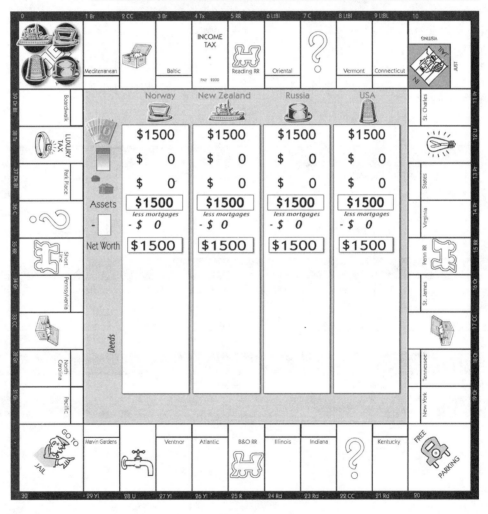

ROUNDS ONE TO SIX

In these early "buy 'em" rounds, the four semifinalists accumulated the following properties, penalties/rewards, and rents:

The Iron (Bjorn—Norway)		The Battleship (Geoff—NZ)		The Top Hat (Oleg—Russia)		The Thimble (Richard—U.S.)	
PROPERTIES PURCHASED							
Electric Company		Vermont		Tennessee		Reading RR	
Illinois		St. Charles		Indiana		Ventnor	
Boardwalk		States		Pacific		Park Place	
Oriental		Waterworks				Virginia	
Pennsylvania RR		North Carolina					
		Short Line RR					
($1090 total)		($1030 total)		($700 total)		($970 total)	
PENALTIES/REWARDS							
C. Chest	+$30	GO	+$200	Chance	0	C. Chest	+$100
($10 from each player)		C. Chest	+$20	C. Chest	−$10		−$10
			−$10	GO (inc. tax)	0	GO	+$200
GO	+$200	Just Visiting				Just Visiting	
		Free Parking					
RENTS EARNED/PAID							
Elec. Co.	+$48	States	+$10	Short Line	−$25	Indiana	−$18
		St. Charles	+$20	St. Charles	−$20	States	−$10
		Short Line	+$25	Indiana	+$18		
				Elec. Co.	−$48		
NET CHANGE IN CASH							
−$812		−$725		−$775		−$708	
CHANGE IN NET WORTH							
+$228		+$285		−$85		+$262	

Game 3 Round 6

order of play:
Iron
Battleship
Top Hat
Thimble

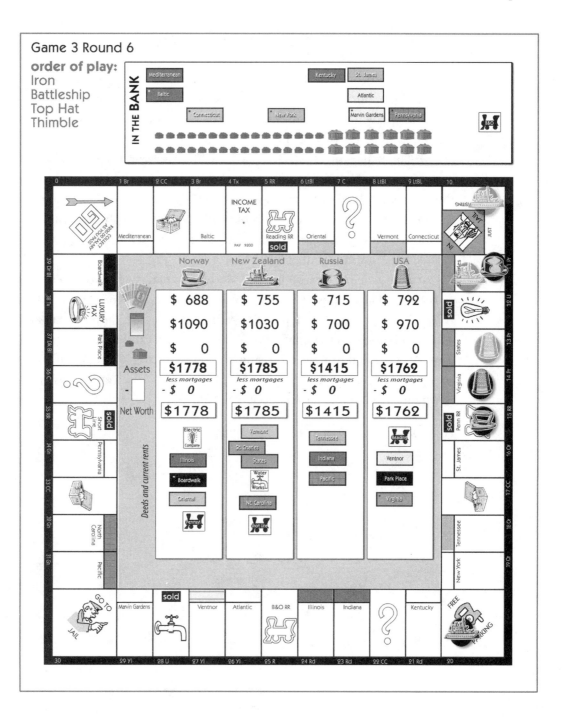

ROUNDS SEVEN AND EIGHT

To begin round seven, the Iron rolled and was rewarded by triples. He gained the opportunity to move to any space and decided to leap to Marvin Gardens, which he acquired for $280. The property-rich Top Hat advanced to Illinois, which he purchased, then acquired the B&O, thanks to Mr. M. The Battleship also rolled triples. (Which was amazing, because it is an extremely unlikely event for two players to roll triples in the same round, the odds being 1296 to 1!) He moved to Pennsylvania Avenue, nabbing the most expensive Green. The Thimble rolled double 2s plus the Bus. He decided to move to St. James, rolled again, and landed on Illinois, which earned the Top Hat a rent of $24.

In round eight, the Iron bought Mediterranean, thanks to a roll of 10 plus Mr. M. The Battleship rolled a 10 and paid Income Tax. The Top Hat rolled double 3s plus Mr. M, paid $26 rent on Pacific, then advanced to and acquired Baltic (after collecting $200 for passing GO). His next roll of 10 plus Mr. M moved him ahead to States and thence to New York, which he bought for $200. The Thimble rolled 2,3 plus the Bus and elected to move to Atlantic Avenue; he purchased it for $260.

Game 3 Round 8

order of play:
Iron
Battleship
Top Hat
Thimble

IN THE **BANK**

Kentucky

* Connecticut

	Norway	New Zealand	Russia	USA
	$ 548	$ 509	$ 431	$ 332
	$ 0	$1490	$1020	$1410
	$ 0	$ 0	$ 0	$ 0
Assets	**$1430**	**$1999**	**$1451**	**$1742**
	less mortgages	*less mortgages*	*less mortgages*	*less mortgages*
-	- $ 0	- $ 0	- $ 0	- $ 0
Net Worth	**$1978**	**$1999**	**$1451**	**$1742**

Deeds

Norway: Electric Company, Illinois, Boardwalk, Oriental, Pennsyl., Marvin Gardens, Mediterranean

New Zealand: Baltic, Vermont, St. Charles, States, New York, Water Works, Nt. Carolina, B&O, Short Line

Russia: Tennessee, Indiana, Pacific, Pennsylvania

USA: Reading, Atlantic, Ventnor, Park Place, St. James, Virginia

Board spaces:

0 — GO COLLECT $200 AS YOU PASS GO
1 Br — Mediterranean
2 CC
3 Br
4 Tx — INCOME TAX PAY $200
5 RR — Reading RR — sold
6 LtBl — Oriental
7 C
8 LtBl — Vermont
9 LtBl — Connecticut
10 — JAIL / JUST VISITING
11 Pr — St. Charles
12 U — sold
13 Pr — States
14 Pr — Virginia
15 RR — Penn RR — sold
16 Or — St. James
17 CC
18 Or — Tennessee
19 Or — New York
20 — FREE PARKING
21 Rd — Kentucky
22 CC
23 Rd — Indiana
24 Rd — Illinois
25 R — B&O RR — sold
26 Yl — Atlantic
27 Yl — Ventnor
28 U — sold
29 Yl — Marvin Gardens
30 — GO TO JAIL
31 Gn — Pacific
32 Gn — North Carolina
33 CC
34 Gn — Pennsylvania
35 RR — Short Line — sold
36 C
37 Dk Bl — Park Place
38 Tx — LUXURY TAX
39 Dk Bl — Boardwalk

ROUND NINE

The Iron's roll of double 5s plus 1 advanced him to the Electric Company. His next roll (a 10) took him to Community Chest, which jumped him ahead to GO.

The Battleship rolled a 10 and paid rent on Marvin Gardens.

The stage was now set for an intense period of negotiation, which resulted in the game's first trades. Their consequences were vast. The Battleship wheeled and dealed and got not one but two color groups: the Browns and the coveted Oranges. The Top Hat came away with the Reds and the Thimble with the Purples. The Iron (Norway) seemed hopeless, locked out of the deal-making. To anyone overseeing the action (like me, the judge), the Battleship appeared to have gained the upper hand. (You gotta go with the Oranges, right?) But he could only gain the $900 required to build this group to the killer third-house level if he drained his cash reserves and drew down all of his borrowing potential. Similarly, the Top Hat could not afford to adequately develop his potentially powerful Reds. Only the Thimble had sufficient cash to aggressively build up his Purples, and while his opponents contemplated, he put up seven houses among them. Before action resumed, the Battleship made up his mind and erected four houses on his Oranges.

At this point, faced with certain elimination without a color group of his own, the Iron proposed a seemingly lopsided trade: he offered to trade a Green to the Battleship in return for a Light Blue property. The Battleship, having won his last preliminary game by virtue of the Greens, likely thought this group would once again bring him a victory. He was clearly excited to own two color groups and accepted the deal without batting an eye. More important, neither of the remaining two players took notice and attempted to warn him of the danger of saying yes to the trade, or even made a counteroffer. Each of these three players had become complacent. *Norway is done, right?* Meanwhile, Norway breathed new life and was back in the game, thanks to his Light Blue group.

Complacency

Success is its cause. Let's talk about its dangers. It feels good to let down your guard after you've surmounted an obstacle or prevailed over competition.

But unless you are constantly vigilant and anticipate where the next threat will come from, you'll be caught off guard. These three players had written off the Iron, believing he was no longer a competitive threat. *I think it is harder to notice the dangers of success than the dangers of failure.* The threat of failure spurs action, while success spurs inaction.

Complacency is a feeling of security while unaware of potential danger. Complacent folks feel little need to change and resist learning anything new. But if you've observed the dramatic churn in the economy during the past several years, you see proof that it is essential to realize and adjust to the impact of new technologies and ideas. How many retailers have gone out of business because their goods are no longer sought? How many manufacturers disappeared because they could not maintain a cost advantage? How many social conventions and cultural beliefs have withered, while the growths of new (some might say strange) offshoots took their place?

Complacency leads to errors of judgment just before "new" replaces "old." It is especially comfortable for those wrapped in the success of a system or enterprise to wear blinders. They become vulnerable and lose out to those who maintain wide vision and see change of fortune out of the corners of their eyes. Examples? Millions of investors were devastated by the 1929 stock market crash. But wise financiers like Joseph P. Kennedy and the father of his daughter-in-law-to-be, Jack Bouvier, both sold out in time. Not so fortunate was Winston Churchill, who ignored the advice to exit by his financial advisor, Bernard Baruch. In 2008, millions more were affected by the financial meltdown. But not hedge fund manager Dr. Michael Burry. He made fortunes for his clients by shorting the very derivatives others couldn't buy enough of. (Note: until the crash, his clients were most unhappy with their lack of profits.) And it is not just investors and financiers who become complacent. When I was young, General Motors enjoyed a nearly 60 percent share of the U.S. auto market. Changing demands by consumers caught GM sleeping, and by 2008 it was bankrupt. The government was obligated to bail it out, and the price tag to U.S. taxpayers will likely be $14 billion.

The moral is: never let down your guard, especially when the skies are blue and the wind is fair. Alas, there's always a storm brewing.

In our game, the storm rose suddenly following a game-changing trade between Norway and Russia. Batten down the hatches. Let's continue with this round.

The Top Hat rolled double 3s plus Mr. M. He advanced first to Just Visiting and then to Kentucky, which he purchased. He next rolled double 3s (again) plus Mr. M. He moved ahead to Ventnor and then to Connecticut, which he quickly purchased. By virtue of his "double double," no properties remained in the bank. But he was obligated to roll one more time. And this time his 7 plus Mr. M landed him on St. James, where a rent awaited him. To pay, he had to raise cash and was forced to sell his house on Pacific and mortgage his Greens. Mr. Monopoly then carries him two spaces forward to Tennessee and a $70 rent.

The round ended quickly after the Thimble rolled a 12 and paid a Luxury Tax of $100.

Game 3 Round 9 - conclusion

order of play:
Iron
Battleship
Top Hat
Thimble

IN THE **BANK**

	Norway	New Zealand	Russia	USA
	$ 748	$ 455	$ 405	$ 67
	$1550	$1030	$1600	$1510
	$ 0	$ 400	$ 0	$ 700
Assets	**$2298**	**$1885**	**$2005**	**$2277**
	less mortgages	*less mortgages*	*less mortgages*	*less mortgages*
-	- $ 0	- $ 100	- $ 460	- $ 435
Net Worth	**$2298**	**$1785**	**$1545**	**$1842**

Deeds

Norway: Oriental, Vermont, * Connecticut, Marvin Gardens, * Boardwalk, Electric Company, B&O, Short Line

New Zealand: Mediterranean, Baltic, St. James, Tennessee, New York, Water Works, MORTGAGED Pennsyl

Russia: Kentucky, Indiana, Illinois, MORTGAGED Baltic, MORTGAGED Nrth Carolina, Pennsylvania

USA: St. Charles, States, Virginia, MORTGAGED Atlantic, MORTGAGED Vermont, MORTGAGED Park Place, MORTGAGED Reading

ROUND TEN

The Iron rolled a 6 and landed on his own property, Oriental. Having moved safely beyond danger, he confidently built ten houses among his Light Blues, with four going up on Oriental. His timing was also based on the fact that his opponents were approaching his color group.

The Battleship rolled double 2s plus Mr. M. Community Chest required him to pay $50 to the bank, while Mr. M carried him to the Short Line, where he paid a $50 rent to the Iron.

The Top Hat rolled 7 plus Mr. M and paid a $25 rent to the Iron and a $28 rent to the Battleship.

The Thimble, however, was not as fortunate. After he picked up the dice and commented on how fast this game was unfolding, his double 6s plus Mr. M landed him on Income Tax (negating his $200 for passing GO) and then Oriental. The Iron's newly built houses paid off smartly. The Thimble owed $400 and had to tear down all seven of his Purple group's houses and mortgage heavily. Obligated to roll again, he tossed a 6 plus Mr. M and landed on Tennessee. He mortgaged two of his Purple properties to cover the $70 rent there and the $80 rent on New York (courtesy of Mr. M).

Before the round ended, the Battleship mortgaged his Railroad. The Top Hat built two houses on his Reds and also two houses on his Greens.

Game 3 Round 10

order of play:
Iron
Battleship
Top Hat
Thimble

IN THE BANK

	Norway	New Zealand	Russia	USA
	$ 814	$ 283	$ 27	$ 1
	$1550	$1030	$1600	$1510
	$ 500	$ 400	$ 400	$ 0
Assets	**$2864**	**$1713**	**$1927**	**$1501**
	less mortgages	*less mortgages*	*less mortgages*	*less mortgages*
-	- $ 0	- $ 100	- $ 460	- $ 685
Net Worth	$2864	$1613	$1467	$ 816

Deeds

Norway: Oriental, Vermont, *Connecticut, Marvin Gardens, *Boardwalk, Electric Company, B&O, Short Line

New Zealand: Mediterranean, Baltic, St. James, Tennessee, *New York, Water Works, MORTGAGED Pennsyl.

Russia: Kentucky, Indiana, Illinois, Pacific MORTGAGED, North Carolina MORTGAGED, Pennsylvania MORTGAGED

USA: St. Charles, States MORTGAGED, Virginia MORTGAGED, Atlantic MORTGAGED, Ventnor MORTGAGED, MORTGAGED RR, MORTGAGED

Board spaces:
- 0 GO
- 1 Br Mediterranean
- 2 CC
- 3 Br Baltic
- 4 Tx INCOME TAX PAY $200
- 5 RR Reading R.R. sold
- 6 LtBl Oriental mortgaged
- 7 C
- 8 LtBl Vermont
- 9 LtBl Connecticut
- 10 JUST VISITING / IN JAIL
- 11 Pr St. Charles
- 12 U sold
- 13 Pr States mortgaged
- 14 Pr Virginia mortgaged
- 15 RR Penn RR sold
- 16 Or St. James
- 17 CC
- 18 Or Tennessee
- 19 Or New York
- 20 FREE PARKING
- 21 Rd Kentucky
- 22 CC
- 23 Rd Indiana
- 24 Rd Illinois
- 25 R B&O RR sold
- 26 Yl Atlantic mortgaged
- 27 Yl Ventnor mortgaged
- 28 U sold
- 29 Yl Marvin Gardens
- 30 GO TO JAIL
- 31 Gn Pacific mortgaged
- 32 Gn North Carolina mortgaged
- 33 CC
- 34 Gn Pennsylvania mortgaged
- 35 RR Short Line sold
- 36 C
- 37 Dk Bl Park Place mortgaged
- 38 Tx LUXURY TAX
- 39 Dk Bl Boardwalk

ROUNDS ELEVEN AND TWELVE

The Iron opened round eleven with a roll of 9, thereby advancing to the Pennsylvania Railroad (mortgaged). The Battleship rolled a 12 and moved to (his own) Tennessee. The Top Hat advanced 10 spaces and got burned by Luxury Tax, which forced him to sell his two remaining houses in order to pay its $100 penalty. The Thimble rolled a total of 12 and moved to Pacific. The Iron now built hotels on his Light Blues, funded by the strong infusion of cash he had received from rents during the prior round. The Thimble offered to buy the Short Line from the Iron, who tactfully declined.

Round twelve began with the Thimble landing on (mortgaged) Pacific. Next, the Iron rolled 1,4 plus the Bus and chose to move to Free Parking. The Battleship followed with double 3s. He moved to Illinois and paid $40 to the Top Hat (who lamented, "If only I hadn't had to tear down my houses"). The Battleship picked up the dice again and rolled 10, landing on mortgaged Pennsylvania Avenue. The Top Hat rolled 6 plus Mr. M. He passed GO, collected $200, and found himself briefly on benign Baltic but finally on deadly Oriental. Its $550 rent knocked him out of the game. Bankrupt, he transferred $117 in cash and $1140 in properties to the Iron. The Greens, which the Iron had forgone to get the Light Blues, were now in his possession, along with the Reds.

The Iron rolled 2,3 plus the Bus and decided to move two spaces to Community Chest. The card he drew took him to GO, and he collected $200. The Iron then mortgaged Boardwalk and the Reds, but unmortgaged the three Greens. The Thimble elected to unmortgage Reading Railroad before the Iron continued his mortgaging spree by turning facedown Marvin Gardens, along with the B&O and Short Line Railroads.

Game 3 Round 12

order of play:
Iron
Battleship
Top Hat
Thimble

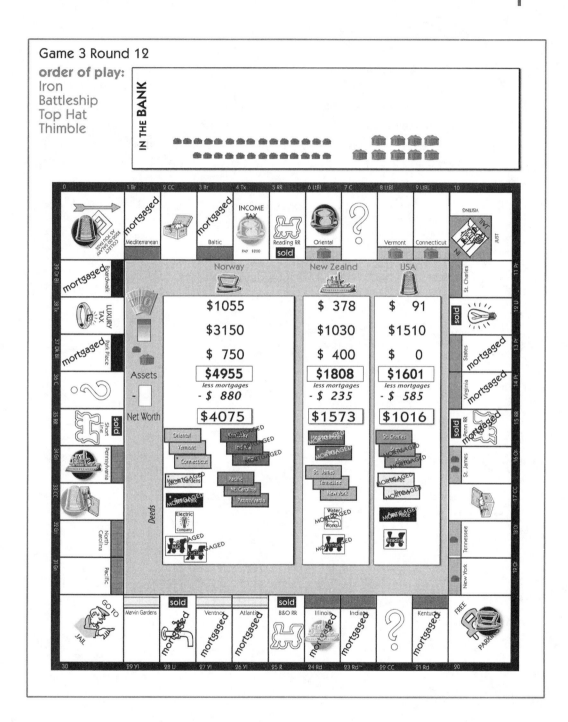

IN THE **BANK**

	Norway	New Zealnd	USA
	$1055	$ 378	$ 91
	$3150	$1030	$1510
	$ 750	$ 400	$ 0
Assets	**$4955**	**$1808**	**$1601**
	less mortgages	less mortgages	less mortgages
−	− $ 880	− $ 235	− $ 585
Net Worth	**$4075**	**$1573**	**$1016**

ROUND THIRTEEN

Now it was a three-player game, with the Iron in the driver's seat.

The Iron rolled 3 plus Mr. M and moved first to Indiana and then to the Reading, where he paid a $25 rent to the Thimble out of his $200 salary.

It was now the Battleship's turn to land on Oriental, by virtue of a roll of 12. He got $200 for passing GO and paid $550 to the Iron.

The Thimble, for the moment, stayed out of harm's way by rolling 2,4 plus the Bus and electing to move to Community Chest, where he earned $10.

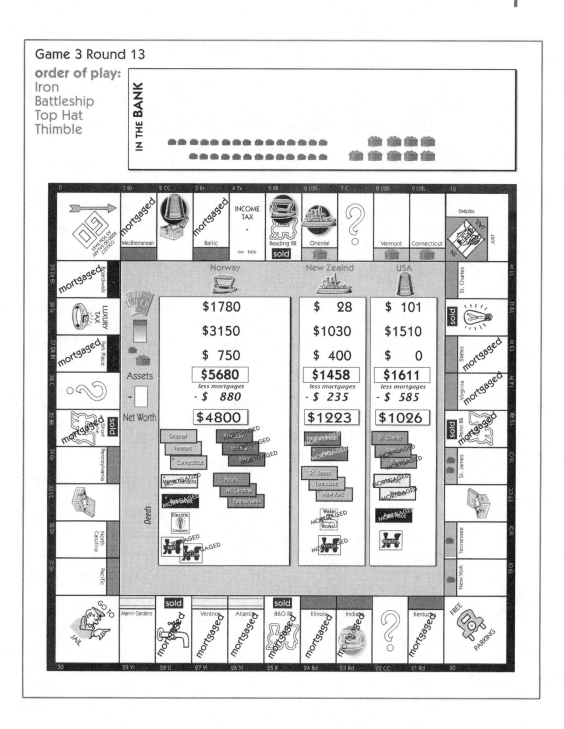

Game 3 Round 13

order of play:
Iron
Battleship
Top Hat
Thimble

IN THE **BANK**

Norway

New Zealnd

USA

	Norway	New Zealnd	USA
	$1780	$ 28	$ 101
	$3150	$1030	$1510
	$ 750	$ 400	$ 0
Assets	$5680	$1458	$1611
	less mortgages	less mortgages	less mortgages
	- $ 880	- $ 235	- $ 585
Net Worth	$4800	$1223	$1026

Deeds

ROUND FOURTEEN

The Iron rolled 2,5 plus the Bus and moved seven spaces to the Electric Company, which he owned.

The Battleship rolled 6 and also moved to the Electric Company where he paid a $24 rent.

The Thimble rolled 7 plus Mr. M and found himself on Connecticut with its hefty $600 rent. Unable to muster this expense, he went bankrupt to the Iron, transferring $101 in cash and $925 in properties. The Iron picked up the Purples and four other deeds. He was obligated to pay $59 in interest on the mortgaged properties and decided to leave them mortgaged. He then built five houses among the Greens.

Only the Battleship stood in the way of the Iron winning the ultimate prize. The Iron decided to go for the win by mortgaging Reading Railroad, St. Charles, and the Electric Company. This left only the Light Blues and Greens in play. On the latter, the Iron built seven houses.

Game 3 Round 14

order of play:
Iron
Battleship
Top Hat
Thimble

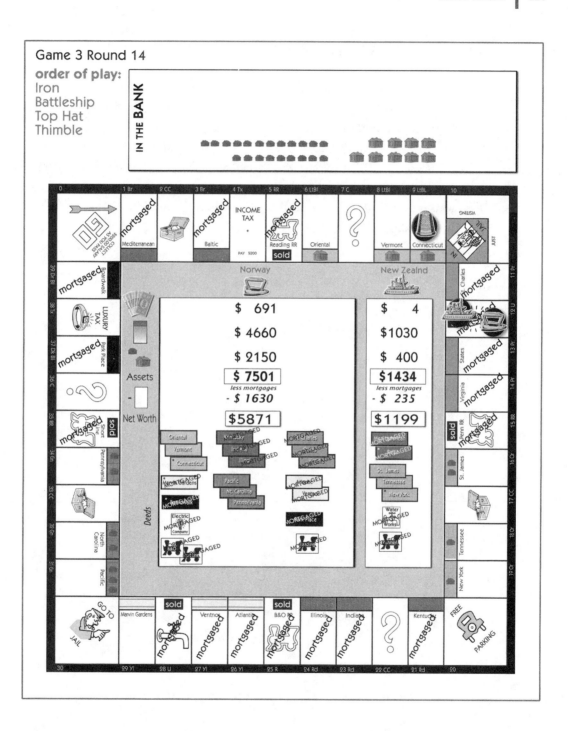

ROUNDS FIFTEEN TO TWENTY-ONE

For the next seven rounds, the Battleship clung to life. During these rounds, the Iron netted a total of $130 for passing GO and paying a $70 rent to the Battleship. The Battleship netted $220 for passing GO, collecting the Battleship's $70 rent, and paying $50 to get out of Jail. Because he built three houses during this time, he was forced to tear one down to pay his Jail expense. But it proved to be a moot point. The Iron had arranged his seven houses among the Greens so that Pacific had the odd (third) house. It was the most likely of the three to be landed upon by the Battleship.

Game 3 TURN 15

order of play:
Iron
Battleship
Top Hat
Thimble

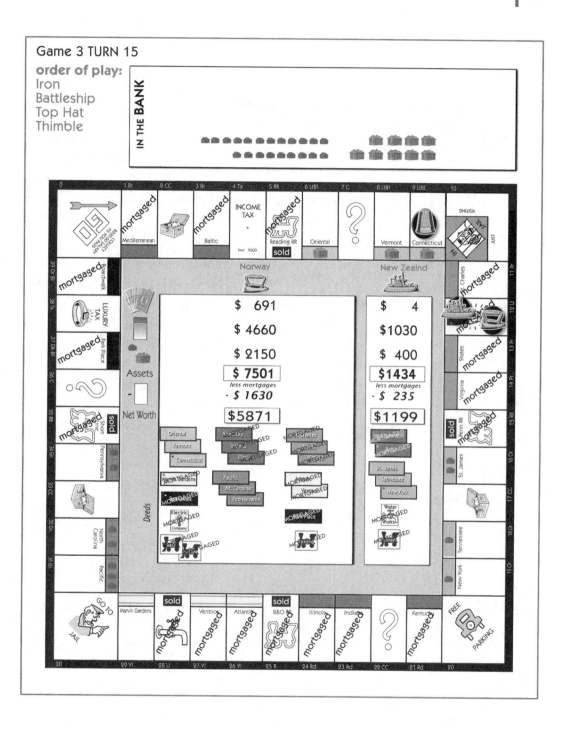

IN THE **BANK**

Norway

$ 691
$ 4660
$ 2150
$ 7501
less mortgages
- $ 1630
$5871

New Zealnd

$ 4
$1030
$ 400
$1434
less mortgages
- $ 235
$1199

Assets

Net Worth

Deeds

ROUND TWENTY-TWO

The odds prevailed when the Battleship rolled 8 plus Mr. M and moved first to Pacific and then to North Carolina Avenue. The $900 rent on Pacific was more than enough to finish the Battleship's journey around the game board. He went bankrupt and turned over $4 in cash among his $1499 in net worth.

The Iron (Norway), with all the game's assets in his possession ($7135), became the 2009 World Monopoly champion. He had relied on a timely trade and immediate development, coupled with his knowledge of frequency, to win. And of course, he caught his complacent opponents napping.

It is worth repeating one other real-world lesson from this intense game: adversity often sparks creative problem solving (in contrast, complacency dulls creativity). Speaking for myself, I don't like to deal with problems any more than the next guy (or gal), but I do admit it shifts my mind into high gear because I am determined not to be unjustly set back or see my business harmed.

There is no more uncomfortable feeling than realizing you lost because you didn't put forth your best effort . . . and no better feeling than knowing you rose to the occasion and came out as well as you could have hoped.

Game 3 Round 22- game end   The Iron (Norway) wins!

order of play:
Iron
Battleship

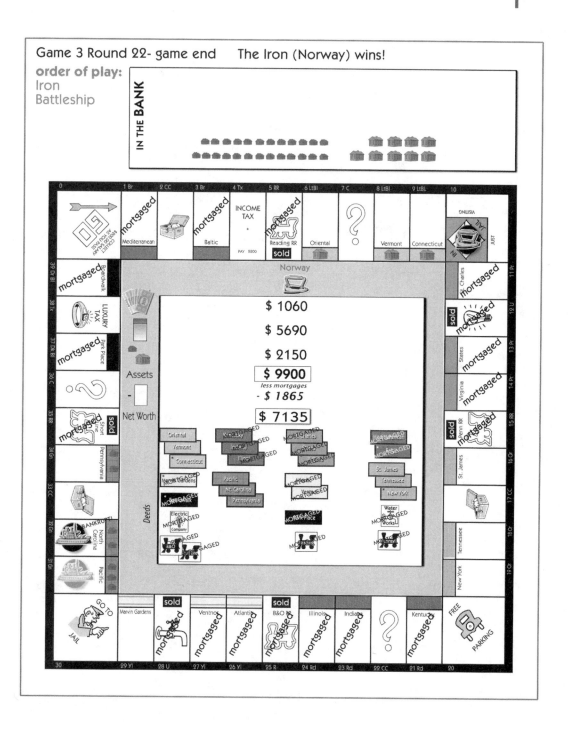

14

FUN

REWARD YOURSELF FOR ACCOMPLISHMENT

It's okay to break the rules once in a while, just for fun, after you learn how to make them work for you.

We don't stop playing because we turn old,
but turn old because we stop playing.
—Anonymous

Have fun. Play the game.

With MONOPOLY, you can own it all as a high-flying trader in the fast-paced world of real estate. Tour the city for the hottest properties: sites, stations, and utilities are all up for grabs. Invest in houses and hotels, then watch the rent come pouring in! Make deals with other players and look out for bargains at auctions. There are many ways to get what you want. And for really speedy dealers, use the speed die for a quick and intense game of MONOPOLY. So get on GO and trade your way to success! For the latest MONOPOLY games, visit www.monopoly.com.

Is anything in life free? Well, there are the coupons typically found in the Sunday paper and online that offer welcome discounts or free goods if you make a purchase. But I want to talk about something bigger—namely, a way to make money for free that anyone who is lucky enough to enjoy the privilege should take advantage of. I'm talking about company-matching of money you save in your employer's savings or retirement plan. Many companies will match your contributions up to 5 percent of pay; some go even higher. Now, this is truly free money.

Let's say that 5 percent of your monthly pay is $400. If you save 5 percent of this, or $20, your employer will give you another $20 *free*. That's an instant doubling of your money, once it vests. It's like landing on Free Parking in Monopoly and earning whatever money is tucked under the space— but I'm getting ahead of myself. Money is never placed under Free Parking, unless you are playing by "house rules," which is the opening topic in this chapter.

Once you've absorbed the key financial lessons offered by Monopoly and have earned your MBA (Monopoly Business Acumen), you're ready to tackle the final lesson I offer: *reward yourself.*

Over the many years I've been pursuing my financial plan, nothing inspires me to the next goal more than celebrating the current goal, be it by doing something my wife and I have held off doing, or acquiring an item we've longed for. (As a gamesman, I couldn't help to apply the concept of gamification even before it was generally known.) My advice is to keep your reward reasonable, so you won't dig too deeply into your gain, but also make it significant enough to make the accomplishment feel palpable.

To that end, this chapter offers you many more ways to just have fun with Monopoly. And we'll begin with the most common way: adding house rules.

THE HOUSE RULES!

My devoted Monopoly friends asked me why would I include these "non-rules" in a book whose aim is to teach how to win the "real" game. The answer I gave them was this: many house rules are so common, and they create so much fun, that they are already assumed to be part of the official game (especially 1, 2, and 3 below). By highlighting them in this chapter, I hope to draw attention to the fact that they are *not* included in the formal rules, and that, yes, they can be fun if the mood strikes to add them. Many of us play the game just for social fun. On those occasions, house rules work well because they tend to keep players in the game longer. As some would say, what pleasure is there in setting aside a few hours to play for fun if you're bankrupt in 30 minutes?

Here are all 14 of the most prevalent house rules. After each one, I've noted its pros and cons. I suggest adding no more than one to two per game. Otherwise, your game will become too unwieldy—and worse, it will drive into your psyche bad habits that you'll need to overcome the next time you play the game the right way.

1. Free Parking Jackpot

This is by far the most popular house rule. Thirty-seven percent of those surveyed say they use it from time to time (and even more use it in conjunction with house rules 2 and/or 3). Rather than deposit taxes and card fines in the bank, the banker places this money under the Free Parking corner. This includes every $50 paid for leaving Jail. (At the game's beginning, some place a $500 bill under Free Parking to initiate this kitty.) The current jackpot money under Free Parking is awarded to a player when he lands on this space. Sometimes it's a small fortune; at other times it's chicken feed.

Pros: Infuses more cash in the game and increases the chance of avoiding bankruptcy. Provides a means for a player who is trailing badly to strike it rich and regain a competitive position.

Cons: Defeats the goal of the game, which is to bankrupt all opponents as soon as possible. Can make the game intolerably long. Adds another element of luck.

2. Double GO Bonus

This is the second most popular house rule. Ten percent of those surveyed use it alone from time to time; even more combine it with house rules 1 and 3. Put simply, whenever a player lands exactly on GO, he collects not $200 but $400.

Pro: Adds more money into the game, making it possible to grow cash and make bigger investments.

Con: Like any rule that infuses money, it lengthens play and adds another element of luck.

3. No Purchases First Time Around the Board

This rule is used by 5 percent in our survey, and even more use it in combination with house rules 1 and/or 2. The idea is this: you may not buy or auction properties on your first circuit of the game board. Once a player completes a circuit, by landing on or surpassing GO, he buys and/or auctions as usual. Variation: no player is permitted to buy property until one player has passed or landed on GO. Then *all* may buy as usual.

Pro: Tends to eliminate the very real disadvantage of going last in games involving five or more players.

Cons: Makes the game longer to play and adds another element of luck.

The next 11 house rules are more specialized and are less frequently included in play.

4. Trading Options

It is human nature to look for other levers to pull in order to activate a transaction (think of what transpired the last time you bought a car). The official rules are very strict on what may be traded in the game: deeds and cash only. But unofficially, players have creatively added a lot more in their trade proposals. The most popular trading option is to include rent "immunity." Namely, you offer an opponent "free rent" the first time he lands on a property that he trades to you. Some players even grant more than one "free rent pass" to sweeten a deal.

Pro: Increases the pace at which color groups are formed.

Cons: Delays the end of the game because fewer rents are collected. Adds another complication and a condition that needs to be tracked in order to avoid disputes.

5. Selling Cards Before Looking at Them

This is not a widely used house rule, but I have seen players attempt to use it during tournament competition. The idea is that after landing on Chance or Community Chest and before you draw your card, you may auction it off to the highest bidder, keeping the proceeds. The top bidder then draws the card and earns the reward, makes the move, or incurs the penalty specified. Thereafter, play reverts to the player to your left, as usual.

Pros: Reduces risk for the seller and adds an element of excitement to play.

Cons: Adds time to the game's play and can create confusion.

6. Moving Houses and Hotels

This rule is rather bizarre. It permits a player to move houses or hotels from one of his group to another, as long as the "build evenly" rule is adhered to *and* the player pays the building cost difference if moving to a more expensive group. Moving to a less expensive group, by contrast, does not earn a refund, and if the buildings are subsequently moved back to a more expensive group, the cost differential must again be paid. The intent of this rule is to increase the odds of collecting big rents.

Pros: Adds to the game's dynamic and leads to more excitement. Might quicken its conclusion.

Cons: Unpleasant confusion often results; leads to aberrant strategy and detracts from mastering the game as it is intended to be played.

7. No Rent While in Jail

The intent of this rule—that a player may not collect rent while in Jail—is to encourage a player to leave Jail quickly and thereby risk paying big rents himself. While he's in Jail, all opponents gain a reprieve and breathe a sigh of relief knowing that this player's properties are rent-free if landed upon.

Pro: Compels a player to leave Jail, which might result in his own bankruptcy, so it could speed up the conclusion of the game.

Con: Takes away the strategic advantage of going to Jail late in the game, which is a core principle of smart play.

8. No Auctions

When a player lands on an unowned property and elects not to purchase it, the property remains unowned rather than being auctioned. When a player goes bankrupt to the bank, the bank does not immediately auction them. They must be landed upon to be eligible for purchase by the landing player.

Pro: Prevents wealthier players from profiting during auctions.

Cons: Lengthens the game and removes one of its most interesting types of interaction.

9. Six Railroads and Traveling by Rail

According to this rule, the two Utilities are treated like additional Railroads. They cost $200 to buy and can be mortgaged for $100. Landing upon them (naturally or by draw of a card) does not result in payment according to the dice, but rather as rent according to the total number of railroads owned. The rent for five Railroads is $300 and for six $400.

Further, whenever a player lands on any Railroad, he may pick up his token and move it to any other Railroad he owns. This player must pay rent if an opponent owns the Railroad first landed upon. Travel is "direct" from station to station, so a player does not get $200 for passing GO. The owner of the Railroads may not prevent the player from traveling. Mortgaging does not hinder this rule.

Pros: Creates dramatic moves and may help a player avoid onerous rents.

Cons: Makes the game longer and adds a complication.

10. Borrowing Money from the Bank

This one is so diametrically opposite to the intent of the game that I was reluctant to include it. But there is a bank in Monopoly, and we all assume that banks do make loans. So while the official Monopoly bank only offers mortgages, here's how some players bend this rule.

When cash is needed to fund a transaction, a player may—one time only—borrow $500 from the bank. The banker keeps tabs of loans on a sheet of paper. Until a debtor repays the bank he only receives $100 when passing or landing on GO. Further, if he wishes to repay the loan before he has landed on or passed GO at least once, he must repay $600 instead of $500. If this player goes bankrupt to another player, that player inherits the obligation to repay the loan and cannot do so until he lands on or passes GO at least once (or repays $600 immediately).

Pros: Keeps a player in the game longer, and enhances funding for development, which could prove vital to win.

Cons: Is contrary to the principles of the game, lengthens play, and requires record keeping.

11. No Limit on Houses and Hotels

This house rule removes another strategic element of play and is therefore a jarring departure from official play. Put simply, the bank has an unlimited supply of houses and hotels (which presumably can be bolstered by pieces from another Monopoly set).

Pros: Lots of building, without restraint, and perhaps a quicker conclusion to the game.

Cons: Lots of building, without restraint. Loss of a key game strategy.

12. Time Limit

This rule does not affect game play in any way, aside from fixing the moment it will end. Let's say you start playing at 1 p.m. on a Saturday afternoon, and all want to go to a 4:30 movie. You simply decide to end the game at 4 p.m. At the moment the clock strikes four, the player in motion completes his turn. Then all remaining players total the value of their assets (use printed values on the deeds for houses and hotels and the deeds themselves). The player with the highest asset total is the game's winner.

Pro: The perfect solution to playing a game when time is limited.

Cons: None really. Timed games are used in preliminary tournament competition.

13. Welfare

A simple house rule: if at any time a player has less than $100 in cash and no unmortgaged properties, he is given $100 from the bank.

Pro: Keeps a player alive a little longer.

Con: Lengthens the game.

14. Random Properties

This is actually a fun variation and provides good practice for developing your negotiating skills. All deeds are shuffled, turned facedown, and dealt out before the game begins. Typically, players will need to bargain with each other to acquire a color group, and since no cash has been spent to acquire properties, cash is often a lubricant to facilitate trades, and plenty of money is in play to quickly build houses and hotels.

Pro: Speeds up the game.

Cons: Removes skill and could quickly swing the game in one player's favor.

A variation on this rule is to, rather than deal out the deeds, require each property, when first landed on, to be auctioned. The player landing on the property will offer the first bid.

Use Your Imagination

For many, Monopoly is a toolbox for the imagination. Players have devised house rules for partnership play, uneven building, rent sharing, secret bidding during auctions, a token to represent the bank that pays rents landed upon, bidding to go first (instead of rolling the dice), starting at a corner other than GO, and mortgage foreclosures. (As an example of the last, if you land on an opponent's mortgaged property, he must unmortgage it and charge you rent *or* you can purchase it for its mortgaged value plus 10 percent interest.)

As long as you're having fun, go for it! Let your creativity roam. (Don't forget to come back to the real game when you're done with your adventure.)

MONOPOLY: THE MEGA EDITION

If you're not into a long game filled with house rules, there's a version of Monopoly that offers a dream come true to those who want to enjoy even more of its financial immersion *without* changing the core of the game.

The Mega Edition of the game features more money, a bigger board, nine more properties, new buildings (skyscrapers and train depots), and a deck of strategic Bus Tickets. Yet despite these add-ons, the game takes only 65 to 75 minutes to play because of the inclusion of the Speed Die (which was originally created for this big edition).

Here are Mega's (few) added rules (complete standard Monopoly rules appear in the Appendices):

For Ages 8+   2–8 Players

GAME CONTENTS
Gameboard • 37 Title Deed Cards • Money and Banker's Tray
Tokens • 3 Dice • 16 Chance Cards
16 Community Chest Cards • 16 Bus Tickets
32 Houses • 12 Hotels • 8 Skyscrapers • 4 Train Depots

WHAT'S NEW?

MONEY

Each player begins with $2500, including a crisp new $1000 bill, in addition to the standard five each $1's, $5's, $10's, six each $20's, and two each $50's, $100's & $500's.

THE DICE & HOW TO MOVE

On your turn, roll all THREE dice: the two white dice plus the new SPEED DIE.

- If **pips** appear on all three dice, simply move the total of all three.

- If you roll a **Mr. Monopoly**, you get a bonus move. **First**, move according to the white dice, do what you would normally do on that space; then move again to the next <u>unowned</u> property, which you may now buy. If you roll a Mr. Monopoly after all of the properties are owned, make a normal move according to the white dice, then move ahead to the first property on which you need to <u>pay rent</u>. If all other players' properties are mortgaged, stay where you are. Note: An opponent can't build or trade until your Mr. Monopoly move is completed.

- If you roll the **Bus**, first make a normal move according to the white dice, then decide to either take a BUS TICKET for later use (usually a good idea if any tickets are left in the deck) or move again to the nearest Chance/Community Chest space in front of your token.

DOUBLES & TRIPLES

Refer only to the white dice when determining doubles. If doubles entitle you to roll again, you may use a Bus Ticket in place of rolling the dice. While in Jail, roll only the two white dice (if you pay beforehand to get out, roll all three dice). If you roll TRIPLE 1's, 2's, or 3's, move ahead to ANY space on the board. Do not roll again. You do not go to Jail if you've rolled doubles twice before rolling triples.

NEW PROPERTIES & SKYSCRAPERS

Each color group has one additional property. You may build houses and hotels once you own <u>all but one</u> property in a color group. If you own <u>all</u> of the properties of a color group, and have built hotels on each, you may then build SKYSCRAPERS. Refer to the property's Title Deed for the cost of a Skyscraper as well as the amount of rent you can collect from having one here.

Note: you are entitled to collect TRIPLE rent on any unimproved property in a group once you own all of its properties. You may not mortgage any property of a group until all houses on it are sold back to the bank. If you acquire the final property of a group, after previously building on its other properties, you must un-mortgage this property immediately (if mortgaged) and build it up according to the "even" building rule or, if you can't afford to do so, you must redistribute existing houses among all properties of the group. You may need to break down hotels to do this. You may sell a Skyscraper back to the bank for half its value and revert to a hotel.

A Skyscraper   A Train Depot

RAILROADS

You may improve your Railroads by building a TRAIN DEPOT on it (cost: $100). A Train Depot doubles the rent due for the Railroad. You don't need to own multiple Railroads before building a Train Depot on one. Train Depots may be sold back to the bank for $50 each.

BUS TICKETS

On any turn, you may choose to use a Bus Ticket (if you have any) instead of rolling the dice. If so, move forward to any space on the same side of the board. (Corners are the final space on each side, as well as the first space of the next side.) If you use a bus ticket to move to a utility owned by an opponent, roll both white dice to determine your rent (4×, 10×, or 20× depending on the number of utilities owned by this opponent). You can buy/sell/trade Bus Tickets with other players. Bus Tickets can be used to move to the "Go To Jail" space (thus putting a player in Jail). This can be a good strategic play. After using a Bus Ticket, give the Ticket to the Banker; it is out of play for the remainder of the game. (There are 16 tickets in all. When they are gone, they're gone!) Watch out! When an "All Tickets Expire" card is drawn, all other Tickets in the hands of the players are lost to the bank (they've expired). If a Bus Ticket or Mr. Monopoly roll causes you to land on or pass GO, collect $200 as usual.

Note: All Bus Tickets should be revealed as collected and kept face up.

Additional rules clarifications and answers to frequently asked questions may be found at: http://winning-moves.com/megafaq.

© Winning Moves, Inc.

OTHER NEW SPACES

AUCTION If you land here, pick an unowned property for the Banker to auction off. Later in the game, when all of the properties are owned, you must move ahead to the property on which you need to pay the highest rent (the closer one, if tied).

BIRTHDAY GIFT If you land here collect $100 from the Bank, or draw a Bus Ticket for use on a later turn. Your choice.

BUS TICKET Take a Bus Ticket and keep for use on a later turn. Do nothing if no Bus Tickets remain.

The Mega Edition has developed an enthusiastic following. Top players have already conceived some great strategies to win it, including 2003 U.S. Monopoly champ Matt McNally. Check out his tips:

WINNING TIPS
by Matt McNally
2003 U.S. Monopoly Champion

1. MASTER THE TRADITIONAL GAME OF MONOPOLY.

If you understand the core principles of the standard MONOP-OLY game, you're well on your way to having a great time playing, and winning, MONOPOLY: The MEGA Edition.

2. BUY WISELY.

In the MEGA edition, the location of your color group is often of vital importance. It's best to acquire a color group located after one that may not be developed (because its ownership is split between two or more opponents). Late in the game, these properties will likely be mortgaged and Mr. Monopoly (on the speed die) will deliver many opponents to your group. Thus, if you own the railroad (if any) that precedes this group, mortgage it. In the hands of an opponent, this railroad would rarely be mortgaged because it would gain the benefit of Mr. Monopoly, short-circuiting visits to your group.

3. BUILD IMMEDIATELY.

In MEGA, you can build houses and hotels when you own all but one property of a group. Build them as soon as you can. Beat your opponents to the punch in the housing boom.

4. BUILD IN REVERSE SEQUENCE.

When building unevenly, build your next house on the first property of a group. Why? The speed die will advance opponents' tokens to the nearest rent. This will likely be the first property of a group. At a minimum, try to build three-houses each. Great rents start at this level.

5. EMPLOY YOUR COLOR GROUP STRENGTH.

- Browns and Light Blues: Build these properties to hotels and skyscrapers. Doing so will make your opponents' visits cost them dearly, perhaps even fatally. In cash-rich games, create a housing shortage by only building to the four-house level. This may prevent opponents from developing more expensive properties, due to a lack of houses in the bank.

- Purples, Oranges, Reds, and Yellows: These are the best properties to own. They're hit frequently and have tremendous bankrupting power. Trade for one of these groups when there is little fear of being the first player to pay a crippling rent.

- Greens and Dark Blues: Develop them cautiously. They are very expensive. Do so when: 1) You acquire naturally the three green properties or two dark blue properties; 2) the preceding color group is split and will not be developed; or, 3) the game is slow to reach the trading stage (if so, lots of cash will be in play).

6. DEVELOP ONE COLOR GROUP FIRST.

Mr. Monopoly will move tokens around the board quickly. Thus, it's better to have one highly developed group rather than two lightly developed groups. Build up a second group if you have fully developed your first group and have lots of surplus cash. Ideally, this group will be on the opposite side of the board from your first group.

7. MORTGAGE ALL NON-ESSENTIAL DEEDS.

Once you've acquired a group, raise money from mortgaging in order to generate fearsome rents via houses, hotels, and skyscrapers. Mortgage lone deeds from other groups first. Next, mortgage colored pairs, then single utilities, then single railroads.

8. CREATE "SPEED BUMPS."

Capitalizing on the rapid movement of tokens around the board is important. Mr. Monopoly will be rolled one time out of three on average, and late in the game he will bring about many rents. By mortgaging, and later unmortgaging the same property, you can set up and dismantle "speed bumps." Speed bumps enable you to maneuver an opponent into hitting your heavily developed color group, or if placed adroitly, to prevent an opponent from going bankrupt to anyone but you.

9. OWN TWO RAILROADS; BUILD RAIL DEPOTS.

Build train depots only when you control at least two railroads. Doing so will help you achieve a great return on this investment. This tactic will also avoid the need to sell a depot (at half price, of course) if you have one railroad and wish to include it in a trade.

10. TAKE A TICKET; RIDE THE BUS.

Save a bus ticket whenever possible, unless you anticipate an opponent drawing a bus ticket that will cause all others to expire. Early in the game use a ticket to land on an unowned property—especially one that will enable you to form a color group. Late in the game, use a ticket to bypass opponents' groups or to go to jail and delay the risk of paying a big rent.

MONOPOLY IN OTHER MEDIA

No great game would remain great if it were not available to play electronically.

Imagine playing MONOPOLY while cheering on the sidelines of a soccer game! It's possible! MONOPOLY is available to play digitally on 21 different platforms including Console (PlayStation, PS2, PS3 Wii, Xbox 360, Nintendo DS), Mobile (Android and iOS), and connected hand-held (iPad, Kindle, Nook, Android Tablet, Playbook), as well as online though social networking sites.

And, finally, you can watch the entire story of MONOPOLY on DVD, and through digital downloads, thanks to . . .

Under the Boardwalk: The MONOPOLY Story, narrated by Zachary Levi (*Chuck, Tangled*), tells it all. For over 75 years, the game of MONOPOLY has brought friends and families together on countless occasions and created millions of memories. This documentary captures how the classic board game became a worldwide cultural phenomenon, and follows the colorful players who come together to compete for the title of MONOPOLY World Champions.

Visit MonopolyDocumentary.com. Available on Amazon, iTunes, and Netflix.

OFFICIAL MONOPOLY RULES

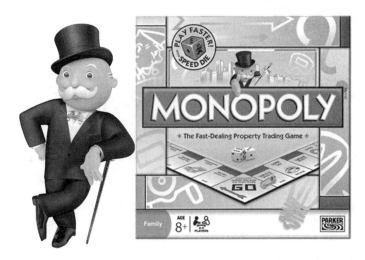

THE MONOPOLY® GAME

Rules of Play

OBJECT The object of the game is to become the richest player by buying, renting, and trading properties.

PREPARATION Place the game board on a table, and put the Chance and Community Chest cards facedown on their allotted spaces on the board. Each player chooses one token to represent him/her while traveling around the board. Each player is given $1500 in cash divided as follows: two each of $500's, $100's, and $50's; six $20's; five each of $10's, $5's, and $1's. All remaining cash and other equipment go to the Bank. Stack the Bank's cash on edge in the compartments in the plastic Banker's tray.

BANKER Select as Banker a player who will also make a good Auctioneer. A Banker who plays in the game must keep his/her personal cash separate from that of the Bank. When more than five people play, the Banker may elect to act only as Banker and Auctioneer.

THE BANK Besides the cash, the Bank also holds all Title Deed cards, as well as buildings prior to use by the players. The Bank pays salaries and bonuses. It sells and auctions properties and hands out their proper Title Deed cards; it sells buildings to the players and loans cash when required on mortgages. The Bank collects all penalties, loans, and interest, and the value of all properties that it sells and auctions. The Bank never "goes broke." If the Bank runs out of cash, the Banker may issue as much money as may be needed by merely writing on any ordinary paper.

THE PLAY Starting with the Banker, each player in turn rolls the dice. The player with the highest total starts the play. Place your token on the corner marked "GO," roll the dice and move your token, in the direction of the arrow, the number of spaces indicated by the dice. After you have completed your play, the turn passes to the left. The token remains on the space occupied and proceeds from that point on the player's next turn. Two or more tokens may rest on the same space at the same time.

According to the space your token reaches, you may be entitled to buy a property—or be obliged to pay rent, pay penalties, draw a Chance or Community Chest card, "Go to Jail," etc.

If you roll doubles, you move your token as usual, the sum of the two dice, and are subject to any privileges or penalties pertaining to the space on which you land. Retaining the dice, roll again and move your token as before. If you roll doubles three times in succession, move your token immediately to the "In Jail" part of the "IN JAIL—JUST VISITING" corner space (see JAIL).

"GO" Each time a player's token lands on or passes over GO, whether by rolling the dice or by drawing a card, the Banker pays him/her a salary of $200. The $200 is paid only once each time around the board. However, if you pass GO on the roll of the dice and land two spaces beyond it on the Community Chest space, or nine spaces beyond it on the Chance space, and you draw an "ADVANCE TO GO" card, you collect $200 for passing GO the first time and another $200 for reaching it the second time by instructions on the card.

BUYING PROPERTIES Whenever you land on an unowned property you may buy it from the Bank at its printed value. You receive the Title Deed card showing ownership of this property; place it face up in front of you. If you do not wish to buy the property, the Banker auctions it to the highest bidder. The buyer pays to the Bank the amount of the bid, in cash, and receives the corresponding Title Deed card. Any player, including the one who declined the option of buying the property at the printed value, may bid. Bidding may start at any price.

PAYING RENT When you land on a property owned by another player, the owner collects rent from you in accordance with the list printed on its Title Deed card. If the property is mortgaged, no rent can be collected. When a property is mortgaged, its Title Deed card is placed face down in front of the owner (see MORT-GAGES). It is an advantage to own all of the Title Deed cards in a color-group because the owner may then charge double rent for unimproved properties in that color-group. This rule applies to un-mortgaged properties even if another property in that color-group is mortgaged. It is even more advantageous to have buildings on properties because rents are much higher than for unimproved properties. **The owner may not collect the rent if he/she fails to ask for it before the second player following rolls the dice.**

"CHANCE" & "COMMUNITY CHEST" CARDS When you land on either a Chance or Community Chest space, take the top card from the deck indicated, follow the instructions and return the card face down to the bottom of the deck. The "GET OUT OF JAIL FREE!" cards are held until used and then returned to the bottom of the deck. If the players who draw these do not wish to use them, they may sell them, at any time, to another player for an amount agreeable to both.

"INCOME TAX/LUXURY TAX" If you land on one of these spaces, you must pay the Bank the amount shown.

"JAIL"

You land in Jail when

   (1) your token lands on the space marked "Go to Jail";

   (2) you draw a card marked "GO DIRECTLY TO JAIL"; or

   (3) you roll doubles three times in succession.

When you are sent to Jail you cannot collect your salary of $200 in that move since, regardless of where your token is on the board, you must move it directly into Jail. Your turn ends when you are sent to Jail. If you are not "sent" to Jail but in the ordinary course of play land on that space, you are "Just Visiting," you incur no penalty, and you move ahead in the usual manner on your next turn.

You get out of Jail by

   (1) rolling doubles on any of your next three turns; if you succeed in doing this you immediately move forward the number of spaces shown by your doubles roll. Even though you rolled doubles, you do not take another turn.

   (2) Using a "GET OUT OF JAIL FREE!" card if you have one.

   (3) Purchasing a "GET OUT OF JAIL FREE!" card from another player and playing it.

   (4) Paying a fine of $50 before you roll the dice on either of your next two turns.

If you don't roll doubles by your third turn, you must pay the fine of $50. You then get out of Jail and immediately move forward the number of spaces shown by your roll. Even though you are in Jail, you may buy properties from or sell them to other players, buy or sell buildings, and collect rents.

"FREE PARKING" A player landing on this space receives no cash, properties, or rewards of any kind. This is just a "free" resting place.

HOUSES When you own all of the properties in a color-group you may buy houses from the Bank and place them on those properties. If you buy one house, you may place it on any one of those properties. The next house you buy must be placed on one of the unimproved properties of this or any other complete color-group you may own. The price you must pay the Bank for each house is shown on your Title Deed card for the property on which you place the house. The owner still collects double rent from an opponent who lands on the unimproved properties of his/her complete color-group. Following the above rules, you may buy and place at any time as many houses as your judgment and cash will allow. You must place them evenly, i.e., you cannot place more than one house on any one property of any color-group until you have placed one house on every property of that group. You may then begin on the second row of houses, and so on, up to a limit of four houses to a property. For example, you cannot place three houses on one property if you have only one house on another property of that group. As you place evenly, you must also break down evenly if you sell houses back to the Bank (see SELLING PROPERTIES).

HOTELS When you have four houses on each property of a complete color-group, you may buy a hotel from the Bank and place it on any property of the color-group. You return the four houses from that property to the Bank and pay the value of the hotel as shown on the Title Deed card. You may place only one hotel on any one property.

BUILDING SHORTAGES When the Bank has no buildings to sell, players wishing to buy them must wait for some player to sell his/hers back to the Bank. If there are a limited number of buildings available and two or more players wish to buy more than the Bank has, the buildings must be sold at auction to the highest bidder.

SELLING PROPERTIES Unimproved properties (but not buildings) may be sold to any player as a private transaction for any amount the owner can get. However, no properties can be sold to another player if buildings are placed on any properties of that color-group. Any buildings so located must be sold back to the

Bank before the owner can sell any property of that color-group. Buildings may be sold back to the Bank at any time for one-half of their printed value. All houses on one color-group must be sold one by one, evenly, in reverse of the manner in which they were built. All hotels on one color-group may be sold at once. Or they may be sold one house at a time (one hotel equals five houses), evenly, in reverse of the manner in which they were built.

MORTGAGES Unimproved properties can be mortgaged through the Bank at any time. Before an improved property can be mortgaged, all of the buildings on all of the properties of its color-group must be sold back to the Bank at half price. The mortgage value is printed on each Title Deed card. No rent can be collected on mortgaged properties, but rent can be collected on unmortgaged properties in the same group. In order to lift the mortgage, the owner must pay the Bank the amount of the mortgage plus 10% interest.

When all of the properties of a color-group are no longer mortgaged, the owner may begin to buy back buildings at full price. The player who mortgages a property retains possession of it and no other player may secure it by lifting the mortgage from the Bank. However, the owner may sell this mortgaged property to another player at any agreed upon price. If you are the new owner, you may lift the mortgage at once if you wish by paying off the mortgage plus 10% interest to the Bank. If the mortgage is not lifted at once, you must pay the Bank 10% interest when you buy the property and if you lift the mortgage later you must pay the Bank an additional 10% interest as well as the amount of the mortgage.

BANKRUPTCY You are declared bankrupt if you owe more than you can pay either to another player or to the Bank. If your debt is to another player, you must turn over to that player all that you have of value and retire from the game. In making this settlement, if you own buildings, you must return these to the Bank in exchange for cash to the extent of one-half the amount paid for them. This cash is given to the creditor. If you have mortgaged properties, you also turn these properties over to your creditor but the new owner must at once pay the Bank the amount of interest on the loan, which is 10% of the value of the property. The new owner who does this may then, at his/her option, pay the principal or hold the property until some later turn, then lift the mortgage. If he/she holds the property in this way until a later turn, he/she must pay the interest again upon lifting the mortgage. Should you owe the Bank, instead of another player, more than you can pay (because of penalties) even by selling off buildings and mortgaging properties, you must turn over all assets to the Bank. In this case, the Bank immediately sells by auction all properties so taken, except buildings. A bankrupt player must immediately retire from the game. The last player left in the game wins.

MISCELLANEOUS Cash can only be loaned to a player by the Bank, and then only by mortgaging properties. No player may borrow from or lend cash to another player.

B

SECRETS OF SUCCESS SUMMARY

Monopoly's 36 Secrets of Success with Real-Life Parallels

Secret		Chapter
1	**The odds of landing on any space of the board are not equal.** *Anticipate game changers in life. They happen to some extent daily.*	2
2	**Buy every property you land on, especially if another player owns a deed (or deeds) in this group.** *It is good to gain influence in the real world. It attracts opportunities. Rely on your character and smarts.*	4
3	**Don't risk an auction early in the game when bidding will most likely be irrational.** *Don't lose your objectivity, like many investors (and speculators), when a market or stock seems to be rising without pause.*	4
4	**Owning the Railroads is like owning a cash machine.** *The Railroads are akin to bonds or high-yield CDs in real life. In normal economic times, their yields are superior.*	4
5	**Caution: the Greens are the most expensive group to develop.** *Decide if you first want to own established blue chips in your investment portfolio, or cheaper potential blue chips.*	4
6	**The Oranges get landed on more than any other group.** *The Oranges are like a great stock that pays a good quarterly dividend and grows steadily in value as well.*	4
7	**Nine Community Chest and only two Chance cards pay you money. Nine Chance and only one Community Chest move you to another space.** *Position yourself for both improved returns on your existing investments with an eye open for a big-move opportunity.*	4
8	**The Reds are landed on almost as frequently as the Oranges. The Yellows are not landed on as much, but are still solid investments.** *Ask yourself: would you rather invest $100 per month in a mutual fund, or wait five years, accumulate $6000, and then buy 100 shares of a $60 stock?*	4
9	**Owning both Utilities is a so-so investment.** *The game's Utilities are akin to very safe, boring, and low-return bank savings.*	4

Secret		Chapter
10	**The Dark Blue properties are more intimidating than rewarding.** *If financial markets are in retreat, buying the best blue chip will likely lose you money for a while. With patience, it should gain in the longer term.*	4
11	**You do not have to pay a rent if your opponent fails to ask for it in time.** *Exercise vigilance. Make sure your bills are accurate before paying.*	4
12	**The Light Blues and Purples are good investments, provided that the more powerful groups are split or underdeveloped.** *There's a time when your nest egg needs easy-to-purchase public investments, and a time when sizable private offerings make more sense.*	4
13	**A player's cash can be increased by as much as half the value of the assets acquired.** *Calculate your real-life personal or business borrowing power; it's an informative exercise.*	4
14	**Draw on your borrowing power, if need be, to acquire a color group.** *It is prudent to take on debt only if the investment you acquire should earn a higher return than the interest paid on the debt.*	4
15	**When you must mortgage, try to do so in this order: single properties first, then a single Utility, then a single Railroad.** *When you incur debt, try to minimize its effect on your income.*	4
16	**It is better to roll before building on one's turn.** *If you can gain more information before making an investment, do so, provided the opportunity doesn't slip by while you dig.*	4
17	**Unmortgage in reverse order of the mortgaging priorities in Secret 15.** *Pay off your most costly debts first.*	4
18	**Build three houses on each property of your color group as soon as possible. Mortgage single properties to do so, if necessary.** *Add to profitable investments until you reach a point where the need to remain safely diversified causes you to halt.*	4

Secret		Chapter
19	When building the next row of houses on a group, place the first house on the property most likely to be landed upon. *When adding to your current investments, pick types with the best chance to rise in value.*	4
20	Take advantage of triples—a rare throw—to move to the space that will bring you the most advantage. *When fortune unexpectedly smiles, try to maximize your benefit. Lightning doesn't strike on command.*	4
21	If you can afford to, bid at least the mortgage value of a property at auction, because after acquiring it you can raise this amount by mortgaging the deed. *If you can buy something of value, which you know you can sell for more than your bid, don't hesitate.*	4
22	When deciding to add to one color group or another, place a building where it will cause the greatest increase in rent adjusted for the likelihood of landing on the property (its "frequency"). *Likewise, it is usually unwise to weight your investments equally. It is usually best to add new funds to those performing the best.*	4
23	A small, innocuous token sometimes goes unnoticed on the game board. *If you allow your ego to draw undue attention to yourself, you needlessly promote adversaries.*	5
24	The most likely total you'll roll with two dice is 7. With the Speed Die added, the most likely total rises to 9. *The power of compound interest makes your money grow faster after a few years of savings. It is as if a money "speed die" was added to your annual earnings "dice."*	6
25	The Speed Die opens up many possible moves and real strategic choices. *The Speed Die makes luck more akin to real life and reflects its faster pace today.*	6
26	Don't rely entirely on luck to help you gain an advantage over your opponents or lead you to victory, unless you are desperate. *Make your own luck by fostering opportunities.*	6

Secret		Chapter
27	**The properties on the second and third sides of the board get landed on more often than the properties on the first and fourth sides.** *Some investments have a higher likelihood of growing their dividends and increasing in value.*	7
28	**There is typically a *big* difference between the apparent rent-earning power of a group (based on its printed rent values) and its real income-producing potential.** *Your investment decisions can be easier to visualize if you create a comparison among the alternatives under consideration.*	8
29	**Not all groups provide increased returns when investing in a fourth house and/or hotel on each of its properties.** *As a rule of thumb, when adding to your investments, add to the investment class that's causing the most growth in your principal.*	8
30	**If you need to mortgage one of two color groups, pick the one with the lower ROI.** *Common sense dictates that among two comparable investments, you liquidate the one providing a lesser return (even if the other is more easily liquidated). Likewise, when paying off debt, first pay off the one with higher interest.*	8
31	**The never-mortgage-unless-you-must properties are those most frequently landed on, especially Illinois, New York, and the Railroads.** *If you have to sell an investment, it is often better to sell the one that is underperforming.*	8
32	**Do not exchange houses for a hotel unless your opponents cannot afford to buy them! Maintain a housing shortage if you can.** *There's a real-life parallel: be patient and don't give up on a promising investment if you believe nothing has fundamentally changed to alter your reason for buying into it.*	8
33	**Houses not only earn you rent, they also drain your opponents of the opportunity to fund their purchases and cause you harm.** *If you chase hot investments rapidly rising in value (because they are in vogue), you risk overpaying.*	8

Secret		Chapter
34	**Memorize all the possible results on the game's 32 cards. Keep track of which have entered play. Know which loom in your future, and when the deck will recycle.** *Think through the annual events affecting your finances that you need to anticipate. Prepare in advance.*	10
35	**When you negotiate, be yourself. Stay on track. Agree to a trade only if it improves your chances of winning.** *Negotiating is not scary if you remember to be yourself. Don't try to sell any harder, or any differently, than you feel comfortable doing. Assert your needs; build trust.*	11
36	**The best way to evaluate any deal, after filtering out negotiating style, is to rely on the numbers.** *Will the deal gain you ROI, frequency, and rent power? Or will it give the edge to your competitor? Only say yes to a real-life proposition if it betters your circumstance or financial return.*	11

BIBLIOGRAPHY

Monopoly,® Money, and You is largely based on personal experience and observations. The following is a list of references consulted.

Gladwell, Malcolm. *Blink: The Power of Thinking Without Thinking*. New York: Little, Brown, 2005.

Gunther, Max. *The Luck Factor*. New York: Ballantine, 1978.

Lewis, Michael. *The Big Short*. New York: Norton, 2010.

Mero, Laszlo. *Moral Calculations*. New York: Springer, 1998.

Orbanes, Philip E. "Everything I Know About Business I Learned from Monopoly." *Harvard Business Review*, March 2002.

Orman, Suze. *Women and Money*. New York, Spiegel & Grau, 2007.

Speed, Breck, and Mark Dutton. *Money Doesn't Grow on Trees*. Nashville: Cumberland House, 1996.

Robert B. M. Barton. Interview by author, January 9, 1988.

---

www.1929anupperclassaffair.com

www.brainyquote.com

www.investorplace.com

www.straightrdope.com

www.thinkexist.com

INDEX